BOOTSTRAPPER'S

SUCCESS

Secrets

151 Tactics for Building Your Business on a Shoestring Budget

KIMBERLY STANSÉLL

CAREER PRESS
3 Tice Road, P.O. Box 687
Franklin Lakes, NJ 07417
1-800-CAREER-1
201-848-0310 (NJ and outside U.S.)
FAX: 201-848-1727

Copyright © 1997 by Kimberly Stanséll

BOOTSTRAPPER'S SUCCESS SECRETS
ISBN 1-56414-277-9, $13.99
Cover design by The Hub Graphics Corp.
Printed in the U.S.A. by Book-mart Press

To order this title by mail, please include price as noted above, $2.50 handling per order, and $1.50 for each book ordered. Send to: Career Press, Inc., 3 Tice Road, P.O. Box 687, Franklin Lakes, NJ 07417.

Or call toll-free 1-800-CAREER-1 (NJ and Canada: 201-848-0310) to order using VISA or MasterCard, or for further information on books from Career Press.

Library of Congress Cataloging-in-Publication Data
Stanséll, Kimberly.
  Bootstrapper's success secrets: 151 tactics for building your
business on a shoestring budget / by Kimberly Stanséll.
    p.   cm.
  Includes index.
  ISBN 1-56414-277-9
  1. Small business--Finance. 2. Small business--Management.
  3. Success in business.   I. Title.
HG4027.7.S72   1997
658.15'92--dc21   96-39973
                                                           CIP

To my mother,
Eunice Henderson,
who wrote this book
with me in spirit

Acknowledgments

A heartfelt thank you to the following:

My brother, David Jay Henderson, my hero and biggest cheerleader.

My childhood friend, Jamis Jones Williams, a tireless listener and confidant. Here's to coming a long way from Smedley Junior High.

Fellow authors, journalists, writers and self-publishers who've traded industry secrets with me through the years.

The reference staff at the Loyola Village, Westchester, Marina del Rey and Culver City libraries who've mentored me in the ways of research and granted me so many favors.

Hewlett-Packard and Gale Research for providing me with special tools that made writing this book easier.

All those who subscribed to my newsletter, *Bootstrappin' Entrepreneur*, without which there would not be this book.

All those who generously participated in my various surveys and have shared their strategies for inclusion in this book.

The Career Press publishing family for embracing this idea and giving me leeway to write the book I had envisioned.

And most of all, the Lord, for being true to His word and granting me the desires of my heart.

Contents

What's Your Bootstrappin' IQ?

"Bootstrapper" is a universal term. If you asked a room full of small business owners and self-employed professionals how many bootstrapped their ventures, the majority of the group would raise their hands. Their stories would run the gamut, though. An electrical engineer launched a telecommunications firm using $4,000 coupled with $25,000 from a private investor; it normally takes $10 million to start this type of business. A strategist was able to use unemployment benefits as a self-employment stipend and begin helping companies nationwide reduce their workers' compensation costs. I took $328.21 from my corporate paycheck to create a line of costume jewelry—a business that grew on cash flow and led to other ventures.

Start-up capital isn't the factor that bonds bootstrappers together. It's intelligence. Webster's defines intelligence as the ability to learn from, understand or deal with new or trying situations. Having a bootstrapper's IQ means having the ability to use your mind to move beyond limitations. You become skilled at maneuvering through the challenges of your situation. Tenacity, perseverance and enthusiasm undergird your efforts. Ingenuity becomes your ultimate cash substitute, freeing the mind to rely more on your creative genius than a checkbook balance.

All bootstrappers do not start off so astute in their thinking. They do, however, begin with a willingness to take a risk on themselves. This self-understanding helps them analyze their ability to cope with a bootstrapper's existence. It's a life of ups and downs. Some days you may feel like you're beating your head against a wall. The rewards do come, but only to those who are steadfast in their journey. If you make a commitment to work with what you have and learn what you don't know, then you, too, possess a bootstrapper's IQ.

How to use this guide

Bootstrapper's Success Secrets pierces the heart of the problem: How can I make my business idea work with little or no money? This insider's guide of proven survival tactics has the answers to help you build your business on a shoestring budget. These real-life strategies are gleaned from my experiences of bootstrapping two ventures (a jewelry business and a corporate research, writing and consulting firm), from publishing the national quarterly *Bootstrappin' Entrepreneur: The Newsletter for Individuals with Great Ideas and a Little Bit of Cash* for four years and from networking with and interviewing hundreds of bootstrapping veterans across the country.

The quick-reading format allows you to absorb the guide all at once or selectively by chapter and use it as a handy reference guide. *Bootstrapper's Success Secrets* can help novices or wannabes reach their learning curves faster. Those more experienced can use it as a refresher course and stimulus for new ideas. The collection of 151 tactics is complemented with sidebar articles filled with ideas and case studies of bootstrappers in the trenches. You're bound to find something that'll help you build a more profitable business.

At the end of each chapter is a resource list called the "Bootstrapper's Follow-up File." Once you've finished a chapter, you can scout out the resources available to support you in implementing a strategy. These resources are complete with addresses, phone numbers, fax numbers and e-mail or Web page addresses, depending on each contact's preference. I've also loaded the guide with plenty of **free** resources (with the word "free" always indicated in bold so you can locate them right away) to help you save your cash for the other low-cost resources I've included. I need one favor, though—please be sure to let all contacts know that you found them in this book, as many of these freebies are special offers to my readers.

If you like the book, and I'm sure you will, please tell others about it. I also invite you to e-mail me (Ibootstrap@aol.com) or write me (Suite B261-BSS, 8726 S. Sepulveda Blvd., Los Angeles, CA 90045) with your feedback.

There are no shortcuts to success in business. But there are definitely faster ways of getting there. Those ways, my friend, are now in your hands!

—Kimberly Stanséll,
Los Angeles, Calif.

Chapter 1

The Bootstrapper's Mind-set

*"I've done so much, with so little, for so long,
I can almost do anything with nothing."*

—John Bryant, founder, Operation
Hope, Los Angeles, Calif.

Survival Tip #1: Purge any vestiges of the corporate mind-set.

"Dejobbed" and dissatisfied workers both leave their former workplace with more than a severance package and personal belongings. The workplace culture reinforces philosophies that shape a person's attitude and behavior. When you become self-employed, you're changing cultures and therefore must think and act in alignment with your new environment. A corporate mind-set in a bootstrapper's environment can lead to failure; the two are incompatible. Here's why.

In an employer setting a person usually has work tools in abundance. For example, in every position I held there was top-flight computer equipment, the latest software releases, a well-stocked supply room and a receptionist to man the phone. This land-of-plenty environment helps foster the attitude: "I need a lot of stuff to do the job." As a bootstrapper, what you *really* need is redefined. Subletting an 8-by-10-foot space, haggling over prices at a computer show and outfitting an office with refurbished wares can work as the backdrop to a big contract, too.

Second, the workplace reinforces what you "can't do." People are denied opportunities merely because of office dynamics. If you fail at politicking, you may be left without a clear sense of your talents. A "can't do" attitude is akin to bootstrapper's paralysis. You must be open to experimenting and finding out what you "can do" to make your venture successful. Third, the workplace doesn't encourage you to say "no" (you could end up getting fired). Successful bootstrappers confidently say "no" to unprofitable projects, difficult clients, unwise counsel or anything that's not moving their business in the right direction (see Survival Tip #104).

The workplace does expose people to learning opportunities not available everywhere. Take inventory of what you learned from an employer's marketing strategies, industry, success or failure, customer feedback, contacts and experiences with equipment or furniture. This type of information can help you build a better business, whereas other unsuitable corporate influences will only work against you (see "Corporate mind-set seeping into your business," page 16).

Survival Tip #2: Say good-bye to your spendthrift days.

In my "Six Ways to Stretch a Mini-Budget" workshop, I ask the audience to make "footloose confessions"—to reveal their spendthrift habits that were costly to former employers. Footloose confessions include everything from ordering large quantities of office supplies for personal use (read: stealing), encouraging their friends-and-family circle to call on the company's toll-free line, excessively using directory assistance at 25 to 75 cents per call and sending everything via express mail. Besides being an effective icebreaker, this process helps people zero in on key areas where they may be losing money in their own businesses.

Most employee positions are insulated from cash flow issues. When the purchasing department okays your request, it's approving more than your order. It's validating your behavior, approach and thought process—or lack thereof—about how you spend money. So workers who order whatever they want are just as okay as a manager who spends everything in a budget. Bad habits begin to germinate because employees are not conditioned to think about how much their actions are costing the company. But what was okay back then may not work in your own business.

Many of us carry these spendthrift habits into our own ventures— not recognizing them until the expenses begin to pick our pockets. Managing on a shoestring budget requires that you be able to distinguish between your needs, wants and absolutes (see Survival Tip #25). Remember, you're spending your own money. If you spend money when it's not okay, you'll be out of business fast. So spare yourself the consequences and make your confessions today!

Survival Tip #3: Let go of resentment.

You may have some unresolved feelings about separating from the workplace environment. When I left the corporate environment, I resigned from a position that wasn't in jeopardy of being eliminated. In fact, discussions about a promotion were underway. But I had a secret: A part-time jewelry business was stimulating me in a way that my day job was not. I *chose* to leave the company to pursue other interests. But because I didn't plot my exodus very well, I experienced some hardships. When I would talk to my mother about quitting, she would remind me that I chose this working lifestyle. Her comments were my reality check: *I'm here because of my choices.* The commitment to make my venture work was renewed.

A colleague had a different response. Her spouse was downsized, and she started a business out of necessity. During a rocky time, she said, "I resent struggling so hard to make this work. I wouldn't be doing this if my husband hadn't lost his job." Although the business did become successful, her resentment helped create a love-hate relationship with the venture, affecting her willingness to make sacrifices at times.

Many people who start businesses out of necessity do find fulfillment in the bootstrapping journey. However, a resentful attitude can rob you of your chance to reach that point. Ill feelings can affect your ability to remain committed during tough times. My colleague could have turned her attitude around by changing how she viewed the struggle: "If I continue to work at making this business successful, my family will not be so economically vulnerable." Resentment can also cause you to make half-hearted choices. An adjustment in your thinking will free you to make the sacrifices necessary to keep moving forward.

CORPORATE MIND-SET SEEPING INTO YOUR BUSINESS

Psychologists Maynard Brusman, Ed.D., of Working Resources in San Francisco (workingres@aol.com) and Jessica G. Schairer, Ph.D., of Self-Employment Solutions in Los Angeles (Jgschairer@aol.com) both counsel people who are going through career transition. They share some common areas where former employees have difficulty shifting into a self-employment lifestyle:

Creating your own structure. One of the biggest adjustments for people is having to provide their own structure. In the workplace there's always someone above you structuring your day, whether it be through supervisory directives or a job description. When you become self-employed, you set the priorities and create structure for yourself. You must also become skilled at juggling the multiple demands of a business. Bootstrappers' credo: "Whatever the work is that needs to be done, I do it."

Believing no matter what you do or the results you produce, you'll still get paid. People who are unmotivated, inefficient and occasionally contribute something of value remain on payrolls across the country everyday. Self-employment rewards are based on the ones you produce yourself. Your income is a direct result of your efforts. You must commit to working diligently every day—your livelihood depends on it.

Understanding personal responsibility belongs to you. For years the American work force was lulled by thinking that Mr. Blue Chip employer would take care of them forever. Employers' paternal relationships with workers are gone. We're all affected by society's shifting: from entitlement to earning, from blame and excuses to personal accountability, from people having rights to people being responsible for themselves. Only those who work at creating their own tomorrow will survive.

Balancing what you need to do with doing the job. Unless they were in sales, many people are used to just doing the job and having someone else sell the product. Many bootstrappers enjoy doing the work more than selling and marketing themselves. Failing to market your business will have a wearing affect on cash flow. When business is rolling, you'll be busy making money. When you're not busy, you'll be stalled with nothing on the way. It's a challenge to embrace doing things that you don't like, but it's a necessary part of your survival.

Survival Tip #4: Adopt a successful "money personality."

The Public Agenda Foundation study *Promises to Keep: How Leaders and the Public Respond to Savings and Retirement* identifies four underlying personality traits: planners, strugglers, deniers and impulsives. Although the Foundation's focus was to analyze people's personality traits in relation to how they view saving for retirement, some inferences can be drawn about your survival as a bootstrapper.

Planners are in control of their financial affairs. This group is more likely to know where their monthly budget is spent and make spending adjustments to save more for retirement. Planner bootstrappers should fare well in managing business expenses and identifying unnecessary "extras" in their operations. This group makes less conservative investments and may experiment more with business-building strategies. A word of caution: Planners tend to lean toward riskier investments and have to be careful not to get blinded by a strategy's profit potential. You can better survive any miscalculated payoffs by balancing your plans with some reliable approaches (see Survival Tip #72).

Strugglers are beset by financial difficulties and uncertainty. Their view: "Every time I get my affairs in order, unpredictable expenses set them back." Struggler bootstrappers may stick with their ventures longer than other groups because they're comfortable with being uncomfortable. They make financial decisions based on what they have on hand and have modest expectations about their retirement. Strugglers may find themselves running marginally successful businesses that could be turned around with a goal-setting program to create growth (see Survival Tips #142 and #143).

Deniers have a hands-off approach to savings. They refuse to give up life's extras to save for retirement and believe everything will take care of itself. Running a business requires a lot of give-and-take. The problems or needs of an operation don't magically take care of themselves—rather, the business itself disappears.

Impulsives are driven to seek immediate gratification. This group admits they waste too much money buying things they do not really need, and the more they make, the more they spend. Impulsive bootstrappers create museum offices, which may be fun to browse while you're listening to all their marketing-campaign-gone-bad stories.

Their impulse spending may prevent them from making strategic investments that will build their enterprises.

You may identify with one trait or fall somewhere in the middle. It's important to begin thinking about how you spend money and why. Begin breaking away from patterns that can ruin your business. The sooner you do, the sooner your venture can realize its potential (see Survival Tip #113).

Survival Tip #5: Lace up your boots with determination.

Many attributes contribute to a bootstrapper's success, but determination is the spark plug. You've decided definitely and firmly to pursue your dream or goal. Determination gives you the will to succeed, while other qualities support your desire to make it happen.

Stories from Women of Enterprise Award honorees illustrate determination at work in people's lives. The annual awards program, sponsored by Avon Products, Inc., and the U.S. Small Business Administration, salutes five women entrepreneurs who've overcome hardships to achieve success. What's interesting is that many of the women's determination was rooted in rising above their environment or circumstances, and running a business was a vehicle for doing so.

Marge Gershen Abrams, a 1992 honoree, is a good example. She grew up in poverty as a sharecropper's daughter. She later married a serviceman, and they had three children. When her husband, who sold janitorial supplies, died of a heart attack, Abrams was forced to become the breadwinner. She knew all his customers and asked his boss for her husband's job. She was rejected on the premise that "a woman can't sell." Fearful that she'd lose her children, Abrams offered to clean the buildings of her husband's customers. This cleaning lady is founder of Associated Building Services Company, a Houston cleaning service that grossed more than $40 million in sales in 1995. Abrams's response to her success: "I'm not special. I'm just determined."

Survival Tip #6: The journey can be rocky, so know your personal and professional limits.

Are you willing to walk around the world—or just halfway—to become successful? The road to building a business can take its toll on your life. Establishing some commandments for living and running a business may prevent you from losing more than is necessary.

Business is a family issue. Parameter-setting with your loved ones is a good place to start. You can secure family support by helping them understand what you're doing and how they'll be affected. Family chat sessions should focus on what's motivated you to start a business and the effort level you'll need to sustain—working long hours, missing some family activities or traveling a lot. You should also be clear about how much jeopardy you can put them in. Taking a second mortgage on your house or a loan against the retirement fund may be off-limits, but postponing your Caribbean vacations may be doable. (Single entrepreneurs should adopt similar guidelines for their lives, too.) Your family's perspective of what you're doing can become clearer when they see how it benefits them. Barbie Dallman, for instance, gives her spouse a monthly check for 5 percent of the profits. She doesn't have to do this; it's just her way of saying thank you for his unwavering support.

Business is also a personal issue. When business becomes impersonal, you're more susceptible to compromising your values and integrity. You should define some limits about the type of work, customers and behavior that you're willing to accept. People who earn money in an unhealthy way either lose it or don't enjoy it. Also, make a pact to guard your health. Entrepreneurs are notorious for being too busy taking care of business to take care of themselves. While you're building up your business, your body may become too ragged to enjoy its fruits.

Survival Tip #7: Understand that "more time" is a myth and "different time" will be your reality.

Here's a joke: Owning a business is great because you only have to work half the time, and you decide which 12 hours they are. The truth is, bootstrappers work harder and longer hours than in most day jobs. Small-office professionals usually have a home office, which allows them to work from both places. Home-office folks live a few feet away from their headquarters and have the option of working at any time. Self-employment does give you a chance to have more control over your time, but you have to work at it.

You can set your own hours but the schedule needs to be compatible with your industry. Salon 21 owner Michelle Bell works a four-day week. Her Los Angeles salon caters to professional and entrepreneurial women who keep her door revolving from 7 a.m. to 7 p.m. Bell uses her off-days to be involved with community activities, attend networking functions and recuperate from her work schedule.

It's difficult to run a business with children underfoot. Many business owners maintain day-care arrangements similar to what they had while in the workplace. Many parents, like Barbie Dallman, do find that self-employment makes them more available to their children. Dallman, who runs Happy Fingers Word Processing & Resume Service from her Charleston, West Virginia home, is able to be in two places at once whenever her son is sick. She's able to meet her parental responsibilities and still run the office.

In a bootstrapper's environment the stress of asking for permission to take time off is eliminated. You'll be able to more freely handle emergencies and personal commitments, and plan time off around your family's schedule. You may not end up with more time. However, you will find yourself living and working simultaneously.

Survival Tip #8: Think beyond how you used to perform, and creativity will come to you.

Creativity became award-winning business writer Catherine Wald's companion once she ditched her corporate position. As a communications editor, she wrote straightforward material for internal publications. Wald's creativity was hampered in three ways: She had an image to protect; she didn't want to take the risk of offending someone; and her energy was zapped from trying to anticipate others' reactions. Working independently from her Mohegan Lake, New York, office, Wald felt free to learn new styles of writing. Her writing services now include speeches and company biographies for a Fortune 500 clientele who appreciate the fresh perspective she brings to projects. She's even had success at writing essays that have appeared in *The Chicago Tribune* and *Newsday*.

You, like Wald, may have had your creativity blocked in the workplace. Once you're involved with entrepreneurial work, the biggest creativity squelchers can be self-imposed. Creativity is about creating, not imitating. So you should be careful not to approach your new work as though you're working from an old job description. Most bootstrappers begin by wearing the hats of owner, officer and key personnel. Shifting gears between positions will surely stimulate a dormant mind (or drive you crazy). It's through this process, though, that you're free to experiment with yourself and unlock what's inside.

The smaller your business, the more creative you'll need to be in establishing a marketplace presence and finding solutions to your challenges. The good news: Every person is creative to some degree. You can begin the process by taking some risks. Enrolling in an art class, telling your own joke at an improv comedy club and spending more time with creative people can all work as stimuli. Wald, for instance, began trying her ideas on clients, and their responsiveness encouraged her not to hold back anymore. Begin with a few small steps, and soon you, too, will be bubbling with ideas.

Survival Tip #9: Prepare for a time of self-discovery—you may end up reinventing yourself.

My greatest revelation as a bootstrapper is that I discovered my true self. I was employed as a personnel director, and my job was to interpret labor law. A person managing the position needed to be capable, intelligent, diplomatic and knowledgeable, so I thought of myself in those terms. While I still possess those qualities, they're not the first ones I'd use to describe myself now. Like Sherlock Holmes, I followed the clues to myself. As I rebounded from setbacks, I discovered my resourcefulness. As companies paid for my ideas, I valued my cleverness and creativeness. As people subscribed to my *Bootstrappin' Entrepreneur* newsletter, I expanded my voice in others' lives.

Every experience exposes you to a valuable part of yourself. You may discover a hidden virtue. Your likes may become your dislikes. Time may mean more to you than money. Dixie Darr, a knowledge broker based in Denver, discovered working alone all the time wasn't her thing. She now takes on projects that allow her to work on teams. Darr also realized that handling every aspect of her business isn't enjoyable. Darr concentrates on what she does best—research and writing—and delegates tasks such as bookkeeping and mailings.

Try this self-discovery exercise. Write down five adjectives that describe you and how your business can benefit from each one. Tuck this information away for a year. Before you review the list again, write down the adjectives that describe you now. Compare the lists and see how you've changed. Nurturing your new discoveries may require you to reinvent the business. I went from worker to jewelry designer to publisher to author. Self-discovery can change the complexion of your business—what you start off doing may look dramatically different down the line.

Survival Tip #10: Accept that shamelessness is the name of the game.

Figure out what these bootstrappers have in common: A cosmetics designer convinces a vendor to produce $80,000 worth of product based on an in-hand purchase order, no money down and payment due when the department store paid. A consultant asks an industry giant to endorse his product, thus positioning himself to leverage sales off of the company's customer base. Rather than deplete personal resources to produce a book, a self-publisher solicits $5,000 sponsorship contribution from companies trying to reach the same target market.

These people were very bold in garnering the support they needed to build their businesses.

A bootstrapper is only limited by his or her sense of shamelessness. Bootstrappers are shameless promoters, jugglers of expenses, marketers, salespeople and recruiters to their cause. It's important, however, that you do not confuse this concept with unethical behavior. Shamelessness is not about indulging in shady practices or building your business on a foundation of lies. Instead, it's about putting your bootstrapped venture out there before the public's scrutinizing eye. Sure, you might be rejected, but you're willing to gamble on your chances for acceptance.

Joel McIntosh, of Prufrock Press, has mastered the art of shamelessness. McIntosh's firm sells education materials to teachers. It's a lucrative market, but he has to manage his payables around school districts' purchasing procedures, which slow down during certain months. In his company's startup phase, McIntosh needed printers who would grant him flexible credit terms on orders ranging from $10,000 to $50,000. McIntosh's shameless approach: He brought in graphs outlining Prufrock's cash flow flux and used them to negotiate 90- and 30-day terms. Four printers were won over by his up-front approach and agreed to work with him under these arrangements. Prufrock Press now grosses more than $1.3 million annually, and its relationships with the printers are still intact.

A shameless bootstrapper is open to daring and odd solutions. You're bold in asking for assistance from those who have what you need. You're able to sell others on how your unconventional approach can work out to be a win-win arrangement. It takes guts and courage. It takes a person who is anchored in a healthy self-esteem base.

Survival Tip #11: Nurture your self-esteem.

Bill McGrane, founder of McGrane Institute, Inc., in Covington, Kentucky, defines self-esteem as the respect a person feels for him- or herself; it's an emotion. Self-esteem has everything to do with your success. It affects your belief that you have what it takes to be an entrepreneur, your conscientiousness about money, the level of risks you'll take and how you sell and communicate. Consumers buy from businesses they have confidence in. And your strength as an entrepreneur lies in *your* confidence and satisfaction with yourself. Your positive energy will come through to those who do business with you.

Self-esteem creates a feeling of acceptance so that you can pursue innovative approaches and be open to your own and others' creativity. Operating from a self-*image* base—an imitation, mask or facade of your true self—has the opposite effect. Protecting your image becomes the priority, which prompts you to judge the presentation of ideas instead of their substance. Therefore, you miss out on opportunities with potential benefits.

For example, if you were operating from a shaky self-esteem base, you wouldn't dare ask for supplier financing the way Joel McIntosh did (see Survival Tip #10). You would lack the confidence to even ask for those terms. You might also be concerned about what others think, and you would probably discount this option as a form of begging. Securing the kinds of arrangements you need as a bootstrapper requires you to *sell* people on *yourself*. If you're a low self-esteemer, you wouldn't believe in yourself enough to be able to convince someone else about your potential to deliver. Familiar with the adage "Treat people as you like to be treated"? If you don't feel good about yourself and treat yourself well, you'll probably be off the mark in the way you treat your customers, too.

Developing your self-esteem is a worthwhile investment. Begin by expanding your awareness. Educate yourself about what's going on around you. If you feel deficient in an area, go find information that'll help you (see Survival Tip #118). Reprogram your awareness. Evaluate the way you think about yourself and others. Practice listening to others without judging them. Commit to daily self-esteem action; self-esteem is built by doing—putting your thoughts into action. The more you do, the more energy, passion and excitement you'll create in your environment.

Survival Tip #12: Take joy in progress.

Rome wasn't built in a day, and your business won't be, either. If you understand that big success is the result of little successes achieved over time, then you'll begin to appreciate your efforts. It's easy to become frustrated with the growth pace of your venture, especially when you're eyeing someone who appears to be making great strides. Every business has its own rhythm. Some get off to a fast start while others need constant resuscitation.

Consider keeping a business activity journal, similar to departmental status reports distributed in many workplaces. Divide or categorize it based on marketing activities, cold calling, mailing responses and so forth. Log your entries daily, weekly or (at the very least) monthly. Keeping track of your progress helps you remain focused. When you get weary, glancing back at your entries will boost your psyche. The pages will remind you that the client who just asked for a project bid never used to return your calls. Or the customer who used to frown at your fees now regularly refers people to you. That's progress—delight in the fact that you're still in business to see it happen.

Writing down a personal definition of success and using it to gauge your progress will help you keep a clearer perspective on how you're doing.

Lastly, release the "big-break" mentality; it only keeps you in a state of anticipation. Sometimes we get so preoccupied with what's coming that we miss the moment we're in. I learned to view every opportunity as a stepping stone to another place in the journey. Once I made the shift in my thinking, I was able to joyfully work at my business every day.

Bootstrapper's Follow-up File

American Psychological Association, 750 First St. NE, Washington, DC 20002-4242; 202-336-5500. Provides referrals to local psychologists who specialize in helping people make the transition from unemployment to reemployment or self-employment. Also check the phone directory under your state or county's psychological association.

Fit Facts, NordicTrack Health and Fitness Department, 800-358-3636. A **free** collection of briefs discussing the benefits of various exercises and how to develop a personal health and fitness plan.

McGrane Institute, Inc., P.O. Box 17406, Covington, KY 41017; 800-341-3304; northern Kentucky: 606-341-2216. Offers resources and workshops nationwide to help people resolve self-esteem issues that affect their careers and personal lives. Publishers of *Brighten Your Day With Self Esteem* by Bill McGrane. $26.90 postage pd.

Money Personality Quiz, Olivia Mellan & Associates, Inc., 2607 Connecticut Ave. NW, Washington, DC 20008. A 20-question test ($8) to help you identify five money types from the book *Money Harmony: Resolving Money Conflicts in Your Life and Relationships* by Olivia Mellan (Walker & Company, 1994).

Napoleon Hill's Positive Action Plan: 365 Meditations for Making Each Day a Success by Napoleon Hill (Dutton/Penguin USA, 1995); 800-331-4624. $22.95.

Promises to Keep: How Leaders and the Public Respond to Savings and Retirement, Public Agenda Foundation, 6 E. 39th St., New York, NY 10016-0112; 212-686-6610. A 31-page study identifying the major barriers and attitudes Americans have toward saving for retirement.

The Way of The Guerrilla: Achieving Success and Balance as an Entrepreneur in the 21st Century by Jay Conrad Levinson (Houghton Mifflin Company, 1997); 800-225-3362. $19.95.

To Build the Life You Want, Create the Work You Love: The Spiritual Dimension of Entrepreneuring by Marsha Sinetar (St. Martin's Press, 1995); 800-321-9299. $18.95.

Working Families: Promoting Balance for Today's Working People, The Economic Press, Inc., 800-526-2554. Monthly newsletter providing tips and solutions to tame out-of-control schedules and juggle nonstop responsibilities. **Free** sample copies available.

Chapter 2

Evaluating Your Idea

"Capital isn't so important in business. Experience isn't so important. You can get both of these things. What is important is ideas. If you have ideas, you have the main assets you need, and there isn't any limit to what you can do with your business or your life. They are any man's greatest asset—ideas."

—Harvey Firestone,
American industrialist

Survival Tip #13: Don't let your ideas follow money—let money follow your ideas.

Money is not a stimulus for good ideas but a magnet for bad ones. You may come up with a zillion ways to spend it, but they may not be the best use of your resources. Just look at people who win the lottery. At a reunion of Texas million-dollar-jackpot winners, the group shared experiences and talked about the new realities of their bountiful lives. Many of the winners admitted to spending their money on some indulgences. More interesting were the stories of how financial "advisors" and hucksters would continually try to latch themselves onto the moneybags with suspicious idea solicitations and questionable "investment" opportunities.

It's important for you not to discount an idea because it seems to lack money behind it. Here's an example of this principle at work. When the rights to Patricia Gallagher's book *Start Your Own At-Home Child Care Business* reverted back to her from the publisher, she decided to self-publish a reprint. Gallagher quickly sold 2,000 copies, but she needed $7,500 to print 5,000 more. Rather than deplete her own stash, she paused to figure out another way to do the run. Gallagher spent two weeks calling industry-related companies and professional individuals to see if they'd be interested in financially supporting her idea. For a $5,000 sponsorship contribution, each company's ad would appear in the book's back section. Gallagher had the same target audience as the sponsors: early childhood providers. The companies—a manufacturer of early childhood equipment, an industry magazine, a first-aid manual publisher and a resource and referral service—were all willing to let their money follow her good idea.

Surely, there will be times when money *is* the problem. However, if you first concentrate on substantiating your idea's viability, you'll be clearer on the financing options. Also, this principle will move you away from automatically throwing money at a problem without considering other solutions (see Survival Tip #132).

Survival Tip #14: See yourself as a problem-solver.

People spend money on products and services that solve their problems. Psychologists at Yale University report that the most persuasive words in the English language are *you, money, save, new, results, health, easy, safety, love, discovery, proven* and *guarantee*. People's problems are rooted in these words. They want to save money and time. They want to discover how to become smarter, avoid problems and gain control. They want easier ways to live, do business and get more for their efforts. They want proven health, relationship and safety strategies. The list can go on and on.

If you view yourself as a problem-solver, then you'll focus on developing an idea that's the solution for a targeted audience. Ask yourself what problems are out there that you're interested in, qualified to address and care about solving. That's what Tony Ulwick of Total Quality Group in Delray Beach, Florida, did. Problem: Companies who spend millions developing their products need to be sure they're valuable and profitable. Solution: Ulwick and his staff help pinpoint what's important to the consumer as well as what's cost-effective for the client. Total Quality Group spearheads a three-month process of meeting with the product development team to discuss concepts, gathering data on consumer interests, testing the price market and finding ways to manufacture a high-quality product at an economical price. Ulwick is a qualified problem-solver; he's a former IBM product development employee and credits much of his success to what he learned at the corporation (see Survival Tip #1). At about $100,000 apiece, Total Quality Group has solved problems on more than 100 projects for clients such as AlliedSignal, IBM and Motorola.

Your ideas should clearly be the solution to an existing audience's problem. A problem-solver mentality will help you stay focused on customers and on meeting their needs and wants. It'll also give you an edge in developing your marketing and customer relationships programs (discussed in Chapters 5 and 6).

Survival Tip #15: Use research as a weapon against failure.

F1 Services, a research bureau, has a brochure that captures people's attitudes about information-gathering. "Research" is printed in dirt-like coloring on the cover, and the inside reads: "...doesn't have to be a dirty word." Being in business doesn't require you to be a researcher *par excellence*, but it does require you to do some basic homework.

Research affects every aspect of your business. From evaluating the soundness of an idea and developing a customer profile to determining an appropriate business structure, identifying an immature market and pinpointing short- and long-term growth strategies, research can save you from spending money you don't have or don't need to spend. Your awareness will be expanded. You'll be able to make informed decisions, scrutinize information that comes your way and determine when you need to call in a professional. Research will support your expectations about a business's success as well as uncover potholes in your thinking. For example, someone starting a subscription-supported newsletter reads about an entrepreneur whose publication had 50,000 subscribers after three months, but then basic research uncovers data showing that newsletter businesses experience high turnover—many publishers who begin in January cease operation by June because of lack of subscription support.

Another research advantage: You'll get more substantive help from others. A librarian, industry expert or counselor can work as a conduit to better information when he or she knows what you want. Even if you've done *a little* homework, you've moved from working with nothing to working with *something*, and he or she will be able to point you toward more resources (see "How a local librarian can work as your staff researcher" on page 39).

Experts cite that most businesses fail because of a lack of information rather than a lack of money. People who are willing to do the dirty work usually don't end up in this category.

HOT SOURCES FOR SMALL BUSINESS RESEARCH

Business Research Centers. There are numerous sites across the country that provide low-cost research services to business clients. These facilities are often affiliated with an academic library, such as the Center for Business Research at Long Island University. *Internet-Plus Directory of Express Library Services* (American Library Association, 1996; see page 41 for more information) lists numerous sources for research and document delivery services. There's even a handful of **free** search sources on the Internet, such as the National Museum of Art (on America Online, go to keyword *NMAA* and click on the *Reference* icon) and the Internet Public Library (www.ipl.org). The National Museum of Art anwers questions and provides source referrals on American art, using the Smithsonian Institute and other resources. IPL answers your research questions for free.

Local and community newspapers. Many papers provide expanded coverage of the local small business community. Through *The Los Angeles Times'* Tuesday edition (which is devoted to small business coverage), I discovered that the Technology Conversion Executive Development Program (310-204-1832) offered technology-based businesses a free, 10-week class to upgrade skills in management, marketing, financing and planning and that *Something Ventured*, a 26-part small business TV series, was available in 35

Los Angeles libraries. You can find similar community resources in your area by regularly scanning the business section or calling local papers to find out whether any special sections or editions are devoted to small businesses.

The Internet. It's the network of networks, and once you become skilled at using it, you can level the playing field between yourself and elite corporations. There are many payoffs; you'll find information on competing globally, access industry profiles and government information, connect with groups of people to share information and much more. The key is learning how to maneuver your way through the layers of its offerings. Helpful resource: *Cyberpower for Business* by Wally Bock and Jeff Senné (Career Press, 1996); 800-CAREER-1 (201-848-0310 in N.J. and outside U.S.); $14.99.

State Data Centers (SDCs)/Business and Industry Data Centers (BIDCs). SDCs work with local organizations to make census data available for public use. BIDCs provide an enormous amount of information about product and service development using economic data from the Bureau. You can take advantage of **free** computer access to databases, software and other resources needed to develop a business and marketing plan. *Taking Care of Business: A Guide to Census Bureau Data for Small Businesses* provides a nationwide listing of these facilities. You can also find location information on the Web (www.sbaonline.sba.gov) or by calling 800-U-ASK-SBA.

Survival Tip #16: Make sure your idea has longevity.

For a quick primp before meetings, D'Lauren Kite relied on a small hand mirror tucked into an index card file. After numerous friends remarked how convenient the mirror was, Kite decided to create MirorDex, an unbreakable mirror that fits discreetly in a Rolodex. Kite approached the Rolodex company about piggybacking her invention onto its product line. The company flatly passed on her offer, saying it was too novel. Perhaps it was right. While Rolodexes are not obsolete, people are relying more on electronic information-tracking devices. Kite was able to sell thousands through her Apple Valley, California, mail-order company; however, she wasn't able to generate the type of sales that a mass distribution opportunity could produce. She stopped marketing the product two years ago.

Other novel products *have* fared well in the marketplace. Remember the infamous Pet Rock of the 70s? Unfortunately, a lot of clever ideas do not experience this type of success. Before you throw a lot of money into an idea, be sure it can pass a longevity test. Ask yourself such questions as:

- What sparked this idea? Did it come from something I read or saw somewhere?
- Does it have global, national, regional or local implications, or is it only relevant to my everyday life?
- Who is my target audience, and how will societal changes affect this audience in the future?
- Does the idea solve a short- or long-term problem?
- Does my idea complement the direction society is moving in? (For example, our society is becoming more mobile, more reliant on technology, more culturally diverse, more health-conscious and more pressed for time.)

Many good ideas wilt after close examination.

Remember: The more unique, odd or innovative your idea, the more you'll need to spend on educating the marketplace. It's a shame to spend good money on an idea that doesn't have a future.

Survival Tip #17: Take a risk on your own idea—it may be better than buying into someone else's dream.

There's a perception that you're more likely to succeed if you invest in a franchise or business opportunity package. Well, these investments can be just as risky as setting up shop independently. A recent Small Business Administration study of 138 franchising chains that began operations in 1983 found that only a quarter of them were still operating 10 years later. The study also showed that large corporate franchises did tend to fare better than independent businesses; however, small start-up franchises did not.

Be leery of business opportunity packages that promise you can make a lot of money for a few hours a week. Or those that extol: "We are not just selling you a business; we put you *in* business." Although there are some legitimate opportunities, the bad ones seem to garner all the press. These prepackaged small businesses appear in a variety of forms, including dealerships, distributorships, consulting, multilevel marketing programs, licenses and direct sales programs.

Investing in a formatted business may seem like a good idea, especially when you have limited capital and business experience. A franchise fee buys you an affiliation with an established company, instant name recognition, training and ongoing support. Business opportunity packages come with similar offerings. Neither option is a guarantee for success. Both require investigative legwork to find out if the opportunity is right for you and if it has the potential to yield the financial return you expect.

There is a common denominator between a franchise, a business opportunity package and an independent business startup: the success of each is fueled by the sweat equity of its owner.

Survival Tip #18: Test your idea against the past, present and future.

Determining the value of your idea by examining a variety of information sources can help ensure its success. You can cover the bases more thoroughly by squeezing details from conventional as well as unconventional sources. Here are some strategies to consider:

Scan through books that chronicle history—*American Chronicle: Seven Decades in American Life 1920-1989*, TimeLife's *This Fabulous Century* series, encyclopedia yearbooks and other decade books. These can provide you with information about popular culture, fads, history and major events. Besides being fun to read, you can find clues about how certain events—such as war, recession or high unemployment—affect people's habits.

Eye-openers to trends include books and periodical articles. An online database search using the keyword "trend" will pull up a lot of citations. Also consider research reports from organizations and individuals. For example, someone developing a product or service for family-owned businesses could gain market insights from the *American Family Business Survey* conducted with Family Enterprise Center (800-924-2770) and other reports. Reports such as these are usually referenced in articles and provide some information for you to do follow-up legwork. Perusing government documents such as *Employee*

Benefits in a Changing Economy or *Trends in Aging* can help you conceive of trends. (*Subject Bibliography Index* is a valuable guide to thousands of government publications.) Another good source: conventions. Brand-new products and groundbreaking research are showcased at these events.

Don't overlook a set of old and current phone books. Use them to discover if there's a category heading for your idea, how much competition exists and the movement of other businesses—those who've closed their doors or have grown. Both groups can work as links to finding out about industry ins and outs (see Survival Tip #128). For example, a business with a tiny ad in 1990 who sports the largest one in 1996 may now be the community's heavy-hitter. By talking to such companies directly or undercover, you can use them as a focus group in reverse—using their experiences to evaluate your idea's viability. The books can also help you identify your niche or unserved markets. If you're looking for ways to distinguish your offerings from the competition, scan the pages to see what they're *not* touting as their specialties. Old phone books can be found at public libraries. The Los Angeles central library, for instance, has a collection dating back to 1915 in its history department. You can also adopt this research strategy to product and industry directories.

Survival Tip #19: Know thy business.

As an insider, you'll definitely have an advantage with a business that's a spin-off of your background and experience. Starting a software development firm is a natural for a former computer programmer, for example. This person has a lot of advantages: expert industry insights and competitive knowledge on how to learn about the competition, discover what the market can bear, attract customers and find suppliers and distributors. This person's overall familiarity with the market would be helpful in determining a true need for his product.

What about someone with less impressive credentials who has a good idea or strong interest in an area? Once I fancied the idea of owning a flower shop until my local florist, Stan's Florist, explained the business to me. I discovered my love for flowers was not enough;

the business required a knowledge of horticulture and a flair for flower arranging (my purchases were always prearranged); and successful shops were always open on the major holidays. He offered me a minimum wage apprenticeship on the weekends so I could learn the business. That day I realized my love for flowers no more qualified me to run a shop than a great cook to run a restaurant or a world-class traveler an agency.

Every business has its own nuances and protocol that you must be educated about in order to be successful. Did you know the floral industry carries supplier credit much longer than 30 days? Or that a yellow pages ad is a must for secretarial and office support services firms? In the Small Business Administration report, *How Small Businesses Learn*, respondents cited customers, suppliers and competitors along with industry and professional newsletters and magazines as their frequently used information sources. Although lack of industry exposure doesn't automatically disqualify someone, you'll need to be proactive in qualifying yourself. Bootstrappers who succeed are the ones who know the most about what they are doing.

Survival Tip #20: Know the idiosyncrasies of your target market.

So, you've decided to market to maturity—men and women age 50 and beyond. Did you know they're more receptive to an ad when you show them pursuing a new passion, or with romance in their life, or laughing with their friends? And that they're more likely to buy if you give them a trial period, sample or coupon because they consider their purchases more closely than other groups? They're also interested in more information on products, not 15-second sales pitches; the more information you give them, the better. This information came courtesy of American Association of Retired Persons' *Modern Maturity*. But figuring out other groups' preferences may not be so simple. Every audience has its own set of preferences, which makes it tougher for you to capture its attention and dollars.

Pinpointing your audience's idiosyncrasies may require reading between the lines. Let's say you wanted to reach the small office/home office group. Your database search pulled up *The Wall Street Journal* article "Huge and Diverse Home-Office Market is Hard to Crack." The piece explains how major business suppliers were having challenges marketing to the diverse needs of the home-office market. You move forward in your research and contact national industry associations. The membership numbers surprise you—you thought more people belonged—and you discover that renewal rates are low. You could draw some inferences from this information. Perhaps this group doesn't part easily with money. If big-boy suppliers are having trouble catering to the group's diverse needs, is your idea aimed at a niche segment of the market? And how big is this segment? The group appears to be elusive. How will you be able to get through to them?

Every group has idiosyncrasies. They're the red flags and patterns that you must prepare to market to, through and around. Idiosyncrasies don't go away; the only way to handle them is to figure them out and face them dead on.

Survival Tip #21: Match your personality with the business's personality.

We've all had an encounter with someone and walked away thinking, "She really shouldn't be in this line of work." You know who I'm talking about: the salesperson with the "dry" personality, the customer service rep who doesn't know how to help you. As a bootstrapper, you can't afford for people to perceive you as being in the "wrong line of work," or you'll be out of business! Every product or service has its own personality; its profitability depends in large measure on how it's complemented by your personality.

This was the biggest lesson I learned from my jewelry business. I test-marketed my wares through a home party system such as Tupperware. Although the parties were profitable, they demanded that I be a schmoozer to move my eclectic merchandise. Sure, people were willing to spend the money, but they also wanted to be entertained. They wanted to hear stories about how I ordered the findings from around the world and the creative thought process that went into each design. At times I was more on display than the jewelry, and I didn't like it. In fact, someone suggested that I adopt a more "entertaining" presentation similar to that of a Mary Kay representative. I had the talent to fabricate the designs; I didn't have the personality to market in that particular forum and quickly began looking for other ways to bring the line to market.

You can determine personality matches by talking to others in similar businesses or industries. Ask them what type of personality traits or temperaments they feel have been necessary in their businesses. Traits—such as giving attention to details, being flexible so you don't get bent out of shape or working well under pressure or with other people—are the style you'll need to run the business. Also, how a business must be marketed is another indicator. If your idea will require heavy involvement with people or groups and the thought of socializing drains you, think about how you can handle that—if you can at all. Don't fool yourself into thinking your good idea will sell itself. Even if a business has high income potential, it won't produce the desired results if its owner's personality isn't a fit.

Survival Tip #22: Consider the virtues of patent, trademark and copyright protection.

Ideas may be your greatest asset. When you begin to transfer them into names, inventions, product designs, logos, music, writings or other forms, they become intellectual property. There are intellectual property laws that protect your creative work from being illegally copied and profited from by others.

There are three types of intellectual property protection: patent, trademark and copyright. They serve different purposes and shouldn't be confused with one another. A patent is granted to the inventor of a new or useful idea. It's a grant of property rights that excludes others from making, using or selling the same invention, and it expires after a number of years, depending on the type of invention patented. A trademark protects the distinguishing identity of goods or services. A word, name, symbol, phrase or slogan, or a combination of these items, can be trademarked. A copyright protects original works of authorship such as literary, musical, dramatic, pictorial, graphic or architectural works, motion pictures and sound recordings. It protects the form of expression; it prevents others from lifting from your idea and reworking it for their use and requires them to obtain your permission to reproduce any part of it.

By familiarizing yourself with these laws, you'll be able to factor in their usefulness as you develop your idea. One bootstrapper shared how she wasted $400 getting basic copyright information from an attorney. The Patent and Trademark and Copyright offices of the Library of Congress will send you information on the process at no charge. This overview material will help you determine, for example, if registering a business name with your state alone is sufficient, or if you need broader protection and can benefit from the assistance of a professional.

Survival Tip #23: Use free counseling as a steppingstone to better information.

A bootstrapper can get **free** business counseling from a variety of places. Popular recommendations that come to mind include: Service Corps of Retired Executives (SCORE), Small Business Development Centers (SBDCs), Small Business Institutes, University Cooperative Extension Services, Innovation Service and Export Counseling Centers and local Centers for Economic Development and Continuing Education programs. You'll find that business owners will have varying opinions about how beneficial these outlets were to their businesses. My experience, however, can help you keep all the opinions in their proper prospective.

After deciding to move away from the home party system for my jewelry business, I began researching the idea of a mail-order catalog. I'd done exhaustive research on the subject, but had questions that only a seasoned professional could answer. I turned to a local SCORE office for advice. Armed with all my research and a list of specific questions, the counselor saw I wasn't there for a primer on how to start a business. It was obvious that I needed specific help on effectively designing and promoting a jewelry catalog. Since I was proactive by being prepared, his response was to connect me to another information source—the retired head of catalog operation for Sears Roebuck. Not only did I receive answers to my questions from a one-hour coaching session, I walked away with marketing advice that has served me well throughout my entrepreneurial career.

The information you get can only be as good as the person giving it. Don't expect a counselor to have all the answers or share your enthusiasm about a project. Use his or her knowledge as your connection to more information, people or resources. You can get past first base by being prepared (see Survival Tip #15).

HOW A LOCAL LIBRARIAN CAN WORK AS YOUR STAFF RESEARCHER

Librarians are some of the most knowledgeable people on the planet. I know because they've mentored me through the years. Sadly, though, statistics show that only 3 percent of small business owners ever set foot in a library. Maybe it's because they don't know how to use one. But ignorance isn't an excuse anymore. Mary Hopf, a reference librarian in Los Angeles, has helped hundreds of business owners tap into the system's information riches and shares some strategies you can use, too.

Avoid being the clueless patron. You make it difficult for others to help you when you don't have a clue as to what you need. Think about the type of resources you're interested in finding. Even if you're just tinkering with the idea, what sparked your interest? If it were an article, bring that with you and request more information that expands on the topic. If you're not sure about a business choice, ask for a book that profiles multiple types of ventures. Otherwise, you may end up in an aisle with hundreds of choices.

Hook up with the library's best resources. Small business is a hot topic and many libraries have extensive collections dedicated to the subject. Collections of books, periodicals, audiotapes, videos and other materials targeted at small businesses may be available. Specially funded sections such as these are popping up across the country in an effort to promote self-sufficiency. Call around to find out which local libraries have special small business sections. Ask the reference librarian about the strengths and weaknesses of its branch and the type of tools available—public computers and printers, CD-ROMs, etc.

Get tutored in information-gathering. You get more mileage from a librarian when you ask him or her to "teach you how to find materials" rather than ordering him or her to fetch something. You can learn how to conduct specialized searches of databases. If necessary, make an appointment for a tutoring session. That's how I learned to use the Internet search engines more efficiently. Working with a librarian can help you begin to think like a researcher, and soon you'll be able to independently connect yourself to resources.

Query about special services. Many libraries serve as depositories for government information and offer **free** Internet access and other electronic links such as the CARL System, a **free** modem dial-in access to libraries' electronic card catalogs. Libraries work in systems. You can access their collective riches through interbranching services. You may also find it helpful to take a library tour, if the library offers them.

Establish a rapport with the staff. When the staff knows who you are, they'll pass along information of interest. And when you're in a pinch, your credibility may motivate them to go the extra mile to help you out. Libraries also make purchasing decisions based on the needs or interests of the community. Increased traffic from business owners such as yourself may encourage your local library to make a greater investment in resources you can use.

Bootstrapper's Follow-up File

101 Best Small Businesses for Women by Priscilla Y. Huff (Prima Publishing, 1997); 800-632-8676. $14.

A Consumer's Guide to Buying a Franchise, Federal Trade Commission, Public Reference, Room 130, Washington, DC 20580-0001; Web address: www.ftc.gov. A **free**, 21-page guide that explains your obligations as a franchise owner, how to shop for franchise opportunities and how to ask the right questions before you invest.

American Business Opportunity Institute, Inc., #700, 3 Bethesda Metro Center, Bethesda, MD 20814. A national information clearinghouse specializing in business opportunities and franchise investment and regulation. For more information, send SASE.

Business Opportunity Fraud, Business Opportunities, North American Securities Administrators Association, 1 Massachusetts Ave., Suite 310, Washington, DC 20001. A **free** consumer bulletin.

Catalog of Small Business Research, Office of Advocacy, SBA, Mail Code 3114, 409 Third St. SW, Washington, DC 20416. A **free** cumulative listing of the U.S. Small Business Administration's contracted research studies. More than 500 titles covering a broad scope of small business topics and issues.

Center for Business Research, C.W. Post Campus, Long Island University, Brookville, NY 11548; 516-299-2833; fax: 516-299-4170; e-mail address: cbr@titan.liunet.edu; Web address: www.liunet.edu/cwis/cwp/library/cbrhome.htm. Offers fee-based services for business clients.

Copyright Office, Register of Copyrights, Library of Congress, Washington, DC 20559-6000; 202-707-3000; 202-707-9100 (hotline for ordering forms); Web address: lcweb.loc.gov/copyright. **Free** copies of Circular 1, *Copyright Basics*, and Circular 2, *Publications of the Copyright Office*, available from this office.

Export Counseling Center, International Trade Administration, U.S. Department of Commerce, 800-872-8723. Provides a variety of information on exporting products overseas.

Information Solutions, Gale Research, 800-347-4253; Web address: www.gale.com. A **free** catalog listing all of the publisher's library reference directories.

International Franchise Association, 1350 New York Ave. NW, Suite 900, Washington, DC 20005; Web address: www.entremkt.com/ifa. Provides information on selecting and investigating a franchise.

Internet-Plus Directory of Express Library Services: Research and Document Delivery for Hire (formerly titled *The FISCAL Directory of Fee-Based Research and Document Supply Services*), FYI Information Services of the Los Angeles Public Library and Information Researchers, University of Illinois (American Library Association, 1996); 800-545-2433. Lists more than 500 libraries nationwide that provide low-cost research services.

Manufacturing Extension Partnership, Bldg. 301, Room C121, National Institute of Standards and Technology, Gaithersburg, MD 20899-0001; Web address: www.mep.nist.gov/centers. A nationwide network of affiliated technology extension centers that provides hands-on assistance to small and medium-sized manufacturers to help them adopt new technologies.

Patent and Trademark Office, 800-786-9199; Web address: www.uspto.gov. A **free** copy of *Basic Facts about Patents* is available from this office.

Small Business Administration, 800-827-5722. Provides prerecorded messages about its various programs and services, including referrals to your local SCORE and Small Business Development Center (SBDC). The *Resource Directory for Small Business Management* lists SBA publications and videotapes. Request a **free** copy from SBA Office of Business Initiatives, Mail Code 7110,

409 Third St. SW, Washington, DC 20416. Many of these publications and other information are available online at: www.sbaonline.sba.gov.

Small Business Institutes, Small Business Advancement National Center, University of Arkansas, College of Business Administration, UCA Box 5018, 201 Donaghey Ave., Conway, AR 72035-0001; 501-450-5300; fax: 501-450-5360; Web address: www.sbanet.uca.edu. Program provides **free** management counseling to small businesses. Contact for information on local programs.

Small Business Profiles, Gale Research, 800-347-4253. A two-volume series of library reference books providing step-by-step guidelines for more than 100 business ventures.

Small Business Sourcebooks, Gale Research, 800-347-4253. A library reference guide to more than 17,000 small business information sources.

Something Ventured, Intelecom, 150 E. Colorado Blvd., Suite 300, Pasadena, CA 91105; 818-796-7300. A 26-part video series on owning and operating a small business. Descriptive listing available.

Subject Bibliography Index: A Guide to U.S. Government Information, Superintendent of Documents, U.S. Government Printing Office, Washington, DC 20402; faxback service: 202-512-1716; Web address: www.access.gpo.gov/su_docs. A **free** listing of more than 12,000 different material resources available through the government.

Taking Care of Business: A Guide to Census Bureau Data for Small Businesses, Customer Service Branch, Bureau of the Census, Washington, DC 20233; Web address: www.census.gov. A **free**, 26-page guide explaining how to access and use the demographic and business-related data offered by the bureau. Also includes a listing of State Data Centers (SDCs) and Business and Industry Data Centers (BIDCs).

The Small Business Resource Guide, IBM Corporation, Mail Drop 340, 1133 Westchester Ave., White Plains, NY 10604. A **free**, 144-page small business reference guide.

Thomas Register of American Manufacturers, Thomas Publishing Company, 800-222-7900. A comprehensive library reference guide listing thousands of product manufacturers.

University Cooperative Extension Services (part of the Department of Agriculture; check the government section of your phone book for a local program listing). Provides counseling and training to small businesses, usually in conjunction with an area university.

Wisconsin Innovation Service Center, 402 McCutcham Hall, University of Wisconsin, Whitewater, WI 53190; 414-472-1365. Provides a comprehensive and confidential evaluation of your invention or idea at a relatively low cost.

Chapter 3

Setting Up Shop

"As a general rule, the most successful people in life are those who have the best information."

—Benjamin Disraeli, British
writer and prime minister

Survival Tip #24: Understand the value of a business plan.

Before she launched the Brooklyn-based Lupien, Ltd., a computer consulting firm, Debbra Lupien combed dozens of startup books. They all touted business plans—written documents explaining how you will execute the startup, operation and growth of an entity—as tools to obtain financing. Since her company was self-financed, Lupien discounted the value of a business plan and operated seven years without one. Then, needing to hone her marketing skills, she signed up for an entrepreneur's class. Lupien got more than she bargained for: The class curriculum required everyone to complete a business plan by session's end. Only 12 of the 25 first-night attendees completed the course with a business plan in hand, and Lupien was one of them.

The assignment had forced Lupien to reflect on the state of her business; she realized it was stagnant and lacked focus. She revamped her business by specializing in custom database development, which supported her goals of concentrating on more enjoyable work, doing more work in less time and serving her clients from her own office instead of at the clients' location. The result: Her profits are now up 50 percent.

Whether it's fear or mere resistance that hinders you from creating a business plan, you must understand that a business plan's value goes beyond its ability to secure a loan package for you. You gain an advantage by building your business on paper first. The business will become crystallized as you describe in writing your company, its products and services, competitors, customers, management, operations, marketing and sales plan, industrial outlook and long-term goals. The economics of your undertaking—how much is needed to get going, stay afloat and move to the next level—will be spelled out for you. Besides a lack of money or good information, many businesses fail because of poor planning. A written plan will force you to think about how to prepare for opportunities as well as difficulties.

And, like Debbra Lupien, you may find that using your business plan as a working document will help make operational decisions easier.

Survival Tip #25: Distinguish between your needs, wants and absolutes.

Every tool for operating a business can be grouped into these categories. Absolutes are what you legally need to run your business. They can include a checking account, fictitious name filing (also called DBA, which means "doing business as"), state or city permits, professional and occupational licenses, an employer identification number or state sales tax and resale certificates. Your particular absolutes will depend on your location and the type of business you're running. Hawaii, Iowa and Rhode Island, for instance, are the only states that regulate the activities of tattoo parlors and require a special permit to run such establishments. Absolutes are often linked to one another, such as presenting your DBA paperwork to open a bank account or a business license to apply for a resale permit.

A need and an absolute can be confused when it comes to your tools, equipment, services, office space and people resources. Although how much you need will depend in part on the nature of your business, the determining factor should be efficiency. Ask yourself: What do I absolutely need to run an efficient operation? Standard office arsenal includes a combination of telephones and special features or equipment, fax machines, e-mail capabilities, pagers, cell phones or computers and their peripherals. A fax machine in my office is an absolute. Many of my faxes need to be filed, so buying a plain-paper fax was a better efficiency investment. See how the thought process works?

There are a few ways to get your wants. First, you can work towards them. If you're desiring a 200Mhz processor computer or a Herman Miller deluxe chair, then devise a savings plan for those investments. Also, Survival Tip #37 may help advance you more quickly toward your wants.

The key point: Successful bootstrappers avoid indulging in their wants while ignoring their needs and ending up too broke to handle their absolutes.

Survival Tip #26: Track down your city's one-stop business startup package.

Working through the regulatory maze in a community may feel as if you're on an egg hunt. Don't despair. You can simplify the process by contacting the office of your state's department of economic, business or community development.

Most state information packages for startups include state and local operational requirements along with contact information. The primary benefit of these packages is that they take the guesswork out of figuring out the legal requirements in your state. They also provide you with links to local Small Business Development Centers, Federal Information Centers and special entrepreneurial training and financing programs. If your area has a one-stop permit filing center, that'll be indicated as well. A one-stop permit filing center allows you to file and pay for all your business licenses or permits through one office—as opposed to running around to several different offices to get everything taken care of. If your city has one, you should take advantage of it.

Packages are usually **free** or available for a nominal fee, but each state's package will vary in substance. One phone call to the Arizona Business Connection or Missouri Business Assistance Center, for instance, will get you a customized package for doing business anywhere in the state. Delaware's business kit includes details on occupational licenses, specifying the types, cost and renewal schedules. Washington's package includes a schedule of **free** business information workshops along with the *Business Resource Directory: For Financial and Technical Assistance*. Some packages will even include a how-to resource and business plan guides.

You can also contact a "first-stop" business information center. There may one directly in your city or in another part of your state (you can check the government listings in your phone book). A first-stop office can provide (by phone or fax or in person) information about licensing, permits, your particular business type and running a business in your state in general.

Beginning your search in reverse—starting on a state level and working your way down—can connect you to more information and resources. Plus, it can give you an overview on doing business throughout the state, which may come in handy should you decide to expand or relocate. So, how should you begin tracking down your centralized source? Turn to this book's Appendix (the Directory of State Resources for Small Businesses, which begins on page 237)—I've started the legwork for you!

Survival Tip #27: Aim to legitimize yourself on every level.

As mentioned in the previous tip, you may believe that finding out all the legal requirements for running your business is a daunting endeavor. Or perhaps you're reluctant to file the necessary applications and pay the required fees because of the expense. Or maybe you feel you'll never get caught. Then again, you might not even realize you have violated a regulation (see Survival Tip #30). Whatever your reasons, if you operate a business without obtaining all the permits or licenses in a jurisdiction that requires them, you're running an illegitimate business, one that does not comply with governing regulations.

You may have to prove your business's legitimacy when you least expect it. For example, a person whose first and last name are included in the name of his operation—"John Doe Fitness Training Service"—isn't legally required to make a fictitious name filing (see Survival Tip #25). John Doe can open a business checking account and start receiving payments for his fitness services. But the city in which he lives may classify a personal training service as one that needs a business license. John Doe may be tempted to bypass the requirement because he already has a business checking account, plus he provides workout services to individuals who probably won't ask to see a license. But let's say an opportunity to lead in-house workout sessions for the employees of XYZ Corporation comes along. If the corporation needs to see John's business license, he could lose out on the opportunity.

Companies, large and small, are carefully scrutinizing who they do business with. No business wants to get caught misclassifying workers as independent contractors and face the IRS's costly penalties (see Survival Tip #121 and #122). If you get caught in the middle of a reclassification battle, you come out a loser, too. You'll lose tax deductions, your credibility and clients' business.

Your illegitimacy may never become so obvious as when you start working with government agencies or corporate vendor programs, attempt to have your business certified as a woman- or minority-owned firm or try to claim your prize in a business contest. Part of proving that you have a legitimate, independent business begins with creating a paper trail, which may include any of the following documents:

- Proof of ethnicity and citizenship or permanent residency.

- Equipment rental and purchase agreements.

- Management service or lease agreements.

- Applicable licenses or permits.

- Bank signature card.

- Fictitious business name filing.

- Tax forms with Schedule C attachments for itemizing the expenses of your operation against the profits of the business.

- Proof of capital invested.

If you've been winging it, it'll be difficult to obtain this information on a moment's notice!

Further, consumers are advised to verify that the contractors they hire have insurance protection before they begin any work. Companies outsourcing work are adopting this practice, as well, and requiring their suppliers to have liability insurance coverage before they will even shake hands with them. In light of this, you should make it a priority to thoroughly research the insurance coverage requirements for your type of business (see Survival Tip #29).

This is also important if you become involved with a "virtual corporation," a group of independent professionals who work together on a specific project and disband once its over. More independent businesses are leveraging the talents of many by teaming up and forming virtual corporations. They take advantage of big-dollar projects without the official ties and commitments of actually running a corporation. These collaborative efforts help independents obtain larger and more profitable projects. But if you, as an independent professional, haven't obtained the necessary insurance coverage (such as liability or errors and omissions), the whole team could possibly lose the project. The reputation of the whole team is at stake.

Don't allow your negligence to disqualify you or others from opportunities. Additional ways to legitimize your business include building a multiple customer base (see Survival Tip #98) and maintaining a business identity. One way to accomplish the latter is by becoming incorporated (see the next Survival Tip).

Survival Tip #28: Pick the business structure that'll best manage your liabilities.

Your legal structure—sole proprietorship, partnership, corporation, Limited Liability Company—can make a big difference in how you pay taxes, handle lawsuits or dissolve or pass on the business. A sole proprietorship is simple to organize, and you, as the owner, have complete control over the business and its profits—which are filed as part of your personal tax income. You also assume all risks and obligations of the business, making your personal assets attachable to cover debts and liabilities. Unless your heirs decide to carry it on, the business ceases when you do.

Two or more people can join together and contribute money, property, labor or skills to form a partnership. Each partner shares in the profits, losses and obligations of the business. So, if your partner makes a bad deal, you carry the baggage, too. You'll both pay personal income tax on your share of the profits. You should have a written partnership agreement, stipulating how the business shall be run, decision-making authority, distribution of monies and provisions for continuing should one partner die or want out. Otherwise, should a legal or dissolvement dispute arise between partners, your formation will be governed, in most states, by the Uniform Partnership Act, which states that each partner shares equally in the profits regardless of the contribution.

The characteristics of incorporation: Your business operates as a separate entity; you're granted more liability protection because you're not personally responsible for the business's debts; you're taxed differently; shares of stock can be bought or sold much easier than in a partnership, making it easier to pass the corporation along to the next generation. Required formalities of a corporation include electing officers, keeping separate records and filing separate tax returns. There are two forms of incorporation. Under a standard (or C) corporation, business income is taxed twice—at corporate rate and your salary rate. However, with a Subchapter S, dubbed a small business corporation, you only pay taxes on a personal level.

The new option on the block is Limited Liability Company (LLC). Available in most states, LLCs give the liability protection of a corporation without the double taxation of a C corporation. But the IRS guidelines are ambiguous and in some jurisdictions LLCs are taxed twice, wiping out one of their main benefits.

Before you choose a business structure, make sure you understand the short- and long-term implications of your decision. *Choosing a Business Entity in the 1990's,* a **free** guide from Coopers & Lybrand, is one helpful resource to consult (see page 66 for ordering information). Also, you should consult a qualified professional.

Survival Tip #29: Safeguard your future with insurance.

Your business can be crumbled by a lawsuit or natural disaster, especially when you don't have adequate insurance coverage. Sean Mooney, of the Insurance Information Institute, recommends that all businesses consider five basic types of insurance: property, liability, business interruption, life, disability and workers' compensation. Ask yourself: "What can put me out of business?" If your product touches the public, there's a potential for liability lawsuits. If you have high property exposure, you'll need coverage to recoup from perils that result in losses of inventory or other assets. When unthinkable events affect your operation, business interruption insurance will cover your income for an extended period of time. If you work from home, you'll need additional riders or special coverage beyond your homeowner's policy limits.

A standard business owner's policy (BOP) will typically cover you for property, liability and business interruption. BOP plans vary widely in cost, coverage and exclusions. Some plans, for example, cover named perils, all risks or risks tailored to the industry type. Although BOPs weren't originally designed for people who work from home, home-basers can get full BOP or specialty coverage. Under CNA Insurance Companies' HomeWork endorsement, for instance, the scope of your coverage expands. The business property limits are comparable to your personal property limits, plus you pick up off-premises and product liability exposures.

Be sure any policy you buy is providing you with adequate coverage based on your business type, setup or size. You may need to have special clauses written for employee dishonesty or other crime/theft incidences. Businesses in which "errors and omissions" or malpractice could result in litigation should investigate getting coverage in addition to the standard BOP coverage. Partnerships and corporations should consider "key man" coverage. It insures the lives of principals, buying you time to reorganize or replace the person or purchase his or her interest. These coverages, along with life, disability, workers' compensation and business auto, are sold separately from BOP policies and each other (see Survival Tip #116 for health insurance).

Begin your coverage search by talking with an experienced agent. It's important to work with someone who has expertise in your situation. Your homeowner's insurance agent may not be very conversant on a BOP policy. You can get referrals from your colleagues. Your industry or trade association may also be able to provide you with sources as well as offer coverage to its members. The Small Office/Home Office Association, for instance, has BOP coverage available through its benefit provider, ITT Hartford. Insurance companies, like most industry suppliers, are competing for small businesses' dollars, so you're bound to find a good deal when you shop around.

Survival Tip #30: Be aware of other legalities that affect your operation.

When I received an invoice from my graphic designer, I thought the tacked-on sales tax was an error. It wasn't. Since the service and labor cost resulted in the creation of tangible personal property, Got-A-Vision Graphics was required to collect the tax. Even if your business doesn't sell a tangible product, you, too, may be required to make the collection. If I was surprised by the charge, imagine how you'll feel to discover that you should have been collecting it from day one—and that the money's still due. This is one of many legalities where ignorance will not exempt you from compliance.

Governing regulations go beyond your basic license or permit. If you're running a mail-order firm, for example, your business must comply with the Federal Trade Commission's (FTC) Mail Order Rule. Unless you state otherwise in an ad or order form, you're required to ship an order within 30 days after you receive a properly completed order. Under federal warranty law, you can also get into hot water misusing "satisfaction" or "money back" guarantees—saying that merchandise can be returned unconditionally and then refusing to honor your promise. Another example: The California Business and Professions Code requires catalogers to include in all their mailing information the true address where their business is conducted.

Start your search with the licensing bureau, asking for a copy of the business and professions code. Order compliance guidelines for your type of business from the local State Board of Equalization and the FTC's *Best Sellers*, a listing of **free** publications that explain laws governing business practices. Industry and trade associations can offer you some pointers, as well as "how to run your type of business" books. It's an exhausting process, but you'll save money and possible heartache.

Survival Tip #31: Let Uncle Sam educate you.

Part of running a legitimate business is complying with Internal Revenue Service (IRS) regulations. Recordkeeping is the number-one nagging problem for small business owners, according to Barbara Jenkins, director, the IRS's Small Business Affairs Office (SBAO). You'll need to invest in a system that allows you to track sources of income, expenses, inventory and payroll. When you're working on a shoestring budget, recordkeeping becomes even more important. One, you'll have a clearer picture of your financial position; two, every saved receipt could translate into tax deductions; and three, you'll avoid having your profits wiped out by late penalties because you were too disorganized to file the payroll taxes on time.

The IRS has a variety of **free** programs and information that can help you get set up properly. Even if you use an accounting professional, attending a Small Business Tax Education Program (STEP) workshop is well worth your time. You'll get information on starting a business, recordkeeping, preparing business tax returns, self-employment tax issues and employment taxes. The program also maintains a **free** lending library of films and videotapes on a variety of subjects and publishes the newsletter *Tax Tips: A Newsletter for New Businesses*.

The SBAO's job is to recommend changes to the federal tax system as they affect small businesses. In 1995, for example, the IRS commissioner and SBAO director conducted seven town meetings with small business professionals across the country. The attendees voiced that there needed to be a centralized way to get information on recordkeeping requirements. In response to their feedback, the IRS created publication 583, *Starting a Business and Keeping Records*. The SBAO does not handle individual taxpayer problems; however, they are interested in hearing about tax law, regulation and policy concerns raised by small businesses.

Survival Tip #32: Pick a name you can live and grow with— and that's your own.

Your business name can give you a competitive advantage. Effective names establish your marketplace presence, convey what you do and create a memorable impression. Clever names, like Glove Me Tender, turn a half-second glance into a three-second look-see. First, you need to be clear on what you would like the name to accomplish. When a lot of people do what you do, you'll need a name that helps people remember you. If the focus is to ensure that people understand what you're offering, you'll need to create a name that complements the word or phrase identifier. If you are well-known in your community or field, then incorporating your own name can work well.

Begin the naming process by pinpointing each key characteristic, benefit or personality trait of your business. This would include the range or specialization of your inventory or qualities that customers appreciate such as skill, friendliness or innovation. Hire Expectations, Inc., Affordable Electronics Store, Accurate Patent Search and Rapid Plumbing are effective monikers. You should also consider names that inspire confidence. If you needed a resume prepared from scratch, who would you be inclined to call just by the mere reading of the name— Archer Resume Service or Resume Wizard? Or what if you had an arduous research project—Aspens Systems Corporation or Research Done Write! ?

You may find naming inspiration in words' origins or shades of meaning through sources such as *The Synonym Finder* or *Dictionary of Word Roots*. Merriam-Webster's Language Research Service will answer questions about words **free** of charge (see page 69 for contact information).

You'll need to be thorough in checking out names already in use or similar to your ideas. The last thing you want is to be forced to stop using your name because it belongs to someone else or to have yours confused with that of another business. Leaf through library or public resources such as phone books, DBA filings, industry and trade association directories and *The Trademark Register of the United States*. Also, think about how you plan for the business to grow. Professional Typing Service may require a name change when you begin offering an array of secretarial or office support services. You want the public to be responsive to your name, so be sure to test it out on colleagues or associates.

There are some basic do's and don'ts. Avoid names that are difficult to spell or pronounce, too short to make sense or too long to remember or that have some introspective meaning that only you understand and that confuses people. Aim for alphabetical positioning when your business is fueled by yellow pages inquiries.

You should consider a state or federal trademark when the entire identity of your business is wrapped up in the name, you plan to do business nationally or globally or you plan to franchise your business.

Survival Tip #33: Operate your home suite on the right side of the law.

Working from home is not a fad. The work-at-home-universe continues to swell every year, with its size estimated at more than 20 million. Big-business notables like Hewlett-Packard, Hallmark, Microsoft, Apple Computer and Hershey Foods all started out as home-based businesses. Today, there are fewer barriers to setting up a home office. The affordability of essential technologies such as computers, software, cellular phones and access to the Internet make it easier for you to run a competitive operation from home. Whether your home is a starting base or choice destination, there are a few things to consider before hanging out a shingle.

Don't neglect to check out local zoning ordinances. Home businesses are prohibited in some communities or governed by local regulations. Ordinance guidelines may affect your daily customer-visitor count, square footage space allowance, permissibility of non-resident employees, hours of operation, advertising your home address and the type of business activities you conduct. You can find out how your property is zoned by contacting the zoning board, building inspector, planning department or city clerk's office. If you live in an area with covenants that regulate the neighborhood, be sure home business activity is permitted. Even if a city's zoning ordinance permits home business activity, it can be overridden by bylaws of a planned community or townhome or condominium association. Study the information and proceed from there. Your compliance may mean operating from a P.O. box—working solely with no visitors—or using a corporate identity program (see Survival Tip #34). Also, the American Association of Home-Based Businesses offers guidance on how to comply with local regulations.

Next, you should consider if a home suite will professionally accommodate your business choice. Is your work space set up so you can privately meet with clients or is it mixed in with the other furnishings and activities of your home life? Do you have adequate space for you or employees to work efficiently? Working from home may require that you to invest in a separate entrance, remodel parts of your house, meet at clients' offices or make other a-la-carte arrangements (see Survival Tip #34).

Survival Tip #34: Consider other "suite-ID" options.

If your business dictates a "full-floor" tenant look, then check out executive suites. A low-end amenities package can get you an interior office (no window), meeting room access, telephone answering, word processing, fax, photocopy and courier service. Prices, of course, will depend on whether you need to be uptown, downtown or somewhere in between. Most facilities offer deals by the hour, day, week, month or year. By using a suite's services, equipment and furniture, you may be able to get up and running faster while keeping your initial capital investment minimal.

The nurturing environment of a business incubator is another option. These facilities house new and growing business under one roof at below-market rates, along with access to technical assistance, counseling and a support network. The amenities are similar to an executive suite. Incubators give you an opportunity to save money through shared costs with other tenants. At the Pasadena Enterprise Center, for example, you can get a 200 square foot space, including services, for $400 per month. But cash in hand won't guarantee your entry. You'll need to submit an application, supporting documents and a business plan (see Survival Tips #24 and #27) and be interviewed by a selection committee. Many incubators and executive suites now offer corporate identity plans, providing you with a professional address, telephone secretary and conference room by appointment (this could be an alternative for someone with restrictive zoning laws).

Then there's always the shameless route. Back in his salad days, Joel McIntosh of Waco, Texas, didn't have a nice place to meet with clients. What the education-market book and magazine publisher did have was a relationship with a local school. The university's board room, an impressive place free of charge, became host to McIntosh's meetings with out-of-towners. Now, McIntosh's firm has reached million-dollar status, and he's not ashamed to meet folks in his current digs.

Survival Tip #35: Focus on professionalism rather than looking like a big shot.

You should always aim to present your business as a skilled, efficient and reliable operation. That's the mark of a true professional. You should focus on setting up your office accordingly. It's the lack of professionalism that has many businesses plodding along. They could, however, operate on another level with a little tweaking.

Professionalism includes visible and invisible impressions. A dirty or disorganized work space or a storefront with a dingy sign all work in souring others' impression of you. Snazzy stationery or fancy furnishings do not cover up unprofessionalism for very long. Amateurish work, poor phone presentation or follow-through systems or overbooking clients can cost you business. Professionalism means operating with some standards of conduct and having the necessary tools in place to support you. A professional operation has adequate phone lines or services that enable clients to receive a business-like greeting and leave messages, faxes or electronic mail hassle-free. The use of office and computer equipment and software will allow you to produce quality work in a time- and cost-efficient manner. Your focus isn't on showing off the mere fact you're in business, but showing that you own a *professional* business.

When you deliver what you promise *when* you promise, you'll inspire customer confidence in you. As you set up your office, take time out to consider the resources and materials you'll need in place to give you a competitive advantage. Any money you spend today will give you a professional advantage tomorrow.

Survival Tip #36: Design your collateral around the identity of your business.

Contrary to popular belief, you should not fall into the trap of creating an "image." An image can be expensive to maintain because you must continually finance the trappings associated with the facade. Also, when you decide on a business "image," you run the risk of misrepresenting yourself to the marketplace. Remember, people do business with those they like, trust or have confidence in. If prospects see that you're not who your image portrays you to be, you'll lose credibility and possible sales. Before you spend a dime on stationery, you should think about how to communicate your true identity.

Every business has one. It's a quality or characteristic that sets you apart from your competition. It often stems from the personality of the business or its owner. In his seminars, self-esteem expert Bill McGrane encourages participants to anchor themselves in their unique factor. Here's how it worked for one entrepreneur. After being cheated out of commissions by an employer, a sales executive in the printing industry decided to open up his own shop. His firm produced cutting edge annual reports for Fortune 500 companies. This savvy salesman, however, needed to distinguish himself in a competitive market. Through the personal history intake in McGrane's workshop, it was revealed that he was also a talented drummer who began playing to deal with certain pains in his life. The tie-in to his business: an instrument logo with the service slogan "We help you drum up business."

Next, you should focus on the presentation of your message, choosing an effective graphic presentation that'll sell. Your package will include the colors, paper, typeface and layout you use. It's important to avoid graphical choices inappropriate to your industry or that'll steer business away from you. For example, studies have shown that the color blue is an appetite suppressant—just ask the M&M's folks. Begin by collecting cards from other professionals and comparing them against your ideas. You can also use paper samples from a local self-service dealer to begin experimenting with some concepts. Don't rush through the creative process. The more time you spend on developing your graphic presentation, the longer you'll be able to use the materials in your business.

Resources that'll help you achieve a coordinated look: *Color Selling: Using Color Psychology to Increase Sales* by Lea Brit (Spectran Publishers) and International Paper's *Pocket Pal: A Graphic Arts Production Handbook* (see page 69 for more information). Using resources like these as a primer will help you work more cost-effectively with graphics and printing professionals. You'll also save money by supplying a printer with your own paper and using a graphic artist who lays out your designs on a computer.

Survival Tip #37: Use out-of-the-way sources to buy quality furniture and equipment.

Your shoestring budget may not allow you to mirror the "ultimate office" as pictured in a magazine, but you can certainly try to mimic it. You should always buy quality merchandise. Every business is fueled by a primary work tool. For a manufacturer it may be a piece of machinery; for me it's my computer. By first determining your primary instrument, you'll be clearer on what the best sources are for getting quality at a good price. In some instances, a brand new tool is more feasible but can be supported by other used or refurbished items. For example, buying a new computer system and printer with expandable memory, yet purchasing used furniture to hold that equipment, would be wise.

Consider some out-of-the-way vendor sources. For example, computer shows offer you extraordinary deals on new PCs (see Survival Tip #38). Discontinued merchandise is another option. Local office furniture outlets, superstores or catalogs offer deals on clearance items. If you opt to buy discontinued equipment, make sure that you'll be able to get replacement parts in the future. Refurbished items can be bought at a fraction of the original cost. Two top-of-the-line furniture manufacturers offer some more affordable options: Miller-SQA's AsNew and Steelcase's Revest have launched separate divisions that sell restored furniture repurchased from customers. Recycled furniture dealers are popping up all over the country. They buy, clean up and resell used furniture. Check out the National Office Products Association's Web page (www.recyclefurn.org) for a listing of dealers nationwide.

Looking for industry-specific equipment or dependable, standard-use items, such as store fixtures? Scan your local paper for auctions. Facilities managers coordinate events for downsized corporations and the SBA and other government agencies handle repossessed items. And then there's leasing companies. Besides being a source to finance a major purchase, many companies sell expired-lease furniture from their warehouse. Check the yellow pages for a local firm.

Survival Tip #38: Buy a computer that you won't outgrow tomorrow.

A computer can be your best or worst business investment—it depends on how you go about it. Unless you plan to buy the latest annual release, accept the fact that whatever you buy will soon be considered dated. But outdated doesn't mean useless. By creating a technology plan, you can ensure that you're purchasing a system that's right for your business today as well as tomorrow.

Your plan should be built around the answers to these questions. What do I need the computer to help me accomplish? Possible answers: to streamline work activities, handle tasks in-house or provide better service. What type of software and accessories will support my objectives? This area is critical because it will dictate your processor and modem speed, memory capabilities, disk storage, printer and monitor choices. If you plan to run graphic-intensive programs or industry-customized software, you'll need a speedy system that can run the applications smoothly. Also, be sure your application choices match your operating systems environment—Windows, Macintosh or DOS. Remember to think forward. Your needs may change as your business grows. Will the system, for example, be able to accommodate network software or multimedia programs? Equipment with expandable slots and memory upgrade capabilities will allow you to grow with a system without having to reinvest from scratch. Use this information as you begin to shop around for a system and deal with a salesperson.

There are a few ways to get your hands on a dream system. Catalogs, local computer superstores and Home Shopping Channels all offer competitively priced equipment. My favorite: shopping at a computer marketplace. They offer new, brand-name hardware, software and peripherals at wholesale prices. Many of the vendors will price-haggle, especially when it's a cash offer. These shows are open to the public and advertised in local newspapers and computer journals. Used computers are another option. Dealers such as Boston Computer Exchange or RTI sell used or refurbished equipment; some of which come with warranties. You may find what you need from an outlet, such as the IBM PC Factory Outlet, which sells overstocked, refurbished, new and withdrawn equipment.

Whatever shopping avenue you choose, you should comparison-shop for the best deal and clearly understand the usage potential as well as limitations of any system. This will prevent you from buying equipment that'll quickly outlive its usefulness in your business.

5 OFFICE SETUP TIPS TO REMEMBER

1. Keep your eyes peeled for nonterminable contracts. Let's say you lease equipment or enter into other contract service agreements. There may be a contract clause that locks you into paying for something even if you decide not use it anymore. Small business attorney Sarah Calvert of Calvert & Associates in Fairfax, Virginia, says there are vendors who prey on new startups because they know most startup business owners don't understand contractual language and usually review the contracts without legal assistance. Just because a contract has printed terms doesn't mean it's not negotiable. If you're uncomfortable with contract negotiations, consider using a legal professional—even it means you have to barter or join a prepaid legal plan.

2. Test-drive items before you buy them. Would you buy a car without taking it for a spin? Treat your equipment, software, furniture and other items with the same attitude. Help salespeople earn their keep and ask them to walk you through a demonstration of a product. Touch, feel and adjust furnishings as they will be set up in your office. Higher-priced software sometimes comes with working models which allow you to test it at no cost, so always ask for them. You can buy yourself some testing time by understanding the return policy periods on your purchases and actually using the merchandise during this time. Also, make sure stationery paper is compatible with your in-house printer; some paper is too textured and doesn't print cleanly on laser printers. Get samples from your printing company and do a test run on the printer before you make your final paper selection.

3. Make investments with your tax deductions in mind. Under the Section 179 deduction, you take a sizable deduction on your taxes for business computers, office furniture and other equipment. It's important to educate yourself on the eligibility, limits and exclusions of your business expenses. By understanding tax deductions, you can strategize when and how you make purchases for your business, thus positioning yourself to stretch out your dollars.

4. Don't ignore the importance of ergonomically friendly workspace. You'll be logging long hours in your business, so it's wise to invest in tools to help you work smarter and prevent injuries. One bootstrapper regrets not spending more time thinking through her office setup—she's unhappy with her desk and the overall setup of her workspace. Your work space should be well-lit, and your furniture and equipment should be designed to provide maximum comfort. Ergonomic product sources: AliMed Ergonomics (800-225-2610) and Ergosource (800-969-4374), or for safety information, call the National Institute of Occupational Safety and Health (800-356-4674).

5. Avoid being a sole proprietor by default. This business structure form is truly the best for many small businesses. However, the more money you make, the more people you deal with and the more assets you accumulate, you should consider other options for protecting yourself. When you start off and aren't making much money, it may seem implausible to worry about such things. But as you grow, do yourself a favor and reevaluate the benefits of other structure options.

Survival Tip #39: Conserve your cash through bartering.

Bartering your know-how can be the key to valuable products and services for your business. You can preserve your cash by swapping your services or wares with other businesses. There are two ways to use this ancient trade method. One is to join an organized bartering exchange—an organization of professionals who trade or exchange products and services in lieu of cash. For an annual membership fee, you have access to a ready network of offerings from office supplies to printing to legal counsel.

Here's how it works: When someone uses your services or products, you get credited in your account for the purchase. For example, if I charge $100 an hour for my small business coaching services and another member of the exchange comes in for a two-hour session, I will have earned a $200 credit in my account. I can use the credit toward something from that person's product line or from anyone else's in the exchange.

The organization keeps a record of your exchange activities with others in the network. You receive monthly statements detailing who used your offering and whose offerings you used. Records also indicate how many trade dollars, or credits, you have available toward other members' products or services. The organization will also send you a 1099-B form to file with the IRS, which considers bartering a form of income. You are required by law to file this form. (If you barter on your own, independent of an exchange, you will be responsible for keeping records of your exchanges and reporting them to the IRS.) I have listed two organized bartering exchanges in the Bootstrapper's Follow-up File for this chapter—the International Reciprocal Trade Association and Itex.

Before you join an exchange, be clear on who's in the exchange, exactly what's available and payable commissions. Make sure there's a proportional number of members in each category. Finally, consider whether the offerings are fairly priced.

Another way to swap your services or products with other businesses is to solicit deals independently. A partnership firm, for example, subletted warehouse space from a soda manufacturer. Their deal: stuffing rubber washers in bottle caps for four hours daily in lieu of rent. William DeNeen got extra mileage from a paid placement advertising his new business, TELE-COR, a telecommunications maintenance coordination service in Waterford, Connecticut. He negotiated with the paper to run his "Residents in Business" profile for two extra weeks—with minimal editing—in exchange for six telecommunication service calls. With her "no fear in askin'" attitude, Got-A-Vision Graphics owner Julia Tavis swapped desktop publishing services for free admission to 10 chamber of commerce mixers. Again, independent deal makers are still required to comply with IRS reporting guidelines.

If you're making deals independently, you should focus on exchanges that ideally suit you and another. Remember, your exchanges aren't being credited toward a network of other choices. Also, be specific in your arrangements and discuss any restrictions up front. If you choose to barter, you should start off slowly and leave yourself room to cash out quickly should you decide trading isn't for you.

A BAKER'S TALE

Becky and Mike Busath's entrepreneurial inspiration came from watching their friends' rags-to-riches success. Their two friends went from selling everything they owned to open a franchise business to being able to buy amenities they had never previously been able to afford. Becky had always loved baking bread, and Mike had always wanted to own a business. The couple married their two desires together and decided to pursue opening a specialty whole-grain bread store in San Antonio. After investigating a franchise bakery, the Busaths became dismayed by the franchise and ongoing royalty fees. Their research showed that the trend back to fresh, milled breads was growing, their targeted community had households with money to spend and there were no other specialty bakeries in the area. Their own independent setup had promise.

Still, the Busaths needed the business training that a franchise would offer. So, they struck a deal with the California-based Campbell Baking & Milling, one of the leading independent bakeries in the country. For a one-time fee, Campbell would provide the Busaths with recipes, three weeks of training, a vendor list for the product and a year of ongoing support. The Busaths found a space not far from their home. What's more, the property's leasing agent was anxious to get a foot-traffic business such as theirs into his center and agreed to pay for 100 percent of the build-out (the remodeling of the space into a bakery). It appeared that Becky and Mike were on the right track until everything started to go wrong.

The city business bureau didn't clearly explain to the Busaths the compliance regulations for a food establishment. Becky mistakenly called out the building inspector before any work had been done on the interior rather than waiting until the facility was ready to welcome the public. (She didn't know that only the first two visits of a building inspector are free.) Other inspections followed later, each one bringing bad news: Either the completed work didn't pass or other new work was needed. The build-out tab began to escalate. Since their leasing contract didn't address the specifics of additional work, the lessor began to pass the costs onto the Busaths. Becky made another costly mistake: She didn't understand that the cost of their food permits ran in accordance with the number of employees. Becky paid a higher fee when she could have saved money by reducing some of her part-timers.

In spite of all this, the Stone Ground Bread Company did open as scheduled, and it is a thriving enterprise today. Becky's advice to other firms:

1. **Ask a lot of questions, even if they seem dumb.** (Had she been more persistent with the city, she could have worked more cohesively with the inspectors.)

2. **Make sure any contracts you sign have details spelled out.** (The Busaths' build-out specifications should have been detailed more thoroughly.)

3. **Only work with licensed and bonded professionals whose reputation you can check out.** (They were stuck with the real estate agency's contractors, many of whom didn't know what they were doing.)

Bootstrapper's Follow-up File

Achieving the Competitive Edge Through Office Ergonomics, Quill Corporation, 800-789-6640; Web address: www.quillcorp.com. A **free** guide on setting up an ergonomically-friendly office.

American Association of Home-Based Businesses (AAHBA), P.O. Box 10023, Rockville, MD 20849-0023; 800-447-9710 (202-310-3130 in the Washington, D.C. area); Web address: www.aahbb.org.

Auction information: *How to Buy Surplus Personal Property*, a **free** guide from the Defense Department, DRMS, National Sales Office, P.O. Box 5275-DDRC, 2163 Airways Blvd., Memphis, TN 38114-5210; the Department of Treasury Public Auction Line, 703-273-7373; the Internal Revenue Service's 24-hour Auction Hot Line (call your local IRS office for the number in your area); and the Small Business Administration (call your local office and speak with the liquidation officer).

Best Sellers, Federal Trade Commission, Public Reference, Room 130, Washington, DC 20580-0001; Web address: www.ftc.gov. A complete list of hundreds of the FTC's **free** consumer and business publications.

Boston Computer Exchange, 800-262-6399. Maintains a database of used equipment for sale and serves as a matchmaker for buyers and sellers.

Business Plans Handbook: A Compilation of Actual Business Plans Developed by Small Businesses Throughout North America, Gale Research, 800-347-4253. A library reference guide.

Choosing a Business Entity in the 1990's, Coopers & Lybrand, National Tax Services, 1800 M St. NW, Washington DC 20077-5984. A **free**, 71-page guide explaining the advantages/disadvantages of business structures.

Compac Works, 800-318-6919. Sells quality reconditioned computers at outlet prices.

Developing Your Business Plan Workshop, Small Business Administration, Web address: sbaonline.sba.gov. A **free** business program you can download from the "Starting Your Business" section of SBA's Web site. Shareware programs for starting a business also available.

Environmental Protection Agency Small Business Office, 800-368-5888 (703-305-5938 in the Washington, D.C. area); Web address: www.epa.gov. Provides resource materials and information to help your business comply with applicable EPA regulations.

Ergonomics and Office Design, Haworth, Inc., 800-344-2600. A **free**, 38-page publication and computer disk which contains ergonomic and ADA information that can help you adjust your office environment for more comfort and greater productivity.

Executive Suite Association, 800-237-4741. Provides referrals to facilities in your area.

First Step Business Plan, National Business Association, 800-456-0440. A software program offering a simple format to help develop a working plan for your business. $5.

Glossary of Leasing Terms, Advanta Business Services Corporation, 800-255-0022. A **free** guide to help you understand the language used when negotiating a lease.

Hewlett-Packard Advantage Center, 800-637-7740. Sells remanufactured business computer systems and printers.

IBM PC Factory Outlet, 800-426-7015. Sells overstocked, refurbished or new and withdrawn systems at 15-25 percent of original price.

Insurance Survival Guides, Insurance Information Institute, 110 William St., New York, NY 10038. **Free** guides that provide valuable information to help protect your business: *Insuring Your Home Business, Insuring Your Business Against a Catastrophe* and *Insurance for Your House and Personal Possessions*. Send SASE with first-class postage for one guide; add 23 cents for each additional guide.

Insuring Your Business: What You Need to Know to Get the Best Insurance Coverage for Your Business by Sean Mooney (Insurance Information Institute Press, 1992); 800-331-9146 (ask for publications department). $22.50.

Internal Revenue Service, Taxpayer Education Coordinator, 800-829-1040. Provides information on the Small Business Tax Education Program (STEP). Other helpful IRS resources (call 800-TAX-FORM to order, or download from www.irs.ustreas.gov): *Your Business Tax Kit; Starting a Business and Keeping Records* (Publication 583); *Tax Guide for Small Business* (Publication 334); *Taxable and Nontaxable Income* (Publication 525) (information on bartering); *Business Use of Your Home* (Publication 587); *Free Tax Help on Video* (Publication 1237); and *Guide to Free Tax Services* (Publication 910).

International Facility Management Association, 1 E. Greenway Plaza, Suite 1100, Houston, TX 77046-0194; 713-623-4362; fax: 713-623-6124. Provides used office furniture information.

International Reciprocal Trade Association, 6305 Hawaii Court, Alexandria, VA 22312; fax: 703-914-9677. Send SASE or fax request for a **free** list of bartering exchanges in your state.

IRS Small Business Affairs Office, C:SB-Room 1211-ICC, 1111 Constitution Ave. NW, Washington, DC 20224. Works with other government agencies, trade associations, small business owners and their representatives to address ways the IRS can better serve the needs of entrepreneurs.

Itex, 800-213-5496; faxback: 800-426-5777; Web address: www.itex.net. A nationwide organized bartering network.

KeyLease Plus, Inc., 800-800-3671. Provides small businesses with flexible leasing options for equipment.

Lighting in the Healthy Office, Steelcase, 800-777-0330. A **free**, 17-page publication that discusses how lighting affects performance and productivity. Also includes instructions for adjusting the lighting in your office.

Major Laws Administered by the U.S. Department of Labor Which Affect Business, U.S. Department of Labor, Room S-1004, 200 Constitution Ave. NW, Washington, DC 20210. A **free** guide with short summaries of major laws which impose requirements on business. Send a self-addressed mailing label with your request.

Merriam-Webster Language Research Service, P.O. Box 281, Springfield, MA 01102. Provides **free** answers to questions about history or origin of words. Send SASE to receive more information about service.

Miller-SQA AsNew, 800-253-2733. A line of restored office furniture.

National Business Incubation Association, 20 E. Circle Dr., Suite 190, Athens, OH 45701; 614-593-4331; fax: 614-593-1996; Web address: www.nbia.org. Provides information on incubators that may be located in your community and an information sheet on how to evaluate an incubator.

National Directory of State Business Licensing and Regulation, Gale Research, 800-347-4253. A library reference guide comprised of licensing and regulation information for more than 100 businesses.

National Insurance Consumer Hotline, 800-942-4242. Answers questions about various insurance matters, offers referrals for consumer complaints and sends out **free** consumer brochures.

National Office Products Association, 800-542-NOPA. Publishes a directory of office furniture recyclers. $10.

Nolo News, Nolo Press, 800-992-6656; Web address: www.nolo.com. A quarterly newsletter of legal information and updates from this publisher of self-help legal books and software. Two-year subscription: $12.

Plan Write 4.0 for Windows, Business Resource Software, 800-423-1228 or 512-251-7541; Web address: www.brs-inc.com. Business plan software.

Pocket Pal: A Graphic Arts Production Handbook, Print Resources Group, P.O. Box 770067, Memphis, TN 38177. A 233-page guide. $7.25.

Pre-Paid Legal Services Inc., 800-775-7582; Web address: www.pplsi.com. Offers small business plans for handling a menu of legal situations, including contract or document review, incorporation, partnerships, intellectual property and more. (Check yellow pages under heading "legal service plans" for similar programs.) Cost: $59/month.

RTI, 800-RTI-TRADE. A computer liquidator; sells used and reconditioned computers.

Small Office/Home Office Association, 888-SOHOA-11; Web address: www.sohoa.com.

Small-Time Operator: How to Start Your Own Small Business, Keep Your Books, Pay Your Taxes, and Stay Out of Trouble by Bernard Kamoroff (Bell Springs Publishing, 1995); 800-515-8050. $17.95 postage pd.

Software for Your Small Business Success; National Business Association, 800-456-0440. This guide teaches you how to choose the right software for your business needs. $2.50.

Staying on the Right Side of Zoning Laws, Home Business Institute, 800-DIAL-HBI. A **free** report on dealing with zoning issues in your community.

Steelcase's Revest, 800-333-9939. A line of restored office furniture.

Tax Tips: A Newsletter for New Business, Internal Revenue Service, Attn: Editor, M:C:DP, 1111 Constitution Ave. NW, Washington, DC 20224; 703-914-9677. A monthly publication for first-time business owners. Send a postcard with your name and address to receive a **free** subscription.

Telecom Made Easy: Money-Saving, Profit-Building Solutions for Home Businesses, Telecommuters and Small Organizations by June Langhoff (Aegis Publishing Group, 1995); 800-828-6961; Web address: www.aegisbooks.com. Filled with tips on how to get the most out of telephone products and services. $19.95.

The Naming Guide: How to Choose a Winning Name for Your Company, Product or Service, The Namestormers, 2811 Declaration Circle, Lago Vista, TX 78645-7523; 512-267-1814. A **free** guide with an abbreviated checklist of steps to follow in developing a new name.

The Official Guide to Buying, Connecting and Using Consumer Electronics Products, Electronic Industries Association/Consumer Electronics Manufacturers Association, 2500 Wilson Blvd., Arlington, VA 22201. A 173-page book guiding readers through the prepurchase and postpurchase phases of making computer and other electronic purchases. $9 plus $6.95 shipping.

Chapter 4

Financing Your Idea

"We never understand how little we need in this world until we know the loss of it."

—Sir James M. Barrie, Scottish playwright
and novelist, *Margaret Ogilvy* (1896)

Survival Tip #40: Be realistic about your options.

The options for a small business startup are limited. It is very difficult for a new startup with no track record to get financing through a traditional lender. The SBA doesn't lend directly to individual businesses anymore; its function is to back or guarantee loans that are made through traditional lenders. So, the average bootstrapper uses piecemeal financing. As a bootstrapper, you will find that your funding puzzle will be influenced by several factors:

- **Discretionary cash:** the amount of money you have that isn't earmarked for other obligations.

- **Personal assets:** your possessions that can be liquidated.

- **Creditworthiness:** your available credit lines or your ability to borrow more.

- **Moneybags connections:** people who'll make you a loan.

- **Character appeal:** people who'll lend you unconventional support based on their belief in you.

There are several ways to piece together your funding puzzle. Dipping into personal accounts or rechanneling wages, bonus or unemployment checks are capital options. Also, foregoing some lifestyle comforts can help your account balances swell. Some people make loans part of their investment portfolio. But remember that well-heeled folks will be more receptive to your asking for a loan if you present it as a business opportunity proposal rather than a beggar's request. And although a small enterprise with no track record will have difficulty securing a commercial bank loan, more banks have begun marketing specialty loans where approval of a one-page application can land you an unsecured credit line or loan ranging from $2,500 to $50,000. Wells Fargo, for instance, has teamed up with the National Association of Women Business Owners (NAWBO) to assist creditworthy females nationwide. If you have a good personal and business credit record and have been in business for two years, you may qualify for a $5,000 to $100,000 loan from this program.

Most business loans do require your business to have been in existence for a while, so tapping your personal credit line may be more appropriate if your business is still in the startup phase. Options could include taking out a home equity loan, borrowing against or liquidating a retirement fund or using a credit card. (Remember to carefully weigh the pros and cons of each of these options before forging ahead. If you pull money from a retirement fund, for example, the penalties and tax liability you incur may not be offset by your business's profit gain. If you use credit, it's important to understand that it's not always easy to juggle the payments. If you decide to pull funds earmarked for something else, make sure that putting them toward your business is a better use of these resources.)

Your possessions may be hidden sources of cash. Selling a car or hosting a neighborhood garage sale can help you raise cash quickly. Lastly, a business can be funded on your personal integrity. The vendor who releases supplies based on a handshake or the landlord who gives you a lease with no money or deposit are financing their confidence in you.

Survival Tip #41: Don't spin your wheels chasing down "free money."

A persistent lie is traveling through the entrepreneurial community: There are millions of dollars in grants available to start a business. This false notion has many talented souls wasting time trying to track down government agencies, private foundations and organizations who will fund their dreams. The truth, however, is that few groups give individuals money to finance a startup.

While researching business grant sources for an article, I became curious about how this myth got started. Well, it started (and continues) with ads, infomercials and books that promise to help you: *Rake in $1,000,000 per year by getting free grants* or *Milk Uncle Sam's free business grant programs*. These ads ask readers to send in money to get information on free money that doesn't really exist. Don't be duped, my friend.

Essentially, the companies that place such ads will provide you with the names of organizations that are listed in directories of foundations and sources of grants. The companies and organizations in these books provide fellowships, scholarships and grant money to other organizations. The majority of the available grant money is really targeted at nonprofit organizations and government agencies, according to Norton Kiritz, president of The Grantsmanship Center in Los Angeles. These groups use the money to fund a variety of special projects such as community revitalization, job training or research. A limited amount of money is granted to individuals for scholarships and financial aid or to fund artistic activities or fellowships.

Now, the reality of what's available to *you*. The well-known Small Business Innovation Research (SBIR) program awards grants to established and qualified enterprises to develop new technologies. The competitive program funds projects that could lead to significant public benefit. For example, Berkeley Systems, creators of the After Dark Screen Saver, received an SBIR award to develop software that helped visually impaired people use Macintoshes. They created "in-Large," a program that made everything on the screen look bigger.

Other options for cash-strapped entrepreneurs include cash awards, prize money or mini-grants offered by a dwindling pool of organizations. Some of the legitimate ones are listed at the end of this chapter. You may find something you're qualified for in Gale Research's *Awards, Honors and Prizes*, a library reference directory of more than 20,000 sources. You should also check various entrepreneurial magazines, such as *Entrepreneur* or *Home Office Computing*. Some of them have their own contests and award programs that come with prizes. Otherwise, read on. This section will show you other funding solutions to consider.

Survival Tip #42: Understand what interests venture capitalists—opportunities with multimillion-dollar potential.

You may be thinking: "If I could just get my hot idea connected with a deep-pocketed financial guru, everything would be okay." Think again—it's not that easy. Venture capitalists—a group of wealthy individuals, government-assisted sources or major financial institutions—are in the business of making equity investments. While they receive thousands of hot propositions annually, they ultimately invest in only a handful. The likelihood of you and their dollars becoming coupled will depend on how closely your opportunity matches the venture fund's goals.

Capitalists generally specialize in one or a few closely related industries; they're interested in opportunities with the potential to become major regional or national concerns and expect to earn 10 times their initial investment in less than 10 years. While some capital funds look for exciting opportunities to kick into high-gear the next America Online, Staples or Federal Express, many invest in household names unknown. Some are interested in startups while others are only interested in those with an established track record. They're not merely your source of funds; they work as part of your management team, bringing hands-on assistance and business experience.

Your business plan will be critical in piquing an investor's interest. A venture capitalist will scrutinize how thoroughly you address the opportunity's potential in your business plan and will also examine the background and skills of those who manage your business to determine if they are capable of making it grow to the level projected in your plan.

If you feel venture capital is an ideal source for your business, you'll need to find the kind that funds the type of opportunity you're offering and grants the dollar amounts you need. Don't spend your time courting a mismatch. You should begin your search locally and branch out from there. Venture capitalists are known to make investments through referrals. You may find some connections through Small Business Investment Companies (SBICs) and venture capital associations.

Survival Tip #43: Match your qualifications with a microloan.

Hundreds of community-based organizations are helping to promote entrepreneurship through micro lending. Private and SBA-backed agencies make loans to qualified individuals from a few hundred dollars to $25,000. The loans can be used for startup, expansion, working capital or equipment or supply purchases. The borrowing criteria is based on the lender's belief in your integrity and the soundness of your idea.

Matching your needs and qualifications with a local lender may be your biggest challenge. The lender programs do not operate under uniform practices. Many of the programs have target audiences, such as women, minorities or low-income groups. Working Capital, for example, lends only to existing businesses in New England's rural areas. Some programs do not impose set income restrictions on borrowers. Their focus may be to stimulate job growth for the community. You'll find that some lenders make loans directly to individuals while others make peer-group loans. In a solidarity circle, people work together to obtain financing, determine the loaning order and influence each other's ability to borrow more based on the group's repayment history. Also, most programs offer you technical assistance, and some may require individuals to complete a business training course as a loan requirement.

Mike Stamler of the SBA public affairs office points out some common misconceptions surrounding the programs:

1. Although women and minorities may be the targeted audience, the programs are open to others, as well.
2. People think the dollar amounts are too minuscule to make a difference, when, in fact, a small cash infusion can be a lifesaver.
3. Your business doesn't have to be full-time to qualify; many of the recipients are running part-time ventures along with regular employment.
4. The money is not a character grant—you will be expected to pay it back.

You can find out if there's a program in your area by contacting your local SBA or economic development office or small business development center.

BOOTSTRAPPIN' MICROLOAN STRATEGIES

It's a misuse of your time to pursue unlikely sources of funding. You can redirect that same effort into creating your own microloan fund. Consider these strategies—they may net you a few hundred to a few thousand dollars in cash or goods:

Cash in on focus groups. Market research groups are always on the prowl for willing participants to evaluate products or services on behalf of their corporate clients. Business owners and entrepreneurs are ideal candidates for many of the products. Marketing consultant Pamela Carden-V. was part of a computer-literate, home-based business owners' group who evaluated multiple-use office equipment. The two- to three-hour sessions pay anywhere from $75 to $150 cash for your time, depending on the group. Interested? Look in the yellow pages for market research firms in your area.

Align yourself with a corporate or government benefactor. If your offering includes the use of special materials, some companies will actually loan or give you items from their product line to support you in your efforts. For example, someone developing an aluminum or energy product could approach respective manufacturers or government agencies. In exchange, you would acknowledge the use of their product on your labeling, promotional materials and so forth. Approach a company's public relations or community outreach department with your request. Prepare a presentation letter explaining what you're doing and how both of you would benefit from the arrangement. Make it clear that you're not asking for money but for product or material support.

Call in your deposit markers. Retrace any security deposits you've made. If they were refundable after a specific time period, you should follow up to get them—requesting cash instead of credit. A law in Los Angeles, for instance, requires landlords to make interest payments at least every five years on security deposits. Depending on the deposit amount and interest rate, you could have a nice chunk of change.

Take advantage of home computer loan programs. Many employers offer interest-free loans to their workers to buy computer equipment. The loans are usually paid back through payroll deductions. This could be an ideal way to buy equipment for a new or existing business. Check with your spouse's or loved one's employer.

Demand compensation for others' mistakes. In 1995, Pacific Bell took out ads explaining to customers that they were conducting billing audits. The telephone carrier encouraged people to contact them if they felt they had been overcharged through late payment charges, returned check charges or service restoration charges. Credited amounts were tabulated with 12-percent interest. If you had been overcharged, you had the option of credit or cash, totaling several hundreds of dollars. Be on the lookout for ways that *you* can initiate the process of making businesses accountable for their blunders. You may have some money due you, too.

Replace vanity gift requests with business ones. For your birthday, anniversary, graduation, retirement and even your wedding, don't be shy about making your requests known. This is an excellent way for others to support your venture. My brother, David, and I started this tradition years ago. We've exchanged everything from software to transcription recorders to professional organizers.

Survival Tip #44: Incur debt in moderation—it'll save your sanity.

Imagine yourself in this situation. Bootstrapper Nicholas desperately needed Consumer Credit Counseling to help him. He was buried under $60,000 in credit cards and business debts. He had two choices: to file bankruptcy or to come up with a repayment plan. Nicholas viewed filing bankruptcy as the easy way out, so he opted to pay back his obligations. First, he was able to get his partner to assume most of the debt and assets of their failing business, which reduced Nicholas's obligations to $30,000. Next, he committed to a debt management plan. It took him four years to work his way through the indebtedness—he now only chooses unsecured debt he can afford to pay back in full.

Running a business comes with a built-in stress factor. When you become heavily leveraged, the pressure is multiplied a hundredfold. Sure, your business may need to carry some debt for startup, growth or expansion. But don't be foolish. Incurring bills frivolously is bad debt—everything around you will be owned by someone else. Good debt helps you take advantage of opportunities. Bad debt: using credit as a regular substitute for income. Good debt: financing a copier to eliminate frequent trips to the corner copy shop. A casual attitude about debt is bad. Strategically and thoughtfully approaching debt decisions is good—you accept the financial responsibility based on your realistic comfort zone.

Overextended bootstrappers make business decisions out of desperation, not savvy. Your flexibility will be hampered because you'll be too indebted in an area to pursue a new or better direction. Growing on cash flow while managing moderate debt is okay. It may take you longer to build, but your business may last longer, too. You just have to decide how you want to spend your nights: going to bed a little hungry or dreaming endlessly about all your bills.

Survival Tip #45: Refine your juggling skills before you begin the credit card financing act.

You've heard the stories before. The movie director who used dozens of cards to finance his first film. Or the three partners who applied for 100 cards simultaneously and got $500,000 in credit lines to jumpstart their company. Personal credit cards are one of the top three vehicles for financing a business. They're easy to get for a person with an unblemished credit history who receives solicitations regularly. And they're easy to use. Where else can you get instant money with no questions asked? Before you begin flirting with the card system, consider a few points.

Plastic is expensive money. If you use it as a short-term loan, say to make a badly needed purchase, and are able to turn around and zero the balance out quickly, that's fine. It's when you use it as your sole source that things can get complicated. When you have little or no cash flow, you'll be unable to pay down a high (or increasing) balance. You, in turn, may need to have more cards to finagle around the payments. You know, robbing plastic Peter to pay Paul. Low introductory rates don't last forever, so you may find yourself scurrying around just to cover the interest payments. Even worse, when you have a personal emergency, your cards will already be tapped out, with no plastic to depend on.

There are future implications as well. Even if your credit remains intact during the card juggling process, you may have problems obtaining other types of loans later. The lending world uses the five C's of credit analysis: capacity, capital, collateral, conditions and character. Along with evaluating your capacity to pay back a loan, lenders look at your potential to run up other debt. If you have five open credit card accounts with limits of $10,000 each, you can potentially run up $50,000 in obligations that could interfere with your paying back the loan in question. So if plastic is your only option, use it judiciously.

Survival Tip #46: Consider the pros and cons of unconventional sources.

The best capital source may lie within your intimate circle. It may be a parent, relative or friend. They're unconventional sources because you can get amounts equal to what you'd get from a traditional lender (such as a bank), but you can work out the terms of the loan with the person, plus there's no scrutiny of your credit history.

You'll need to be careful—nothing can sour a relationship faster than a misunderstanding about money. Approach only those who you like and who can afford to lose some money or will not need it back right away. It goes without saying that a loan from someone you find difficult to get along with will only put more strain on your relationship with that person.

In *More than Money*, a newsletter forum for people with financial surplus, the readers discuss success strategies they use in making personal loans. You may find the suggestions adaptable to your situation. If the loan is $5,000 or more, one reader requires that a small percentage of the amount be placed in an escrow account. The reasoning is that it forces borrowers early on to begin using outside professionals in their businesses. There are power issues associated with a loan situation, and you can flush them out through candid conversation.

You should thoroughly discuss how you feel about asking for the loan and how the other person feels about granting it, the previous loan history between you and the type of communication required if things go awry, then define what mutual respect will mean throughout the relationship. You can then solidify the deal with a written agreement drawn up by a professional, stipulating a repayment schedule and other agreed-upon points.

Diverting funds from other accounts is another unconventional strategy. If the money is intended for something else—an emergency or college fund—you need to consider whether your plan is a better use of the dollars. For example, a bootstrapping couple in New Jersey received a $5,000 windfall. Based on their investment preferences, a planner advised them that putting the money to work in their candy store was a better investment at this time. By taking time out to mull over your moves, you'll avoid ending up on the downside of the choices.

Survival Tip #47: Attract angels of support by selling them on your vision.

Although venture capitalists can be considered angels, the title can be bestowed upon other sources, too. It may be a supplier, colleague or pillar in your community. Your best help will sometimes come from people who don't even know you but are willing to help. You need diligence to find them and courage to ask for their support. Here's an example of someone who was touched by an angel.

Just call Naimah Jones, of Naimah Cosmetics, a visionary. Based on 15 years in the beauty industry, she envisioned a niche line aimed at women of color. Her dilemma: a great idea with no money to finance it. Instead, she coordinated a consortium of professionals who could benefit from being a part of this ground-floor opportunity. Working from an illustrated picture of her concept, Jones secured a tentative commitment from a major Southern California department store. Her angel circle included a manufacturer, who produced samples based on the store's mere interest and later more goods worth $80,000. What's more, he agreed to wait six months until she got paid. The other players included a photographer, who charged her material costs, and an artist, who accepted delayed payment terms.

Their deal: make us your primary supplier when the company gets off the ground.

You can solicit the support of others by involving them in your vision. Be your own best salesperson and show them the potential of your idea. It's important, though, that you accept help from the right people. Someone who has reservations or lacks enthusiasm may be committing for the wrong reasons. Also, consider angels who can function as mentors and can afford to remain committed to the arrangements. Besides their product, service or money, you'll need their emotional support.

FULFILLING A WISH TO EDUCATE A COMMUNITY

Atlanta seemed like a profitable place for a specialist in the business of helping companies set up telecommuter programs. The city had air quality problems, and the 1996 Olympic Games were on the way. In 1991, Michael Dziak decided to package his 18 years of telecommunications experience into a business. He formed InteleWorks, Inc., a training and consulting firm that helps clients maximize the use of existing and emerging communications tools. When Dziak began marketing his services, he discovered the community wasn't educated enough to embrace the benefits of teleworking. If InteleWorks was going to make it, he needed to invest in educating his marketplace.

Rather than going about the task alone, Dziak decided to pinpoint stakeholders in the area who could benefit from being a part of the telecommuting movement. First stop: the Georgia Department of Natural Resources, the agency responsible for writing the State Implementation Plan for Atlanta to meet the requirements of the Clean Air Act. Dziak was effective in getting the agency to understand how telecommuting was a viable transportation control measure. An education program, however, was needed to help employers understand the concept. After submitting a proposal, Dziak was awarded a $10,000 grant from the agency—not to fund his business but to invest in the community's education. The monies were used to publish *Georgia Telecommuting Times*, an outreach newsletter for organizations and individuals. Dziak was also able to form Metropolitan Atlanta Telecommuting Advisory Council (MATAC), a nonprofit group that coordinates educational workshops. Both parties benefited: the state department by fulfilling part of its public outreach responsibilities, and Dziak by participating in the education of his targeted market.

Dziak's involvement with the outreach has paid off. His company has landed various consulting contracts with area employers, MATAC (www. matac.org) has hosted five annual telecommuting education conferences with big-name sponsors, and Atlanta did benefit during the Olympics. There was a 50-percent decrease in peak-hour traffic. The Olympics' Director of Traffic estimated that one-third of the reduction was attributed to people telecommuting.

Survival Tip #48: Put your creative energy to work.

Your biggest challenge as a bootstrapper will be to graduate from a cash-dependent to a wit-dependent business person. It's the only way shoestringers make it on their budget. When you listen to stories about how people came up with creative alternatives to their funding problems, it's because there were no boundaries for believing an option was possible. It stems from your imagination. Children have incredible imaginations. When you were a child, you automatically were able to use your mind to envision yourself in all types of situations and places, even though you were far from it. Remember? It's through free-flowing thoughts that you'll be able to see yourself through your situation.

Jot down exactly what it is you want to do with your business and what you need to get it done. Ponder your notes and allow your imagination to scan the possibilities. Imagine the most unusual and blessed alliances or strategies you can think of. Then begin to connect the dots with people, resources, events or actions that can make it happen. If you're offering a fresh twist on a standard service or a product others have neglected to deliver, then your newness makes you a candidate for unique opportunities. If you imagine yourself with a benefactor to your cause, you'll stir up energy as you talk to people who can lead you to one. Your imagination may point you in unheard-of directions, but don't squelch it because your hope may lie in the thought.

A plastic visor manufacturer convinced a mold-maker to build a $20,000 mold for no money down. He agreed to finance the project through payments of 2 cents for each unit sold. In the unlikely event the product demand was fewer than a million, the company would pay the remainder in bulk. That's creative financing. See what's possible when you take the ceiling off your brain? Now get going and begin imagining unorthodox solutions for your situation.

Survival Tip #49: Take inventory of your possessions.

People don't hesitate to refashion a spare room or home area into a workspace, but rarely approach their other possessions with the same zeal. Go through everything you own and determine what can be reused for your business. Everything has potential—furnishings, appliances, entertainment equipment, old vehicles and more. Your discoveries can either be sold to generate more cash or recycled as equipment capital.

A little paint, polish and dusting can give new life to a forgotten item. If you're an exhibitor, look for old standbys in your garage. Tables and chairs can be camouflaged to decorate an exhibition area. If you're a professional caterer, look for fine table settings tucked away in your linen closet. If you're an event planner or exhibitor, you can probably find good uses for unused wedding gifts such as table-cloths, clocks, vases and frames that weren't purchased from your registry. Don't forget to scour rental storage space. Bidding on abandoned storage stalls is big business. So if people are willing to bid on unknown items in a space, imagine how much value you may find in your own. If you dabbled in various hobbies or relocated before, you probably have some gems packed away. And if you come across an item that's worth repairing, have it fixed and reuse it.

When Kay Young needed money to launch her *Secretarial & Office Support Services (SOS) Quarterly* newsletter, she decided to part with an inherited item. She took a silver set to an auction house and it sold for more than enough to launch the publication. In Young's heart, "SOS" has another special meaning: sold old sliver! There is also another upside to the inventory-taking process. You may be inspired to simplify your life and donate your stuff to a worthy cause.

Survival Tip #50: Start right where you are.

Don't use a lack of money as an excuse not to go out and pursue your dream. Remember, it's commonplace for a bootstrapper to operate undercapitalized. Venturing out on your own is risky business, and it'll start with putting yourself out there for public scrutiny. When you introduce your offering in small steps, your efforts will begin to generate more money to put back into the business.

When I started my jewelry business, my startup money only covered a modest amount of supplies and business cards. I was able to fabricate about six designs, not an entire collection. I didn't have the fancy jewelry trunks to display my wares in. Instead, I created a display box by removing all the dividers from a regular wooden and glass jewelry box and lining it with a silk scarf. I started showing my products to potential buyers and within three weeks I had jewelry orders exceeding my initial capital.

Everything big starts with something little. A professional organizer who now commands $1,500 per day started by organizing people's garages. A millionaire mail-order guru started with one product and one ad. A cookie mogul started with a very short menu—one type of cookie. And the infamous computer giants all started by tinkering in their garages. You, too, can start today and watch your activities multiply.

Bootstrapper's Follow-up File

Access to Credit: A Guide for Lenders and Women Owners of Small Businesses, Federal Reserve Bank of Chicago, Public Information, P.O. Box 834, Chicago, IL 60604. A **free**, 41-page guide offering advice to entrepreneurs and bankers.

American Express Small Business Centers, Web address: www.americanexpress.com/smallbusiness. Pilot program in Phoenix, Los Angeles and Chicago, with centers providing cardmembers with loans as well as access to American Express experts in credit, small business tax planning, cash flow analysis, financial reporting, employee and retirement benefits planning.

AT&T Small Business Lending Corporation, 800-707-0609. Provides assistance with obtaining a loan through the SBA's LowDoc Loan program.

Awards, Honors and Prizes, Gale Research, 800-347-4253. A library reference guide listing 20,000 sources.

Best of America Awards, National Federation of Independent Business Education Foundation, 600 Maryland Ave. SW, Washington, DC 20024. Recognizes firms with fewer than 250 employees at least three years in operation for their excellence in business. First prize of $25,000; three runners-up prizes of $5,000 each.

Elizabeth Lewin Fund (ELF) Award, National Chamber of Commerce for Women, 10 Waterside Plaza, Suite 6H, New York, NY 10010. Makes grants each year to male and female entrepreneurs who want to promote their companies. The ELF awards range from $500 to $15,000 in cash, products, services or any combination thereof.

First Step Software Series, National Business Association, 800-456-0440. **Free** program providing you with an orientation to the SBA-guarantee loan program and assisting you in determining the likelihood of receiving a loan. DOS, Windows and Macintosh versions available.

Guide to the National Endowment for the Arts, National Endowment for the Arts, Public Information Office, Room 803, 1100 Pennsylvania Ave. NW, Washington, DC 20506-0001; 202-682-5400. **Free** resource containing information about various grant programs.

In-Kind Mini Grant Program, Operation Hope Inc., 800 W. Sixth St., Suite 1200, Los Angeles, CA 90017; 213-891-2900. Offers **free** office furniture and equipment to small businesses in designated Los Angeles county communities.

Money Hunt TV Show, fax: 203-0866-4099; Web address: www.moneyhunter.com. Half-hour program giving entrepreneurs a chance to talk about their business opportunity and receive a critique from a venture capitalist. Show guidelines are available by fax. Web page offers a downloadable business plan template.

More than Money, The Impact Project, 2244 Alder St., Eugene, OR 97405-9964; e-mail address: impact@efn.org; Web address: www.efn.org/~impact. A quarterly newsletter to help people with financial surplus take charge of their money and their lives.

National Association of Small Business Investment Companies (NASBIC), 1199 N. Fairfax St., Suite 200, Alexandria, VA 22314; 703-683-1601; fax: 703-683-1605; Web address: www.envista.com/ nasbic. Represents firms licensed by the SBA as small business investment companies (SBICs). Publishes *Venture Capital: Where to Find It*, a book listing venture capitalists and their investment interests. $10.

National Foundation for Consumer Credit, 800-388-2227. Provides referrals to local Consumer Credit Counselors (CCC). CCC centers provide **free** counseling and advice to consumers having financial difficulty and help consumers pay back their debts through a debt management program.

National Inventor of the Year, Intellectual Property Owners, 1255 23rd St. NW, Suite 850, Washington, DC 20037. Programs recognizing outstanding achievement by an inventor. Inventions must be either patented or first commercially introduced in the previous calendar year. Honor includes a $5,000 cash award.

National Self-Published Book Awards, *Writer's Digest* magazine, 800-283-0963, x. 633. Accepts entries of self-publishers' books in the categories of life stories, cookbooks, children's, fiction, nonfiction and poetry. First-place overall winner receives $1,000 plus promotion in *Publishers Weekly*. Other winners receive $250.

National Venture Capital Association (NVCA), 1655 N. Fort Myer Dr., Suite 700, Arlington, VA 22209; 703-351-5269; fax: 703-351-5268; Web address: www.envista.com/nvca. Membership of venture capital organizations, corporate financiers and individual investors.

Rural Information Center, 800-633-7701 (301-504-5547 in the Washington, D.C. area and outside U.S.); Web address: www.nal.usda.gov/ric. Provides information and referrals on federal rural development programs. **Free** information package includes *A Guide to Funding Resources* and *Federal Funding Sources for Rural Areas*.

Ruth Chenven Foundation, 7 Park Ave., New York, NY 10016. Awards up to $1,000 annually to craftspeople and artists engaged in or planning a craft or art project. Applications available from January 1 to May 1 only. Send SASE for an application.

Small Business Administration (SBA) Financial Programs, 800-827-5722; Web address: www.sbaonline.sba.gov. Contact for phone number of your local SBA office, which can give you more information on guaranteed loans to small businesses that have been denied financing from a commercial lender. Such loans include

LowDocumentation Loan (LowDoc), FA$TRAK Loan, Microloan Demonstration, Women and Minority Prequalification Pilot Loan and Certified Development Company programs.

Small Business Innovation Research (SBIR) Grants, Office of Innovation, Research and Technology, 202-205-6450; Web address: www.sbaonline.sba.gov.SBIR. Program giving small businesses the opportunity to develop new technologies to meet federal research and development needs. Awards are made through the Departments of Agriculture, Commerce, Defense, Education, Energy, Health and Human Services and Transportation; the Environmental Protection Agency; National Aeronautics and Space Administration; and the National Science Foundation.

Telecommunications Development Fund, Office of Communications, Business Opportunities, Federal Communications Commission, 1919 M St. NW, Washington, DC 20554. The Telecommunications Act of 1996 authorized the Telecommunications Development Fund to provide a source of loans and investment capital to small communications businesses. Loan applications and investment guidelines are under development. Contact the commission to receive update mailings about the fund.

The Credit Process: A Guide for Small Business Owners, Federal Reserve Bank, Public Information Department, 33 Liberty St., New York, NY 10045. A **free**, 26-page workbook offering guidance to people who are seeking outside financing for the first time. Discusses the sources and types of funding typically available to small businesses along with a business plan section.

The Small Business Financial Resource Guide: Sources of Assistance for Small and Growing Businesses, MasterCard International, 800-821-6176. A **free**, 150-page book discussing various funding options and sources.

The Top Small Business Lending Banks in the United States, SBA Office of Advocacy, Mail Code 3114, 409 Third St. SW, Washington, DC 20416; fax: 202-205-6928. A **free** study identifying the banks that do the most small business lending. Write or fax your request.

Wells Fargo Bank/NAWBO Program, 1413 K St. NW, Suite 637, Washington, DC 20005; 800-359-3557 x. 120; fax: 301-608-2596. A loan fund for women entrepreneurs whose firms have been in business two years. To apply for a loan under $25,000, call. For larger amounts, contact the office in writing.

Women of Enterprise Award, Avon Products, Inc., 9 W. 57th St., New York, NY 10019. Annual program awarding $1,000 in cash, an all-expense-paid trip to New York City, speaking engagements and national publicity to six outstanding women entrepreneurs who have overcome hardship and achieved success. Applications available every October through January. For application package, send 9 x 12 SASE with $1.01 postage.

Chapter 5

Marketing Your Business

"Marketing is always a work in progress."

—J. Daniel McComas, Advertising
Ideas, Inc., Silver Spring, Md.

Survival Tip #51: Gear up to become a lifetime marketer.

Marketing is an activity that you'll be involved with for the entire life of your business. So brace yourself. In various surveys, small business professionals frequently cite two nagging challenges: (1) getting new business or clients and (2) promoting and growing their businesses. The prescription: marketing.

Marketing is much more than advertising the fact that you're in business. It involves everything you do to obtain and keep a customer, from conducting market research, developing a customer profile and positioning your identity in the market to selecting marketing devices to determining your location, how your phones are answered and how you handle customer complaints. (You will learn more about each of these aspects of marketing in this chapter.)

Staying in business also requires that you continually educate the market about your offering. Even when you have a solid, steady customer base, you need to keep them informed as to how you're growing, improving and preparing for and responding to marketplace changes—and, more important, to their needs. You can do this through a systematic marketing program.

A marketing program consists of the strategies and devices you use to communicate to your target audience. Your program may look a little different from mine or from that of a shop owner across the street. We all have dozens of tools available to us—direct response mailings, TV and radio spots, newspaper and yellow pages ads, brochures, community involvement, public relations, billboards, advertising specialty items and more. Which tools you use—and how—will be influenced by market research (see Survival Tips #15, #18 and #54). Market research may indicate that a television repair service's marketing program should be undergirded with paid placements in the phone book, since "television repair" is one of the most often looked-up headings by homeowners. Consultants, on the other hand, may find that an aggressive public relations campaign will sell people on their expertise.

Marketing shapes every area of a business. Your business's life span is controlled by how effectively it's marketed. Marketing helps you penetrate a place in your audience's mind, positioning your business at the top of their mental awareness. They in turn automatically identify your business as the solution to their problem or need, thus creating your share of mind (see Survival Tip #73). It doesn't happen by osmosis. You have to work continually at communicating your marketing message.

Don't let your inexperience frighten you. You can become a savvy marketer with practice and commitment. The average small business owner does not start off with marketing smarts—especially those of us coming from workplace positions in which we didn't have to worry about such things. You can learn how to market yourself by observing others, heeding basic principles (such as targeting your marketing to ensure that the message reaches the people you want to attract to your business's product or service), adopting strategies appropriate for your business type and sticking with a marketing plan (a step-by-step approach for communicating your message to a defined buyer).

Small businesses that flourish in today's marketplace are operated by individuals with a marketing mind-set—people who use creative, cost-effective ways to attract and retain business. A restaurant owner is profiled in the paper for making daily donations of leftovers to homeless shelters. A graphics designer, photographer and printer use a three-way promotional approach by pooling their talents to create a customer giveaway calendar. A business owner takes advantage of being listed in various industry directories free of charge. Learn from these people. They've all learned how to be bootstrapping marketers. It's an ongoing process—and it's a commitment for life.

Survival Tip #52: Don't make your investments around misconceptions.

Marketing is a business investment. Its greatest dividend: prompting clients and prospects to think of you first when it's time to spend their money. You'll fare best by investing your resources—time, creativity or cash—in strategies that work. Before you begin, listen to these misconceptions about marketing that you'll want to sidestep.

One of the biggest misconceptions is that marketing results are driven by your budget. Quite the contrary. High-impact strategies are usually low-cost ones fueled more by creativity and time rather than money (see "Bootstrappin' marketing strategies that will leave your competition in the dust" on page 100-103). As you develop your marketing program and weapons, shift your focus from "how much" to "how effective."

Another mistake people make is failing to recognize the true importance of *frequency* in marketing. Consider this: Research shows that consumers need to hear a message at least three times for them to have name recognition and recall and nine times before they become a customer. A one-time ad or mailing is rarely enough to generate even a 1- to 3-percent response rate. You must invest in strategically repeating your message to capture people's attention and ultimately sway a buying decision in your favor.

A third misconception relates to the number of marketing vehicles people may believe are necessary. The truth is, most businesses do not rely on a *single* tool. Even a business that thrives on yellow page advertising complements that tool with other weapons. Marketing isn't a single activity. It includes a combination of tools and techniques, such as a strong word-of-mouth referral program, direct response, exhibitions, distinctive business cards and stationery, community outreach, program tracking, customer service follow-up and more. Investing in a marketing mixture yields results similar to those achieved by business professionals who have multiple income sources; should one source slow down or evaporate, you'll have other options to fall back on.

Survival Tip #53: Chart your course with a marketing plan.

Many operations plug along without a business plan. However, few of them survive without a plan of attack for marketing their businesses. A marketing plan works as a survival as well as a preventative tool. It'll keep you on track when you're tempted to react impulsively to a dip in business or fall into the deadly trap of lowering prices to keep pace with your competitors. Successful businesses are proficient at attracting and keeping customers by satisfying their needs. A written marketing plan provides you with the methodology for doing so.

Pull out the research you've gathered on your customers, marketplace, competition and trends (see Survival Tips #15 and #18). Use this research as your cornerstone to help you spell out each area of the plan. A simple, effective marketing plan can be created around these four components:

1. Objective: What is it that you need to accomplish? Clearly articulate the purpose of your marketing in terms of specific goals, quantifiable results and timetables. Example: *Best Cleaners' marketing plan will help increase customer referrals and repeat business by 50 percent in 12 months.*

2. Marketing mix: How will you position your business in the marketplace? What should your marketing message communicate about your identity or niche to a target audience? Your marketing mix should work in concert with your product or service, price, place, promotion and position. Clarifying each of these areas for your business will help you select the most complementary approaches and tactics for your marketing program. Define your:

- Product and/or service: *Best Cleaners is a specialty dry cleaner whose treatment process keeps your clothes looking new.*

- Price: *Best Cleaners is value-driven as we save customers thousands in garment replacement costs.*

- Place: *Best Cleaners is conveniently located near a commuter intersection, with ample free parking.*

- Promotion: *Best Cleaners is the town's quality cleaner.*

- Position: *Best Cleaners is the only operation that offers pickup, delivery and drive-through service.*

3. Execution strategies: Which marketing vehicles are the best to deliver your message? Example: *Best Cleaners will use two-for-one specials, neighborhood coupons, season-end customer postcard mailings and special offers in community newcomers' packages. We will mail out coupons every month, run a weekly ad in the local paper and offer a back-to-school special in August. We'll begin to develop our mailing list from information we pick up from the personal checks customers pay with, and our ads will reach people within a 7-mile radius. We've earmarked 30 percent of our annual revenues for this program.*

4. Results tracking: How will you determine the effectiveness of your activities? Whether it's through sales, customer base activity or profits, you'll need to audit each device continually. For example, Best Cleaners could code their newspaper coupons by geographical distribution.

These base components can be expanded or retooled for any business. Don't ignore gray areas; they may be a signal for more market research. Your marketplace position should set you apart from your competition. You should be able to substantiate your position with the competitive research you've done. Best Cleaners, for instance, knows that it's the only one offering all the available convenience services, based on snooping on other cleaners in the area. Although you should make a commitment to execute the plan, feel free to revise or update it as your goals or business needs change.

Survival Tip #54: Choose the right marketing vehicles.

The effectiveness of any vehicle will depend on what you're marketing. Survey responses from my newsletter network substantiate this point. When asked to share their best and worst marketing strategies, readers discounted some popular tools and heralded some unpopular ones. For example, for one computer consultant, joining the chamber of commerce was a dud while volunteering to lead a special-interest group's monthly software roundtable led to referral success. Cable television advertising drained another bootstrapper's pockets, but presenting free seminars produced desired results. Before you dispatch any marketing vehicle, ask yourself three questions:

1. How compatible is the tool with your marketing goals? Let's say that you're aiming to build customer loyalty that leads to repeat business and referrals. Your market research leads you to the Promotional Products Association International. Their studies show that advertising specialties—merchandise imprinted with your name or message and given free—are effective in this area. Furthermore, the more useful the item, the more likely customers will keep and use it. In this instance, the item's usefulness would directly effect its compatibility with your marketing goal.

2. Does your type of business use one particular marketing tool more often than the others? You must know the nuances of your business first (see Survival Tip #19). For example, classified ads fuel some businesses while others use flier distribution effectively. For restaurants, local newspaper ads are effective because most restaurant clientele come from a 3- to 5-mile radius. Local store-front shops find success with coupon advertising in community mail packs or on the back of receipts. Scanning a stack of my own grocery receipts reveals ads from such neighborhood regulars as a car wash, a dry cleaner, an auto repair center, a dental center and a storage facility.

3. Is your knowledge of the marketing tool limited? A device will only work when you know how to work it well. Let's say you decide to send out a direct-response mailing. You've read that personalizing letters yields a better response than sending out generic ones, so you try it. But before you send them out, do you have a follow-up system outlined, which may include a series of phone calls, postcards, consultations or premium offers? There's more to this strategy than sending out letters and waiting for the responses to roll in.

If the tool in question is a go on all fronts, make sure it is well-produced. You won't get big results from amateurishly produced materials or presentations. Develop a file of writers, artists, proofreaders or other marketing professionals with whom you can work or barter.

Survival Tip #55: Uncover a niche.

Authors Donald K. Clifford, Jr., and Richard E. Cavanuagh studied 6,117 small companies that had grown four times faster than the Fortune 250. Their research found that 90 percent of these firms competed in small-niche markets. Their success lay in being driven by customers rather than sales—their marketing was aimed at a small, reliable and qualified pool of buyers.

Your business may start off with a targeted audience. Through the years of observing market trends and regularly communicating with your buyers, you may find a niche inside your group. There are few ways to discover a niche market. Niches can be found by unearthing the idiosyncrasies of your target audience (see Survival Tip #20). Perhaps their idiosyncratic behavior is not being serviced in a particular manner or format. For example, for customers who'd like to shop from the comfort of their homes, a clothier could offer private showings in their homes in addition to a boutique operation. You can also find niches by observing what your competitors are failing to do.

Norm Brodsky, a veteran entrepreneur and an *Inc.* magazine columnist, discovered a profitable niche with his storage company, Citi-Storage. When Brodsky first looked into the business, he discovered that records-storage companies weren't responding to industry changes. Clients were looking to store *active* files, as well as dead ones, off-site. With the exception of a few major companies located outside the metro area, nobody was catering to the evolution of the archive retrieval business. Brodsky invested in a huge modern facility in the city. He distinguished himself from the old records-storage companies by designing his facility specifically for retrieval of active files, and he used the latest technology. He also distinguished himself from the giants by his location within the city, thereby creating his niche market.

Be open to experimenting with several niches before finding one that's a perfect fit for your business. As you discover or evolve into a niche, you'll need to refine your marketing messages. You'll need to communicate the differentiating factors that are important to the customer. For example, if serving your niche means having such strengths as speed, service, exclusivity or specialization, everything in your marketing arsenal must cohesively tout those qualities to customers.

Survival Tip #56: Hammer home your message with a focus test.

When you give people a jack-of-all-trades description of your business, you'll only confuse them and make it difficult for others to work as your marketing mouthpieces. Developing a focus statement will enable you to give a clear, concise and intriguing response when people ask what you do. There are other benefits as well. A focus test, an exercise to chisel out a pithy description of your business, will help you define your product or service, clarify your marketing message and remember the business you're in, which is critical as you filter through opportunities that come along (see Survival Tip #103). The more focused your business is, the more responsive people will be to you and your offering.

Begin the exercise by writing an editorial description of what you do in 25 words or less. Write what comes to mind. If it's a little clumsy, don't worry because you'll spiff it up in a minute. Your description should include what your product or service is, how it benefits the user and the problem you solve or action you perform. Read over your description. The next step is to take that description and make it punchy. Here's an example for an advertising specialist: "We create ads that boost your profits in 60 days. We specialize in helping retailers lower overall advertising expenses while generating more store traffic." This 24-word statement captures what the company does. Each sentence can also work as a standalone 7- to 15-word statement to pique the listener's interest in 15 to 20 seconds. It will also inspire the question "How do you do that?"—opening the door for you to go into more detail about your offering.

By keeping your descriptions simple, you can use them to pass the word about your business in discussions with anyone from an associate to your dentist, as well as use them in your directory listings, ads or quotes for media representatives. You can also use the phrasing to develop your slogan—an attention-getting phrase such as "The 60-day Profit Boosters." By using the same or similar phrasing, your message is communicated consistently to the market and helps develop "share of mind" (see Tip #73).

Survival Tip #57: Market your product like a product and your service like a service.

A product is tangible. A service is intangible. Their difference affects how you market each one. A product gives you great flexibility. You can see and touch it, take it home, resell it and even return it for a refund. When you like a product, you might buy it even if you don't like the person selling it. Think about it. The sensory process has helped you determine the product's value to you and your situation, thus you proceed with the transaction. It's nothing personal between you and the seller.

More and more products are being sold in an impersonal way—and it works. For example, people make large purchases over the Internet, through catalogs and through direct-mail advertisements. A product marketer with a selection of quality merchandise can increase its audience's responsiveness to this method of selling through clear descriptions, good photographs, stock ready to ship, an easy ordering method and a no-hassles return policy.

Selling a *service*, on the other hand, is personal. The value or perception of a service is connected to the person who's selling it. Buyers don't always know a service's value until the servicing process is complete. Your challenge is to help them see the connection before-hand. As a service provider, you're trying to woo buyers on the intangible promise that you'll deliver what you say, and furthermore, that you're the person for the job. Your presentation must market this promise so that it becomes tangible to your clients. A hairstylist, for example, may gain a new customer because that person saw the haircut he or she gave to someone else. Service providers sell themselves primarily on their past performance or ability to convince buyers of their qualifications. You can accomplish this through testimonials (what others say about your work; see Survival Tip #84), media marketing and public relations placements establishing yourself as an expert in the public's minds, speaking before an audience about your profession and case studies of how you solved others' problems.

Consultant David Calabria says that his marketing needs to inspire confidence in his expertise. Direct-mail letters, for example, were ineffective in building his practice. Instead, his target audience started flocking to him once they began regularly reading his bylined articles and occasional quotes in their favorite periodicals. As you can see, some strategies that work for a product may not be effective for a service. Most services require personal contact marketing, such as a personal consultation or an opportunity to see you demonstrate your work. A computer consultant, for example, may offer the first assessment of your computer needs at a highly discounted rate—or for free.

You can begin to match the right approaches to your product or service by examining your own buying habits. What vehicles make you responsive to buying a service from someone? Or which factors influenced to you buy an item without even seeing it first? Also, evaluating the various tools and techniques that have made certain products and services hot sellers in the past can aid you in the matchmaking process (see Survival Tip #18).

Survival Tip #58: Use flexibility to generate high-quality inquiries.

An overlooked marketing weapon: flexibility. It's an intangible but potent tool. You can put it to work by developing a response menu. Offering multiple response devices so prospects can choose the method they prefer makes it easier for them to respond. For example, some people need your information right away, so they prefer to call. Some like the 24-hour convenience of faxing or e-mailing their requests. Others may opt to sent a postcard or letter or use reply cards. Many people fall into the trap of offering only one response method, such as just a phone number or mailing address. When implementing this strategy you should factor in your professional style and business setup. You'll need to ensure that your infrastructure is designed to respond efficiently to all those requests (see Survival Tip #59).

Next, let prospects choose which follow-up action they would like you to take. Rather than offering inquirers one information option, try a combination of two or more choices, such as pointing them to your Web page or offering catalogs, brochures, application notes, a newsletter, a demonstration, a test or analysis, samples, a sales call or any combination thereof. This will significantly increase the number of inquiries you generate.

There are some hidden benefits for you in this tactic. You can determine which prospects require prompt attention by their request choice. Those with an immediate need will probably require a sales call, analysis or demonstration. Those who have longer-term needs, or are not ready for meeting, might ask for literature, application notes, a newsletter or a sample. You can then use this information to code prospects in your database and assign the appropriate follow-up steps. This way, you're pouncing on your hottest prospects while simultaneously coaxing the other ones along.

Survival Tip #59: Develop a marketing infrastructure to carry forth your banner.

You work against yourself when you're not prepared to respond to opportunities that result from your marketing efforts. Scrambling around to piece together requested information will either slow down your response process or deter you from responding at all. The solution: Develop a systematic way to respond to all opportunities. Begin by evaluating all of your response methods (see Survival Tip #58). Let's say that you provide buyers with the option of contacting you by fax or e-mail. In order to respond quickly to their queries, you should have materials that can be sent via those same mediums. For example, when I started including my fax and e-mail address on my newsletter, I developed a faxable promotional sheet as well as a standard e-mail reply file.

Here's an example of a marketing infrastructure at work for an entrepreneur who works as a small-business coach, speaker, consultant and author. A product brochure, which doubles as a flier and catalog (see Survival Tip #72), is printed in lots of 2,000; the master copy is updated as postal rates change or new items are added to the line. A one-page faxable business biography along with hundreds of black-and-white photos are maintained on file. The consultant keeps an updatable resume on computer to include in consulting and seminar proposals. Customized Post-it notes are used to write notes that accompany a flier or newsletter. The entrepreneur's mailing list is ever growing because contacts made through seminars or networking events and all information-requesters are entered on the list. This provides a ready database of recipients for a direct-mail campaign.

Your infrastructure may include a portfolio of your work, quality reproductions of articles about or by you, or an informational sheet of frequently asked questions. One bootstrapper developed a standard packet for customers that included coupons for referring new customers to her business, along with extra business cards. When you use this type of strategy in your business, you deliberately (not just by relying on a few loyal customers as your mouthpieces) pass the word about your business at every opportunity.

A marketing infrastructure positions you to cherry-pick your opportunities and seize the most profitable ones. If you don't pursue an opportunity, it'll be because you *chose* to bypass it, rather than because you missed out since you weren't set up properly to respond in time to get additional consideration for the job.

BOOTSTRAPPIN' MARKETING STRATEGIES THAT WILL LEAVE YOUR COMPETITION IN THE DUST

Befriend an office building concierge. Many high-rise business complexes employ concierges. Their job involves providing tenants with convenience services and maintaining a referral network of local businesses. One building concierge spotlights area businesses in a monthly newsletter and allows each one to come in to give demonstrations to tenants. For example, one week tenants could try in-office massage services or attend a lunchtime debt management seminar presented by a financial planner. Businesses that are mobile, such as an auto detail service that works on your car while it's parked outside the building, a dry cleaner with a pickup/delivery service or a notary public, have particular appeal for tenants. The building concierge arranges these kinds of conveniences for them.

These high-rise buildings often host other events, such as transportation fairs, which could be a fit for your business. (Transportation fairs are popular in cities that are trying to comply with clean air regulations. Businesses such as the local transit authority, bike shops, health and fitness organizations and auto repair shops exhibit at these events to educate attendees about the alternative ways of commuting to work and how to reduce air emissions.) The concierge coordinates all the promotion for such events. Your participation would give you invaluable exposure—tenants may infer that you must be worth checking out if the XYZ Building is allowing you to exhibit there.

Steer foot traffic into your store. An open door is not enough to bring in customers. You need clever approaches that invite people in. In *Chase's Annual Events: The Day-by-Day Directory to 1997* (Contemporary Books, 1997), a directory that's available in most libraries and updated every year, there are more than 10,000 events and observances listed—translating into foot traffic opportunities for you. For example, October is National Breast Cancer Awareness Month. The American Cancer Society (ACS) and various organizations host a tremendous amount of public outreach activities during this time. The ACS provides businesses with **free** literature to distribute. If you ran a boutique, a health and fitness club or a beauty salon, you could chime in, too. A press release announcing your participation would surely pique the media's interest and result in positive press. People who come into your store to pick up the health material may not have dropped by otherwise. Of course, you should be prepared to encourage them to browse your shop while they're there. No matter what kind of business you own, you could find a similar event tie-in for your business by looking through *Chase's*.

Get on bidders' lists. Arrange to get on the lists of city, state, government, corporate or other agencies to receive request for proposal (RFP) solicitations. By doing so, you'll be kept abreast of changes taking place in your local community that will affect job growth and economic development. You can also use the information to spot trends or new markets to exploit. You'll be privy to the names of companies who are awarded the contracts and can possibly align yourself to receive some outsourcing work.

Claim the co-op advertising dollars you're due. Cooperative advertising is a cost-sharing arrangement between a manufacturer and a retailer for customers' advertising programs. The money is earmarked to help businesses stretch their advertising dollars. Yet studies show that billions of dollars go unclaimed each year. Whether you're a full-time retailer or own a service business with a retail center, you should pursue co-op opportunities.

Let's say you carry XYZ brand in your business. You can become a registered dealer of XYZ company, and when you feature them in your ad, you get cash rebates or credits to your account toward more product purchases. Also, by including that brand in your ads, you're helping customers find an outlet based on brand recognition. Co-op opportunities are available in every medium, from yellow page listings to print ads to radio and TV spots.

You can search for co-op opportunities by referring to a copy of *Co-op Source Directory* (National Register Publishing, 1997) at the library; this book is updated each year. Another information source is Sales Development Services (1335 Dublin Rd., Suite 200A, Columbus, OH 43235; 614-481-3530). It sponsors Co-op Awareness Month every October. Kathy Winston, a spokesperson for the Yellow Pages Publishers Association, suggests that small businesses also contact vendors or manufacturers directly and ask if they'd be willing to sponsor a program with you.

Nab an award. Being recognized as a distinguished professional in your industry is an honor and can be used to market your business. A landscaping firms spends 10 percent of its marketing budget on vying for a variety of accolades. The firm also uses the strategy to gain recognition in niche markets it plans to pursue. There are countless opportunities for your business to win an award. At the library, check out the listings in *Awards, Honors and Prizes* (Gale Research, 1996). Like the landscaping firm, you'll need to make an effort to get double the publicity value by publicizing your win yourself in addition to the award-giver's publicity. Several entrepreneurs who've won awards have confessed that they were negligent in using the honor to gain more momentum in their businesses.

Outsmart do-it-yourselfers. Inevitably there are going to be people who either can't afford your prices or believe that after picking your brains through a free consultation, they can handle the job themselves. You can turn the situation around by selling your knowledge in digestible bites. Creating a series of how-to booklets, special reports or fact sheets may be just what a do-it-yourselfer will buy. Avoid pricing your item too low, hoping to convert the person into a sale and make up the cost difference. Instead, price it based on its value, with a decent profit margin. Otherwise you'll end up losing money because some do-it-yourselfers will only be interested in the item, period.

Use your alumni muscle. I regularly send in information to my alma mater, Loyola Marymount University. The alumni publication has a "class notes" section where people send in all types of news. Some of the blurbs are quite lengthy and you can subtly promote your business. Just think: The publication goes to just about everyone who graduated from the University. Exposure such as this can lead to speaking engagements and other business or networking opportunities.

Scout out all free advertising opportunities. If you're online, have you set up a profile for others who are online to read so they can learn about you? It's doesn't cost anything extra to do. On America Online (AOL), for example, you can create a "member profile." I've filled mine with information promoting my business and this book. I've received countless inquires from people who decided to contact me based on the profile information. AOL also lets you place **free** classified ads in the Business Strategies area. There are also some industry directories that offer **free** profile listings. For example, newsletter publishers can receive a listing at no charge in *Oxbridge Directory of Newsletters* (Oxbridge Communications, 1996; 800-955-0231) and *Newsletters in Print* (Gale Research, 1996; 800-347-5253). You may find other opportunities in *Directories in Print* (Gale Research, 1996).

Another idea: Consider setting up a window display of your wares in a library or another city building. Many libraries and government buildings have display cases that they allow local businesses to use. This arrangement works very well for artists, photographers, clothiers and craftmaking businesses. (A library display of my jewelry line once brought me some business.) In a library, all you may need is the head librarian's approval before you set up your display. Be sure your exhibit includes a sign or a card with the name of your business and how people may contact you. It'll start working the moment you set it up, without your even being there.

Use family as your marketing mouthpiece. One entrepreneur's son is so conversant about her practice that several of his friends' parents have become customers. It's happened so many times that she now gives him a referral bonus besides his allowance. It's important that your loved ones have a good understanding about what you do, so when asked, they can respond with a subtle sales pitch. They can also let you know about opportunities they hear about that sound like a fit.

Pounce on newbies. Families and businesses new to a community are excellent targets for certain businesses. Since many town newbies don't know anyone, they rely on referrals from Realtors, employment services, chambers of commerce or the "welcome wagon" committee. You can use these organizations as sources for contacting newcomers as potential customers. Also, if another business is relocating, you could offer to serve the customers being left behind.

Survival Tip #60: Focus on being competitive, not just a low-baller.

Terrible things can happen when you operate a price-driven business. Getting and keeping business will be based on lowering your prices, which cuts into your profits. You'll also create an unreliable customer base. People who buy based on price alone will abandon your business as soon as a cheaper offer comes along. Competitive businesses don't always tout the lowest price in town. Instead, they build up their businesses by offering better solutions to their audience's problems, providing quality service consistently, marketing strengths that show why they're better than the competition and investing continually in components that help them build up their businesses (see Survival Tip #146).

Here's a case in point. A few years ago, someone highly recommended me to a company that needed people to work on a subcontracting project. My project fees were considerably higher than those of the other contractors used by the company, but the client divvied up the work among myself and the others. Each assignment period my work portion steadily increased, and within a year I became the company's sole contractor for the outsourced work. I didn't worry about my competition—I just outshined them. The quality of my work and the ease, reliability and flexibility (all components of my business identity) of working with me more than justified the client's paying my higher fees. Had I lowered my fees to get more work, another savvy professional may have come along and used my strategy.

You can determine your ability to compete successfully with other businesses by being aware of—not worrying about—your competition. You don't want to fall into the trap of copying others, but you should definitely know what's going on in your industry and how others are faring. Scouting can be as simple as checking your section in the new yellow pages book or other professional directories to see who's coming and going or what's being offered. Regularly reading business and trade materials can give you great insights into the tools and technologies that are helping businesses compete. Staying aware of the movement in your industry will enable you to present your competitive offering to the marketplace with confidence.

Survival Tip #61: Strategically spend and place your advertising dollars.

Paid ad placements are vital marketing sources for some businesses. Bear in mind that when customers refer to a directory or advertising section, they've already qualified themselves as someone who needs what you and your competition are selling. Whether you're paying for a display in the phone book, newspaper or church directory, you need your dollars to work effectively in steering people's attention over to your message.

Before you spend one dime on such a placement, keep the following considerations in mind:

- Does the medium allow you to communicate your message as often as you need?

- Will the format allow you to communicate enough information to prompt people to call for an appointment, send in an order or request additional information?

- What is the medium's cost in terms of the number of people it will reach?

- How many of the distribution recipients will actually be your target audience?

Your paid placements should work in concert with your other tools. Let's say, for example, you pay for a yellow pages display along with special ads in a supplier directory and the newspaper. Which of the vehicles generates the most responses throughout the year? If you depend on one type of placement more than the others, you should consider staggering your placements to stimulate movement during any work gaps. For instance, you may opt to go with a placement that comes out a few months before your slow season. Also, consider a placement's life span. Short-lived placements need to be supported by a series of other ones to maintain a flow in your business.

Test runs will help you determine which options are best for your business. Marketing experts recommend that you test paid placements, such as classified ads, for three to six months to get a feel for their effectiveness. Rarely is the response of a one-time placement a cut-and-dried indication of how well an ad works. Start with a few small placements and slowly graduate to a more extensive advertising program. Track the results of any placements. By having prospective customers dial a special number or enter a department code when they call you, or asking every caller how they heard about you, you can monitor the effectiveness of your strategy. You'll also ensure that you're not paying for something that doesn't work. (You can get more information on creating yellow pages ads from the Yellow Pages Publishers Association. For more information, see page 125.)

Survival Tip #62: Incorporate the "media" into your program.

Dancing with the media has many advantages. However, through the years of regularly providing expert quotes, having my business featured in articles and on TV and providing lively conversation on radio shows, I've narrowed its advantages down to two: (1) Media exposure is effective in helping you be first in people's minds even when you're not first in the marketplace and (2) it sows credibility seeds that can't be planted through paid advertising. Although you shouldn't rely on the media as a sole tool, you should reserve some marketing energy to land publicity for your business. You can factor media activities into your overall marketing plan. In comparison to a series of paid advertisements, a series of media appearances can actually be inexpensive and a very cost-effective investment over time.

Media representatives are always looking for interesting stories and useful information to present to their audience. You can steer them your way through carefully crafted press releases. If you have interesting information from an industry survey you've conducted, participated in the development of your community, received an award or special recognition or have some useful tips to share, you are a candidate for publicity. A house-painting service, for example, sent a press release announcing its involvement in giving a facelift to a community landmark. It was newsworthy because the facility serves as host to an annual celebration and completion of the renovation was scheduled around the big day. The service was mentioned in all materials promoting the event and the new exterior, thus drawing attention to the painter's business.

Publicity can help you in other ways. A product manufacturer used responses from publicity as a test-market indicator. Its product was featured in a column syndicated nationwide. Orders poured in but only from certain cities. The manufacturer used this information as it targeted retailers in various areas.

Publicity will often generate more publicity; other media folks will be pointed to you because of past coverage. However, you'll benefit most from media marketing when you can regularly feed media sources with information about your business, which has a cumulative effect (see the following article, "How to woo the media").

HOW TO WOO THE MEDIA

Wooing the media is simpler than you think. When you approach them in the right way and with the right information, they'll be receptive to your message. You can enjoy media marketing success by following these five steps:

1. Learn how to tell it to the press. A large percentage of stories you see, hear and read in the media are generated from hundreds of releases received each month. Unfortunately, most press releases are thrown in the trash because they're ineffective and not written in the proper format. There are a number of materials available to help you learn how to write a press release. I've included some of these references in the Bootstrapper's Follow-up File for this chapter, beginning on page 121. They all provide you with sample releases along with how-to information.

2. Build a targeted media list. A common mistake many people make is sending out releases to any and every media contact they can find. This untargeted approach isn't very effective because your releases are probably going to inappropriate contacts, which is a misuse of your resources. By spending some time developing and building a targeted list, your business will be better positioned to receive some notable publicity.

First, define who you're trying to reach. The answer should be spelled out in your marketing plan. Next, refer to library directories, such as *Bacon's Newspapers/Magazines Directory* (Bacon's Information, 1996), *The Working Press of the Nation* (National Register Publishing, 1996) or *Gale Directory of Publications and Broadcast Media* (Gale Research, 1996). These directories include a description of the editorial content of each media outlet—which will help you find the best outlet for your audience—along with contact names and information requirements, such as new product literature, press releases or how-to information. Compile a list of local or national media, using the most recent directories available, and use this as your mailing list.

Once you start receiving responses from your mailings, you should keep track of those contacts—perhaps coding them in your database as live sources. Get the complete names and follow-up information for any media person that contacts you. In my office it's standard operating procedure to ask for a phone number, fax number, e-mail address and Web address from everybody. You can *develop* a media list by using the directories, but to *build* your list, you must stay in contact with actual media representatives.

3. Send out timely, useful information. Releases that include startling facts or statistics, announce a co-op deal between you and a brand company, offer a free workshop or seminar, introduce a new company catering to an unusual niche market or tell people anything that is unique or out of the ordinary can be considered newsworthy. If you have professional photographs, you can include those with your mailing. Crafting a release on helpful consumer tips can also land you a media placement. For example, a tax preparation service could send out a release titled "10 Deductions

Commonly Overlooked" during tax season. Also, if you publish a newsletter, you should regularly send it to media contacts. It'll keep your name before them and may prompt a call for something they're working on.

4. Make yourself findable. Every placement will not include full contact information about your business. You can, however, be on the offensive and make yourself impossible not to find. Start by having any names by which you do business listed properly with directory assistance. For example, my business phone number can be found under: Research Done Write!, *Bootstrappin' Entrepreneur* and Kimberly Stanséll. This strategy helps ensure that when a feature article only mentions my name or the business name and the words "based in Los Angeles," people can find me. Also, being listed in professional and industry directories can help.

5. Prepare to ride a roller coaster. Sometimes a placement will produce wonderful results and other times it may not yield a single phone call. There may be instances when you spend a lot of time being interviewed for a piece and end up being edited out. As you become a seasoned publicity-seeker, you'll learn to stay focused and move on to the next opportunity, continually sending materials out. It's the nature of the business, but it's an investment worth your time.

Survival Tip #63: Follow the ABCs of making a "free" offer.

Freebies can be an effective or expensive proposition. The offer of a free brochure, special report, tips sheet, product sample or consultation can keep your phone ringing nonstop. It's effective when you're able to convert a high number of inquiries into sales. It's expensive when you're just entertaining freebie junkies.

Your target audience will determine the effectiveness of a free offer. If you've identified the idiosyncrasies of your market, you'll have an idea of how marketing without samples will fly in the face of your prospects. Remember the mature market group (see Survival Tip #20)? Industry protocol may require freebies. For example, it's standard practice for a person to have a free consultation or demonstration before receiving an electrolysis treatment. Some offerings lend themselves to be sampled. Manufacturers send out toiletry, food and cleaning items, and you can sample Boston Market menu items before placing an order. If your offering is expensive, novel and up against heavy competition, freebies can work toward helping people see its value.

If you feel that your budget can't absorb a lot of giveaways, then consider some ways to modify your offer. When Accent on Travel purged its free packets mailing list, they discovered that a low percentage of inquirers were actually booking trips. They switched their game plan by collecting a shipping and handling fee for the packets, which now include a $30 coupon redeemable toward any trip. Selling samples of your offering at a reduced rate can work well. This way prospects get to try the item without incurring a great expense. A word of caution, however. Make sure that your free offer isn't a deceptive lure and complies with the guidelines outlined in the Federal Trade Commission's *Guide Concerning Use of the Word "Free"* (for ordering information, see page 125).

You should also spend time developing a follow-up and tracking system to gauge your results. For example, calculating your sales conversion rates will indicate how well the strategy's working. Some people won't buy right after they sample, so you'll need to invest in follow-up activities to secure an actual sale. Logging all this information can help you create new or better ways to sell your product or service.

Survival Tip #64: Build a tailor-made network.

Networking is also a form of marketing. It positions you to see, hear and be in-the-know without trying Michael Keaton's stab at multiplicity. Instead, other people are at work for you. Your relationship with them creates a top-of-the-mind awareness so that when they see opportunities or information you could use, they pass it on. Networking at its best is the byproduct of reciprocal relationships built over time. It's a critical part of your marketing arsenal. But it only works when you do—you'll get from it what you put into it.

Many people shy away from networking or find themselves in awkward situations because they misunderstand the process. People confess to me all the time: "I'm really not a 'meetings' person." Networking isn't limited to just attending gatherings to pass out business cards. It's not about imposing yourself on someone or only calling when you want something. Networking is about looking for ways to help your professional peers and exchanging resources with them. Great networkers look at people they meet and ponder how they can help them. They find out how by listening to what people tell them about themselves. And when they come across an article or book, they know who to pass it along to because they're familiar with other people's interests or needs.

Your focus isn't just on building up a big pool of contacts—rather, it's on nurturing quality ones and establishing your credibility to the point that when you do need something, people will gladly accommodate you.

You'll benefit most as a networker when you operate within a tailor-made network, a system that's compatible with your style and goals. You'll find yourself moving away from merely mimicking what you see others doing and beginning to focus on strategies that are right for your business. Your system should feel like a well-fit glove, and you'll be more apt to commit to building your network for the long haul. I've relied on five factors to build my "network that works." Here they are (Survival Tips #65 through #69):

Survival Tip #65: Network based on who you are.

You'll gain more ground by pursuing opportunities where you feel most comfortable sharing and giving of yourself. The compatibility of your personality with the business type will be crucial in this area (see Survival Tip #21). You're selling yourself as well as your business. It's important to avoid approaches that make you appear clumsy and choose ones that enable you to shine as a professional.

Here's an example. A psychologist needed to increase the referral stream to his practice. He was already nurturing his network through regular lunch meetings, but he needed to do more. But hard selling wasn't his forte. He was more effective in one-on-one relationships, as he should be, being a therapist. The best way for the psychologist to market his practice was through gatekeepers—people who would refer others to him. Good networkers are attuned to the needs of their contacts. The psychologist knew that his gatekeepers were devoted to their own professional growth. So he began hosting free, intimate professional workshops, to which his "referral club" and their guests could come and learn new techniques and gain new information. The result: His referrals doubled within a few months.

There are a few reasons why this strategy worked. It's important to note that the psychologist's one-on-one preference is compatible with his type of business. Although many practitioners do market through teaching and public speaking, these strategies were not a fit for this psychologist. The issue was to increase his top-of-mind awareness and referral circle. The approach was effective because he was interacting in a manner that was compatible with who he is while exchanging something of great value to his colleagues.

Survival Tip #66: Network based on your business type.

All businesses are not networked the same. Some businesses are best networked through traditional alliances, such as active membership in a chamber of commerce or professional association. Other businesses benefit from faceless networking through the online world. You may also benefit from a combination of traditional and unconventional approaches. However, knowing your business will enable you to more clearly identify the most effective strategies for your situation (see Survival Tip #19).

"Building block" options may include your peer group, competitors, suppliers or folks in your neighborhood. Your network may be built around industry affiliations. A desktop publisher who specializes in business communications, for example, gets a lot of mileage from visible involvement with communications organizations, such as the International Association of Business Communicators. Some businesses benefit through forming a professional team. A florist, caterer, photographer, event planner and disc jockey could exchange referrals or scout out and bid collectively on joint opportunities.

Telecommunication makes it easier for people to become telenetworkers. It's common for businesspeople, particularly those whose businesses have a national scope or are run from a home office, to tell you about reciprocal relationships they've developed through Internet forum groups and over the phone. However, for this to be an effective strategy, your professionalism and enthusiasm must come across in your conversations and writing.

Your business's tailor-made strategies will also determine follow-up methods and frequency. Self-publishers, for instance, often exchange publication subscriptions. Or to establish yourself in online areas, you'll need to showcase your expertise by regularly contributing to a chat forum or posting answers to others' questions. A helpful resource on networking communication links: *52 Ways to Re-connect, Follow Up and Stay in Touch...When You Don't Have Time to Network* by Anne Baber and Lynne Waymon (for ordering information, see page 121).

Survival Tip #67: Network based on what you have to offer and need to gain.

What you know is important in networking. People will only stay connected with productive relationships. If you never appear to know anything, you won't have a network to speak of. Being dubbed as a stingy or tight-fisted networker has the same effect. Think about all your knowledge assets. Maybe you consume a lot of information on an ongoing basis through regular resources. Or you may have access to people or events that your colleagues don't. Then think about what it is *you* need to know. You may not be able to keep up with changes in technology or have problems finding qualified people to outsource with. Once you're clear on what you can exchange, use your networking radar to match yourself with exchange opportunities.

You may be able to network through your work. That's what I do. My projects allow me to regularly discover new small-business resources (many of which I'm sharing with you in this book). I also meet and interview interesting and knowledgeable people for my writing projects. The benefit is that the majority of the people are interested in or involved with entrepreneurship, which makes it easy for us to stay in touch. Adding them to my mailing list for my newsletter or other informational mailings is a cinch; likewise, I'm on their lists. We each appreciate the valuable information, we stay connected and I always have a ready network of sources to draw from no matter what I'm working on. Essentially, every contact becomes a link in my network.

Jan Melnik of Durham, Connecticut, uses another strategy. Through her books and newsletter, Melnik has become a mentor to the secretarial and office support services industry. Her give-and-get networking tool: She produces a summary report of highlights from the annual conference of the National Association of Secretarial Services, sharing the ideas and information presented in various workshops. Melnik's supplement is sent out as an "extra" with her newsletter, and she even posts it in an online forum. It benefits those industry professionals who were unable to attend. Furthermore, it generates an unbelievable amount of word-of-mouth for her as the industry expert.

Survival Tip #68: Develop a three-tier networking system.

It's important that you continue to grow as a professional. Networking with a variety of people who are at various places in their journey can help you. I call it "trilevel networking":

- **Level one: Network with people who are more experienced than you.** These people usually are further along than you or are where you want to be. You get to learn from these individuals. You get to hear how they got from point A to point Z. You also get to hear about the type of projects they're involved with and how they went about landing them. These people are also the most likely to let you in on a trade secret exchange (see Survival Tip #128). By listening to them, you can determine how to go about reaching their level. They serve as mentors in many ways.

- **Level two: Network with your professional equals.** These are individuals who have the same experience or status as you. Since you're pretty much on the same level, you'll have a sort of "buddy system" relationship with these people. You can work to keep each other on track toward your respective goals. If you find it easier to confide in others you view as equals, people at this level can be a good sounding board for you.

• **Level three: Network with professional newcomers.**
They're just getting started and trying to learn. They will
appreciate your knowledge and support and are likely to
repay you later on.

It's through this system that you'll learn the most about reciproc-
ity because on any given day you may find yourself giving or getting
or both.

You may not start off with all these relationships intact. Defining
some goals for your networking activities will help you stay focused on
forming strategic alliances—beneficial to both parties—and you'll be
better able to stay in touch systematically and manage those relationships properly. Don't squelch potential relationships by being careless.
Whenever people show you a professional courtesy always take time
out to follow up with a thank-you or feedback. With so many communication tools at our fingertips there's really no excuse for not doing so.

There are no instant networks. It takes a commitment on your
part to build a network conversation by conversation, exchange by
exchange. It's to your advantage to start building your network today.

Survival Tip #69: Become an exhibitionist.

Showcasing your business at a trade show, conference or networking event can work as a vehicle to reach your target audience.
Whether you pay for a booth or display table, you should always focus
on matching your dollars with the right opportunity. Start by scrutinizing a show's profile package. Your decision to participate will be
influenced by factors such as how the show's theme relates to your
audience; the number and type of exhibiting companies; how the
event will be promoted; and the track record of the event's sponsor. I
was once flown in to speak at a New York City expo that yielded a
poor turnout because it wasn't promoted properly. It was a free trip
for me, but the exhibitors ended up paying to sit around all weekend.

You, too, have a responsibility to bring foot traffic to the exhibit.
You can display show materials and coupons in your business or send
out a special invitation mailing to customers, colleagues and prospects. Make an intriguing offer—lure them to your booth to pick up

some special item or to participate in a drawing and win something valuable.

Look for free exhibition opportunities. That's what Jamis Jones Williams of Chefs in Your Pocket, a catering business in Rocklin, California, did. As a regular Sam's Warehouse shopper, her firm received an automatic invitation to be a debut exhibitor at the Taste of Sam's. The exposure led to dozens of new customers and a contract to cater a company picnic for the community's largest employer—a project she'd been denied a year earlier.

You don't have to spend a fortune on display items either. You can make a professional presentation with second-life items of your own (see Survival Tip #49) or through a used displays dealer.

Survival Tip #70: Be a friend to your community.

Running a business provides you with unique opportunities to contribute to your community in a meaningful way. In the SmartGiving™ seminars, David Calabria of Calabria & Company in Oshkosh, Wisconsin, teaches corporations how to develop growth strategies while strengthening worthy causes. Small businesses can adopt a similar approach and become players in their communities, too. When you lend support through goods, services or time, you're strengthening your community—making it a better place to live and do business. In turn, your business reaps some benefits: You'll stand out from your competition, your product or service is showcased prominently before the public and you'll gain visibility not enjoyed by every firm.

Here are some examples of SmartGiving™ at work in small firms. A hair salon teams up with a nonprofit job referral service and offers unemployed job seekers a free haircut and manicure before they go out on interviews. A graphic design firm donates its services to arts organizations in its community and is now regarded as the quality place for typesetting work. Other affordable contributions can include sponsoring an award, donating a raffle prize or earmarking a percentage of your profits for a designated organization. The National Alliance of Businesses encourages business owners to enhance classroom curriculums by speaking to students about their profession and what it takes to be successful. As employers, they help develop a future pool of laborers by getting involved. According to a survey by the research center of Boston College, eight out of 10 people say they purchased from a business because they approved of its involvement with the community. Your outreach efforts can create a win-win situation for everyone.

You can begin to align yourself with worthy causes by identifying core needs, problems or opportunities in your community. Use your core list to pinpoint organizations and groups that proactively solicit help for a cause. You can then pick an appropriate association for your business based on your own or customers' interest. Either way, your company will be positioned as a community giver and benefit from the goodwill effects that advertising alone cannot buy.

Survival Tip #71: Speak and teach your message.

A surefire way to qualify your business is to speak before an attentive audience. Leading a class or workshop or delivering a message before a group of professionals can help establish you as an expert in your industry. Adult extension course programs, libraries, bookstores, community organizations and trade associations are interested in qualified people to speak at their events or programs. Your challenge will be to match your message with the right audience and venue.

Determine what topics you could speak about that are a natural tie-in for your business. A small business attorney, for instance, teaches a "How to Run Your Business on the Right Side of the Law" workshop. Next, you'll need to match your presentation with a program that your idea will complement and that is able to reach your target audience. The attorney's workshop could be taught through an adult extension program or workshop specialists, such as the Learning Annex. Your expertise may even qualify you to lead a presentation through SCORE.

You can also deliver and promote your message independently. A woman-owned auto repair service offered free one-day seminars that taught women how to check under their hoods for problems. The owner hosted the seminars once a month at her storefront garage. The media loved her story and generously plugged the seminars. Guess who the attendees patronized when they had car trouble?

Sideline gigs can provide you with business research, too. A computer store owner teaches adult education computer courses at local high schools and libraries. Class feedback has helped her develop her customer profile and mailing list and pinpoint niche markets, geographical selling spots and price structures.

Initially, you'll probably present your message for free, a low fee or an honorarium. That's okay, especially if you're speaking before a well-targeted audience that can generate business with resulting profits that would surpass any fee you might have charged. There are other tangibles you can pick up in lieu of cash for your presentation. You can ask for an attendee or membership list to help you develop your mailing list, a free ad in an event program or a prominent mention of your business name or location in materials promoting the activity.

Before you approach any group, you'll need to prepare a proposal for your class or a letter outlining your credentials and the content of your presentation. Should you decide to turn to speaking as a source of income, you should sign up with a local speakers' bureau, participate in a local Toastmasters group and begin reading or taking classes on how to become a professional speaker.

Survival Tip #72: Invest in strategies with a multiplying effect.

Effective marketing strategies always work double time—feeding off of each other and creating a ripple effect. Just like multifunction equipment, your marketing tools should have multiple purposes. Rather than investing in a device that's used to communicate your message in one way, explore the device's potential to be used in other media to get results. The pay-off: You'll get more bang for your buck. Here are some examples:

- A yellow pages ad can be reprinted into a postcard and used as a customer service follow-up tool.

- If you're a guest in an online chat, the transcripts can be posted on your own Web page or provided to media representatives for developing questions to ask you during a live interview.

- A business card can be affixed on the outside of a presentation folder.

- A bylined article has a lot of potential. It establishes you as an expert, and it's a vehicle for educating your market. It can be reproduced for presentation packets, included in promotional mailings and offered as a one-time reprint item in other publications.

- If you've created a quiz or a contest to educate the market about your offering, you could incorporate it into an advertising specialty item. For example, if the quiz had 12 questions, you could put a different question on each month of a promotional calendar you've created for your customers.

- You can use your voice mail service for announcing sales or other appealing information about your company, instead of simply for managing your calls.

Look for ways to repackage your work. A case study about how you solved a client's problem can be printed in a promotional newsletter or work as a supplement to your brochure or proposals. Newsletters are mileage maximizers, too. I took money-saving tips from an issue of my newsletter and turned it into a press release titled "Ten Ways to Save Small Businesses Thousands in 1995." My press release quickly resulted in a spot on a radio show and in citations in a half-dozen other publications.

Strategies with a multiplying effect give you more value for your initial efforts and free you to concentrate on other ways to build your business.

Survival Tip #73: Commit to capturing "share of mind."

You'll cement your place in a market by gaining customers' "share of mind." Your name, identity and offering benefits are systematically repeated before your audience to the point that there becomes an instant association between your company and their need. Share of mind is gained by people seeing and hearing about your company time and time again. It's a process that's nurtured and built over a period of time, and it can only be secured through a commitment to your marketing plan.

Repetition is your power. You'll need diligence in dispatching your marketing efforts. They can start with one ad that is followed by many others. Regularly appearing in the paper and having your expert opinion quoted throughout the media contribute to the process. Nurturing your existing client relationships will translate into word-of-mouth endorsements. Your signs, mailings, phone calls, displays and other weapons help solidify and intensify your share of mind. If you fail or become negligent in your commitment, you'll lose some ground in the building process. It's better to commit and follow through on a few tactics than to occasionally indulge in a bunch of activities.

Share of mind is built slowly. However, you'll feel it is worth the wait when people say to you, "I keep hearing about you and decided to call" or "Wow, you must be doing something right because I see your name everywhere." Besides the resulting financial rewards, the emotional rewards you'll get from hearing these comments will alone make your tenacity seem worthwhile.

Survival Tip #74: Maintain a presence even when you're busy.

A marketing mistake to avoid: ignoring your marketing agenda when you get swamped with work. This is easy to do, especially when you're involved with long-term projects or in the midst of your peak season. Prolonged busy times create a sense of invincibility—you begin to believe that there's no way it's going to end. It's wise, however, to invest in "presence maintenance" strategies, which work when you're not around.

Although you may be operating at a saturation point, you can still engage in marketing activities without generating immediate business. One way is to underwrite a public radio show. National underwriting spots are pricey; however, costs are lower on local levels. Classical stations will acknowledge sponsors throughout different segments of a show and include an 18-word description of each sponsor. Your description can't be a sales pitch, but it will help you maintain your presence of mind in the marketplace. One bootstrapper maintains her presence as an active board member of a local women's forum. She serves as the group's media spokesperson and her name appears on all its press releases. When fielding the calls, she has a chance to talk about her business while serving as a volunteer.

You can maintain your presence by staying within the opportunity loop. For example, if you are unable to serve certain customers but know of other businesses that could, rather than passing on business, set up a referral network. You can even collect a percentage fee from the professionals you refer customers to. You will be inviting queries to still come your way while positioning yourself to take advantage of opportunities should you need the business.

Survival Tip #75: Don't be afraid to do your own thing.

Creativity in marketing can attract people, but it also involves taking some risks and putting yourself out there for possible rejection. People who market their businesses must be confident about putting their own twist on a marketing idea.

A chiropractor actively promotes his practice through what he calls "marketing with a human quality that projects a positive image." His gutsy approach: He rides an elephant in the local 4th of July parade, followed by an entourage of loyal patients who pass out peanuts to onlookers. The community reacts positively to his approach; the number of his patients doubled the first year he did it. Another bold move comes from an author. She caravaned across the country with her three children in a new van custom-painted with animals and the title of her childcare book. She stopped at various cities to do speaking engagements and teach workshops on the subject of her book, as well as some radio and TV appearances and newspaper interviews. Her stunt caught the attention of *Publishers Weekly*, landing her a full-page feature in the magazine. It was great coverage and an impetus for increased book sales.

You can't be afraid to impose your creativity into a situation. Recently a *Chicago Tribune* reporter was prompted to call me by my quotes in a 1993 *Home Office Computing* magazine article. She was working on a technology feature, and she was interested in my buying philosophy: Avoid buying too much, too little or just the wrong thing. We arranged a photo shoot at a local Staples to accompany the article. The photographer explained how he planned to shoot the pictures, which really didn't capture the essence of the piece. So, I pitched him my idea of photographing an overflowing basket of software and technology goodies, showing the readers that this is what will happen if you don't follow my advice. He took a few pictures with my idea and several with his own. When the article appeared, guess whose photo idea was used? You guessed it—mine.

This chapter has provided you with the tools, techniques, safeguards and ideas you need to be a smart, bootstrappin' marketer. Now, go out there and do your own thing!

Bootstrapper's Follow-up File

52 Ways to Re-connect, Follow Up and Stay in Touch...When You Don't Have Time to Network by Anne Baber and Lynne Waymon (Kendall/Hunt Publishing Company, 1994); 800-228-0810. $14.95.

Art Marketing Hotline, 800-999-7013. A **free** marketing advice hotline for artists and other creative business owners.

Cabletelevision Advertising Bureau, 830 Third Ave., New York, NY 10017; 212-751-7770; fax: 212-832-3268. Provides a **free** copy of *Guide to Local Cable Advertising: Tips on Planning and Buying Cable to Generate Maximum Impact from Your Local Media Budget* and a resource list of available publications.

Complying with the 900-Number Rule, Federal Trade Commission, Public Reference, Room 130, Washington, DC 20580-0001; Web address: www.ftc.gov. A **free**, 21-page guide explaining the legal guidelines for marketing with 900 numbers.

Complying with the Telemarketing Sales Rule, Federal Trade Commission, Public Reference, Room 130, Washington, DC 20580-0001; Web address: www.ftc.gov. A **free**, 36-page guide explaining the legal guidelines for telemarketing practices.

Getting Publicity: A Do-It-Yourself Guide for Small Business and Non-Profit Groups by Tana Fletcher and Julia Rockler (Self-Counsel Press, 1995); 800-663-3007. $14.95.

Grammar Hotline Directory, Tidewater Community College Writing Center, 1700 College Crescent, Virginia Beach, VA 23456. A nationwide directory of Grammar Hotline centers, which provide **free** answers to short questions about writing and are staffed by faculty members, graduate students, editors and former teachers. Send SASE.

Guerrilla Marketing Newsletter, Guerrilla Marketing International, 800-748-6444; Web address: www.gmarketing.com. Published bimonthly by Jay Conrad Levinson. $59/year.

Guerrilla Marketing: Secrets for Making Big Profits from Your Small Business by Jay Conrad Levinson (Houghton Mifflin Company, 1993); 800-225-3362. $11.95. Other books in series include: *The Guerrilla Marketing Handbook*, *Guerrilla Marketing for the Home-Based Business*, *Guerrilla Marketing Online*, *Guerrilla Marketing Advertising* and *Guerrilla Marketing Weapons*.

Guide Concerning Use of the Word "Free," Federal Trade Commission, Public Reference, Room 130, Washington, DC 20580-0001; Web address: www.ftc.gov. A **free** guide explaining the legal guidelines when using the word "free" in your advertising.

Incentive: Managing and Marketing Through Motivation, 355 Park Ave. S., New York, NY 10010; 212-592-6400; fax: 212-592-6459; Web address: www.incentivemag.com. A **free** incentive marketing magazine.

Making the Most of Voice Mail and *Voice Mail Tips and Etiquette*, Pacific Bell Information Services, Room 2500Q, 3401 Crow Canyon Rd., San Ramon, CA 94583; 800-954-8477 (in California). Two **free** how-to guides.

Marketability: Bottom Line Strategies for Micro-Business and the Self-Employed, Impression Impact, 369 Lindsay Pond Rd., Concord, MA 01742. A quarterly newsletter filled with marketing tips and ideas. Send SASE for a **free** copy.

Marketing Boot Camp: 85 Profit-Packed Tools, Techniques and Strategies to Boost Your Bottom Line...NOW! by Arnold Sanow and J. Daniel McComas (Kendall/Hunt Publishing, 1994); 800-228-0810. $24.95.

Marketing with Newsletters: How to boost sales, add members & raise funds with a printed, faxed or Web-site newsletter, Second Edition, by Elaine Floyd (EF Communications, 1997); 800-264-6305; Web address: newsletterinfo.com. $29.95.

National Alliance of Business, 800-787-2848; Web address: www.nab.com. Encourages educators and businesspeople to join forces to enhance the nation's educational system; provides information on how companies are contributing to the educational process.

National Speakers Association, 1500 S. Priest Dr., Tempe, AZ 85281; 602-968-2552; fax: 602-968-0911. Membership organization; sponsors workshops, offers training certification program and publishes resource materials for professional and aspiring speakers.

Procurement Opportunities: A Small Business Guide to Procurement Reform, SBA Advocacy Office, Mail Code 3114, 409 Third St. SW, Washington, DC 20416; fax: 202-205-6928. A **free**, 49-page guide designed to help small firms take advantage of government procurement opportunities as a result of changes in federal policy. Offers specific advice on marketing your business to the government. Fax or mail your request.

Promotional Products Association International, 3125 Skyway Circle N., Irving, TX 75038-3526; 972-252-0404 (ask for marketing communications department); fax: 972-594-7224; Web address: www.promotion-clinic.ppa.org. Offers a **free** book, *Make Promotional Products Work for You*, along with other case-study booklets on using advertising specialties and a list of distributors in your area.

Simple Steps to a Powerful Presentation, Quill Corporation, 800-789-6640; Web address: www.quillcorp.com. A **free**, 25-page guide of tips and ideas to help you create your own dynamic written and oral presentation.

Six Steps to Free Publicity: and dozens of other ways to win free media attention for you and your business by Marcia Yudkin (Plume/Penguin USA, 1994); 800-331-4624. $9.95.

Small Business Success, Pacific Bell Directory, 800-848-8000. A **free**, 80-page annual magazine. New volume published every spring in conjunction with the SBA. Filled with marketing strategies and small business management tips. Past volumes available while supplies last.

Speak and Grow Rich by Dottie and Lilly Walters (Prentice Hall, 1989); 800-922-0579. $14.95.

Speaker's Idea File: Quotes, Anecdotes, Humor, and Statistics, Ragan Communications, 800-878-5331; Web address: www.ragan.com. A monthly newsletter of tips, quotes and information to help you make a professional speaking presentation. **Free** sample copy available.

Start Up Marketing: An Entrepreneur's Guide to Advertising, Marketing and Promoting Your Business by Philip R. Nulman (Career Press, 1996); 800-CAREER-1 (201-848-0310 in N.J. and outside U.S.). $16.99.

The Electronic Mail Advantage: Applications and Benefits, Electronic Messaging Association, 1655 N. Fort Myer Dr., Arlington, VA 22209; 703-524-5550; fax: 703-524-5558; e-mail address: 70007,2377@compuserve.com. **Free** case study booklets on e-mail savings and applications.

The Publicity Handbook: How to Maximize Publicity for Products, Services and Organizations by David R. Yale (NTC Business Books, 1991); 800-323-4900. $19.95.

The Publicity Manual by Kate Kelly (Visibility Enterprises, 1995); 800-784-0602. $29.95.

The Small Business Guide to Advertising with Direct Mail: Smart Solutions for Today's Entrepreneur, U.S. Postal Service, Advertising Mail/Product Management Department, Room 5540, 475 L'Enfant Plaza SW, Washington, DC 20260. A **free**, 88-page guide filled with money-saving tips and step-by-step instructions for planning a direct mail marketing campaign.

The Teaching Marketplace by Bart Brodsky and Janet Geis (Community Resource Institute Press, 1992); 510-526-7190 (or write: Community Resource Institute Press, 1442-A Walnut #51, Berkeley, CA 94709). $14.95.

Toastmasters International, P.O. Box 9052, Mission Viejo, CA 92690; 714-858-8255; fax: 714-858-1207. Provides referrals to local Toastmasters groups and offers a **free** copy of *Ten Tips for Successful Public Speaking*.

Tradeshows Worldwide: An International Directory of Events, Facilities and Suppliers, Gale Research, 800-347-4253. A library reference book.

Used exhibit dealers: World Exhibit Brokers, 800-743-0330; Exhibitgroup, 800-424-6224; The Exhibit Emporium, 800-541-9100; SecondLife Exhibits, 617-884-7455; fax: 617-884-0190.

Writing Effective News Releases: How to Get FREE Publicity for Yourself, Your Business, or Your Organization by Catherine V. McIntyre (Piccadilly Books, 1992); 719-548-1844 (or write: Piccadilly Books, P.O. Box 25203, Colorado Springs, CO 25203). $17.95.

Yellow Pages Fraud Hotline, Yellow Pages Publishers Association, 800-841-0639; Web address: www.yppa.org. Provides a **free** tip sheet, *Beware of Bogus Yellow Pages "Bills."*

Yellow Pages Publishers Association, 3373 Cherry Creek Mountain Dr., Suite 920, Denver, CO 80209; fax: 303-320-6999. Publishes resource materials on yellow pages advertising, with information categorized by industry. Specify your business type in written requests to the association.

Chapter 6

Customer Service and Client Relations

"...The least expensive way to make more money and grow faster is to be perceived as a service leader."

—John Tschohl, Service Quality
Institute, Bloomington, Minn.

Survival Tip #76: Embrace customer service truisms.

Listen to what various studies are saying:

Truth #1: A small business that places heavy emphasis on customer service is more likely to survive and succeed than competitors who emphasize advantages such as lower price, convenience, speed of delivery or product performance.

Truth #2: Customers will gladly pay a premium for products or services to companies that differentiate themselves from their competitors with customer-driven service.

Truth #3: The number-one reason American companies lose business is due to poor service. Adopt a treat-you-how-I'm-feeling-today service style, and it may be the last time you see a customer. It's too easy for someone to go elsewhere. Consistently serve customers in the way they'd like to be treated (and better), and you'll keep them coming back for more.

Customers who feel well-served by your business can become priceless allies. Their spirit of cooperation will come shining through when you need it. Well-served customers will gladly brag about your business to others; they'll remain loyal in the face of cheaper or tempting offers; they'll provide you with valuable feedback; and they'll gladly give you their money. Nordstrom, for example, has created a loyal patronage through its legendary customer service. It's been reported that Nordstrom's sales have outpaced its competitors' during recessionary periods. Why? Customers will give their money first to a business that treats them well, and their loyalty will remain constant in lean times.

Most customers have a tendency to patronize businesses with which they are familiar and like. They are slow to change or stray from a business unless they're given a good reason. Once customers buy from you, your job is to serve them in such a way that they'll be inspired to use your services again. Looking for a competitive advantage? Then run your operation by delivering quality service from the perspective of your customer or client. Interested in learning how? Read on.

Survival Tip #77: Court the right customer.

Imagine a scenario when the customer is not "always right." Unconventionally speaking, the customer is not always right when he or she is the *wrong* customer for your business. You've poured resources into developing a profile of the end user of your product or service. You also have marketing tools and strategies at work communicating to that customer. So why court a prospect who doesn't value your offering? A person becomes disqualified as a customer when he or she doesn't have: the financial ability to pay; a real, immediate need for your product or service; and the authority to make a buying decision.

Too many businesses exert energy (and waste money) chasing a "hot" prospect who is really *not* qualified to be a customer. Say your market research has identified your target audience to be women who earn more than $75,000 annually (a select group, considering that only 400,000 women in the U.S. pull in this much dough). Will their perception of your offering differ from that of a woman whose annual income is $25,000? Yes, indeed. What type of mental payoff could you honestly create in a buyer's mind that would convince her to buy something she really can't afford? It's an uphill battle and a misuse of your energy and funds. When you wander away from your customer criteria, there are other effects, too. You'll find yourself trying to be all things to all people, which can result in a haphazard customer service style. You'll end up directing to hopeless prospects attention that could have been used to turn good customers into frequent buyers through follow-up efforts, surveys and other outreach activities (see Survival Tips #81 and #88).

Bob Serling of Stafford Communications in Cardiff, California, advises his clientele of small- to medium-sized business owners to devise a customer screening process. Here's how it works:

Divide prospects into three categories:

- **Group A:** people who meet all the buying criteria; they can afford your offering and have a fairly immediate need for it *and* the authority to make a decision to buy it.

- **Group B:** people who meet part of the criteria, but there's something delaying the buying decision. (You'll want to monitor this group by staying in touch through your customer communications program. See Survival Tip #86.)

- **Group C:** people who don't meet the criteria at all—they don't have a real, immediate need for your offering, they can't afford what you're offering and they don't have the authority to make the decision to buy it. They're wrong for your business.

The results from Serling's screening strategy are worth noting. Tracking businesses that have used this process has revealed that businesses have been able to reduce their customer base by 50 to 70 percent while dramatically increasing their profits by devoting their energy to people who are qualified to buy.

Profitable businesses aren't afraid to alienate segments of the marketplace. They realize that the wrong customer only drains a business, whereas an investment in the right customer pays dividends.

Survival Tip #78: Handle price objections with finesse.

Today's consumers are more price-conscious than ever. Although studies show that customers are willing to pay more for a product or service when there's a perceived value attached, matching your cost with their pocketbooks can be hard work. In large measure, being able to sway a buying decision in your favor will depend on how well you handle price objections. It's premature to automatically deem people as unqualified customers when they say, "Your price is too high." If you understand the meaning of an objection, you can respond with finesse and still get the sale.

First, identify the reason for the price objection. By simply asking why a person feels that way, you may indeed discover that your price exceeds the person's means. However, the question may also lead you to some other valuable insights. You may learn that the person isn't making the right comparisons. For example, a customer who balks at the price of an all-leather shoe because one that doesn't include a leather sole is cheaper is making an off-base comparison. More leather equals more money. If someone is comparing your product or service to one of lesser quality, it's your job to point out the benefits of your offering that are worth the difference in price.

You can also chip away at price objections when you quantify the benefits in terms of price. For example: "You can churn out 3,000 more copies a day with our machine. How much would you save in labor?" Another effective approach: Minimize the difference by showing how insignificant the price difference comes out to be over the lifetime of the product when those extra benefits are taken into consideration. For example: "The difference between the two items is only $50. That's less than $1 a month over a five-year period. But with this product's efficiency feature, which the other item doesn't have, you're really *saving* money in labor costs. How long do you think it will take to save $2 in labor?"

These product analogies can be adapted to service-providing businesses. A printout of what it would cost the client to hire a staffer to handle the project under discussion could be drafted beforehand and presented when the client is having difficulty seeing the price advantages of using an outside professional.

Don't forget to mention the customer service benefits that go along with buying from you. If you're offering 24-hour turnaround or other special services, for example, the buyer needs to understand that those are factors in your premium price. Customers may not need or want this level of service and will not see the value of paying for it; therefore, they may not be the right customers for your business.

You should, however, make a mental note of price objections that you encounter through the years—even when your business is booming. Down the line some objections may be indications of marketplace trends. It may be impossible to eliminate every objection that comes up. However, when you take time out to prepare for those that do come your way, you'll find it easier to close more sales.

Survival Tip #79: Carry some of the risk on your shoulders.

Your sales presentation has to be effective in overcoming a buyer's anxiety. When you coat your offering with a guarantee, you can gain an edge in persuading someone to do business with you. Interestingly, though, most businesses *do* stand behind their product or service but fail to communicate their stance in an up-front, compelling manner. Thus, you inadvertently end up being viewed as a risky proposition in the eyes of potential customers. Samples or demonstrations whet prospects' appetite for your offering. A guarantee—which assures prospects that they have nothing to lose by trying you—can hook them into a full-scale buying commitment.

Here's an example of how a marketing expert secures subscriptions to the newsletter *Marketing Makeover* (800-266-8885). This newsletter is satisfaction-guaranteed down to the last word of the last issue. If you come to the 12th issue of your annual subscription and decide you want a refund, you'll get it. What's more, once you sign on, you immediately receive three bonus reports of real-life profit-building strategies and case studies, in addition to the newsletter. If you don't feel *these* are worth it, you can cancel your subscription and get your $97 subscription fee refunded. The publisher's philosophy: What do you have to lose by trying such a profoundly beneficial offer?

Worried that an offer like this only sets you up to be taken advantage of? Don't be, especially when customer satisfaction is your service mark. Your objective here is to persuasively state—or exploit—what you plan to do to make the customer happy. Guaranteeing your work can help put your company to the test. You'll be kept on your toes as it forces you to be consistent in delivering quality work. You'll be careful not to make false promises, take on too many accounts or indulge in any other overzealous behavior that will interfere with you delivering on your guarantee. For example, the position of my firm, Research Done Write!, is "quality writing, thorough research, on budget, on time—guaranteed." In order to deliver on this statement, I'm forced to manage my workload and time commitments carefully.

Prospects' buying objections (see Survival Tip #78) may provide you with some hints on what to guarantee. For example, the question "How long will this carpet last?" may signal to a carpet manufacturer that a guarantee against staining or fading would ease customers' worries. As you get to know your buyers better, you'll discover what's important to them, and you can adjust your guarantee policy based on these customer-oriented factors.

Survival Tip #80: Introduce clients to your business in smaller bites.

There's another part of buyer's anxiety that poses a problem for business owners. People are more cautious spenders these days. Face it. Some buyers can stare down the most effective marketing ploys and not be persuaded one iota. Others are willing to spend but less likely to commit easily, quickly or to larger expenditures. A countersolution: Sell your offering in smaller bites.

Neal Lubow, a sales-rep-turned-entrepreneur, revamped his Portland-based consulting firm by offering clients a lower-risk method of signing on. Lubow's decision to do this was sparked when a client was unable to devote the time needed to launch a new project using Lubow's services and decided to put it on the back burner. After Lubow made periodic follow-up attempts, the client asked to be removed from Lubow's prospect list. There was a similar pattern with many other clients; they were all reluctant to commit to long-term, big-dollar projects. Lubow began to find that the old sales adage "Get your foot in the door" was not as effective in the early 90s.

In order to survive, Lubow had to make some changes in how he approached the business. First, he changed the business's name to IDEAS By-The-Hour. The name reflected his offering of services in bite-size increments. Next, Lubow adopted a "toe-in-the-door" approach. Lubow, with his repackaged service approach, reintroduced himself to the first client. The client liked it and used an hour of Lubow's time. The first hour turned into another one, which eventually resulted in a large project. The one-hour consultation—the "toe"—resulted in a $5,000 project—the whole body! A no-sale turned into a small sale, which led to a buying relationship.

It'll take creative thinking on your part to devise ways to repackage your offering so that it's accessible from the buyer's point of view. A cataloger or retailer, for instance, can offer a product selection with a broad price range. Or a service provider can work on a smaller project and graduate to larger ones. You'll have to work harder and longer to make more smaller sales; however, this may be necessary in some instances. It's up to you. You'll need to decide when a no-sale is better than a small one in a client relationship.

Survival Tip #81: Assure buyers with postpurchase follow-up.

Whether it's a big or small sale, you can solidify a relationship by following up with the buyer.

Unfortunately, many businesses fall short in this area and miss out on all the potential benefits that a follow-up conversation can yield. First, this is a golden opportunity to show customers you care about them and meeting their needs. A follow-up call can quickly dispel any feeling that you just took their money and moved onto the next sale. Depending on the business, your follow-up window should range from 48 to 72 hours to a week or so after the sale or servicing process. You can use the conversation to thank the customer for his or her business and inquire as to how the purchase is working out. This is also an opportune time to reiterate your guarantee policy. Follow-up reassures buyers that you've not abandoned them and that they can call you if they have any problems or questions later on.

You can also use the follow-up process to gain valuable customer feedback. If you've sold a tangible item, you can inquire about its delivery condition or promptness. If the customer has visited your store, you can question him or her about the shopping experience. If you've designed a program for a client, you should definitely monitor the implementation effects of your work. You can also confirm whether the buyer was satisfied with your service. If there is a problem, you'll be in a position to correct it quickly (see Survival Tip #92) and squelch any dissatisfaction before it starts to mount. Every customer isn't a squeaky wheel, so you'll need to be proactive in soliciting feedback.

Postsale follow-up is also the time to educate buyers about your other offerings (see Survival Tip #82). You can mention your other products or services related to what they've already purchased. Or if they mention a need, you can point out how your business can help in that area, too. You can also tell them about your customer communications program (see Survival Tip #86) or explain that you conduct periodic follow-ups. Then, your phone call or other mailings will be greeted with expectancy rather than with clueless curiosity.

Did you know that seven out of 10 customers who patronize a business only once have no specific reason for not returning? Turn the odds around by inviting a customer into a relationship with you. One bootstrapper, for example, sends new customers a short letter welcoming them to her business and includes a discount certificate toward their next invoice. This type of follow-up shows your gratitude for people's business and invites them to do business with you again. Plus, the discount gives them an incentive to return.

On that note, here's another idea to help you create long-term customers...

Survival Tip #82: Scrutinize the buyer's intentions—it'll help you build relationships instead of one-time sales.

Every business starts off devoting its energy to attracting new customers. How do many businesses err? They get stuck on attracting new customers while neglecting to get more business from their existing clientele. Consider another customer service truism. It costs five to 10 times as much to attract a new customer as it does to keep an old one. Therefore, any effort you expend on developing a loyal patronage base is worth it.

Inevitably, there are going to be folks who patronize your business *one* time—whether that experience was good or bad. You can gain a head start in evaluating a relationship's potential from indicators revealed in discussions leading up to a sale commitment. For example, the manager for a project I was working on gave me a lead on an opportunity in another department. While explaining the project, the other department's manager said, "Our goal right now is to sell products. We're not focusing on relationship-building strategies at this time." My antenna immediately went up. Experience has taught me that this type of attitude toward customer relationship-building would also apply to me—and that steady assignments from this client would be slow-coming. As I listened to her elaborate on the company's priorities, I got a better feel about the company's spending attitude. This company was really only committed to the single project.

You can adopt a similar strategy by creating an "intake" form—a form on which your new clients will fill in information about their plans, goals or future direction. It's your business's version of the questionnaire people fill out the first time they visit a new doctor. Or you can do an informal intake, the way I did, just by listening to what is being said. The information can be used to help manage your communications program more efficiently and pace your follow-up efforts more effectively. As with my client, I wouldn't abandon my efforts to nurture the relationship. However, my communications cycle would focus on staying in touch without pestering her about work that hasn't materialized yet (see Survival Tip #86), and I wouldn't allow my efforts to take away from catering to my better clients.

You can also build relationships by learning your customers' needs and continually educating customers about your business. Often, clients patronize you for one need, not realizing how you could help them in other ways. For example, someone who has a resume written may not know that you provide interview coaching as well. Or a person may buy a cake and be unaware that your bakery provides full-service catering. It's your job to inform clients about everything you offer. Tools such as a customer newsletter, informational postcards or detailed brochures should be strategically distributed (see Survival Tip #86). Case studies describing how your business solved a customer's problem can also help build awareness. (However, you should get customer clearance before you begin sharing such information.) These can be printed in a newsletter or sent out as single mailings.

Survival Tip #83: Squeeze 80 percent of your business from 20 percent of your customers.

Nothing sells better than credibility. Once you satisfactorily service a buyer, you have established credibility and can shift your focus to selling more to the same customer. When you have a pool of satisfied customers, you can use them to run a more profitable business. You already know where your customers are, so you minimize expenses associated with trying to reach them. They're already familiar with your business. If there was a problem, you handled it. They've experienced firsthand how you honor your guarantees. You wowed them by overdelivering on what you promised. Your service style has inspired confidence, and they're ripe to buy from you again, minus the front-end sales lead time. Although they are your smallest market, all of these factors make these customers your most profitable segment.

Consultant Bob Serling shared with me the dilemma of a mail-order camera business owner. The company's leading sales item was an inexpensive 35mm camera; more than 4 million units have been sold. The company wanted to expand its business, but it felt the market had been saturated, plus the current advertising wasn't generating any new business. Mr. Fix-it Serling suggested that the company use a different strategy to expand—relying on its existing mailing list. He advised the company to send a letter to everyone who had bought the camera and offer it to them again, suggesting that customers buy another one as a gift item, or for themselves if the *first* one was a gift for someone else. More than 50 percent of the list responded. Using the existing customer base further, Serling advised the company to offer those same customers a related product. The camera company offered a special flash attachment for the camera, and that, too, sold exceedingly well.

Your current customers can be recaptured by the same product or other related products. You can also facilitate sales through a regular calling schedule. When you monitor customers' purchasing cycles through your database (see Survival Tip #85), you can place calls around the time when they buy. You can use the conversation to discuss their regular order or encourage them to buy something else from you. Also, as you monitor their needs through surveys (see Survival Tip #88) and day-to-day feedback, you can move quickly to introduce new offerings to them. Remember, your best customer is the one you already have, so devote a lot of energy on reselling to them again and again.

Survival Tip #84: Tout your credibility with testimonials.

The first compliment you receive from a satisfied customer should be turned into a testimonial. Most customers will put their words in writing for you, even on official letterhead, if you'd like. In fact, consider collecting testimonials as a regular part of your operation. Testimonials can be effective in putting to rest the doubts of a skeptic who isn't completely sold on your business. It's one thing for you to say persuasively what your business can do, but a third party's input can influence people differently. Testimonials can work as effectively as a media placement (see Survival Tip #62). People trust editorial coverage or customer comments as unbiased opinions.

You can put testimonials to work in a number of ways. You can include them in a portfolio or presentation package. You can excerpt from them and include them on product packaging. You can display them prominently in your office. You can even incorporate them into ads. Sylvia Blishak of Accent on Travel in Klamath Falls, Oregon, put her own twist on testimonials. She took letters and postcards from her clients and created a "testimonial collage" with them. Many of the postcards were sent by clients while on trips the agency had coordinated for them. The top of the collage is titled: "A peek inside Accent on Travel's mailbox...". The agency includes the testimonial sheet inside of travel information packages and as part of regular customer mailings.

Before you start sharing customers' good words, be sure that you obtain their permission in advance and explain how you plan to use the endorsements. You should secure as much leeway as possible from customers so you'll have flexibility in using their quotes. For example, with permission, you'll be able to display a testimonial in your office, as well as excerpt and place parts of it on other items, citing the name and home town of the person who said it. Another advantage: There really isn't a time limit on a great testimonial. You can keep using it for years to come!

Survival Tip #85: Connect to lifetime profits through your customer database.

Saks Fifth Avenue sends regular customers who become inactive a 10-percent discount coupon, along with a letter saying, "We haven't seen you in awhile." A neighborhood dry cleaner sends its regulars a $5 gift certificate for their birthday. These companies are able to monitor their customers closely because they have a database at work. Gestures like these communicate that you're paying attention and listening, and that you're interested in making customers happy and *retaining* them as customers.

Studies show that a good customer list will generate a response that is three to five times greater than that generated by other types of prospect lists. A good customer list is a list of potential customers you've developed yourself with names of people who've bought from your business, who were referred to your business or who responded to one of your marketing devices. Other types of prospect lists include those bought from another party, listing people who are interested in your type of offering but who have never been in contact with you before.

If you began a newsletter aimed at small-business owners, you could reach your potential audience in one of two ways:

1. You could rent a prospect list from another entrepreneurial magazine, which sells the names of its subscribers, or from a market research company that's developed a list from such sources as recent business license filings, the membership data of an entrepreneurial association or the names of people who've attended an entrepreneurial trade show.

2. You could use names of people who responded to an article about your newsletter, who stopped by your booth at a trade show and talked with you for a moment, etc. The difference is you're contacting people who are already familiar with you, even if they haven't bought from you.

With the first type of list, you're dealing with cold contacts. This is where many entrepreneurs get stuck. Just because people have bought entrepreneurial material from other sources in the past doesn't mean they'll be interested in your offering. Your priority should be to develop and maintain a list of your own. With your own list, recipients receive your information thinking, "Oh, I remember him/her from the trade show," rather than "Who is sending me this?"

Scores of businesses don't even have an active database of customer information. Without one, you're disconnected from the source of lifetime profits. A database helps you cater to your customers. The database-building process begins with your first customer or prospect encounter. Collect basic information, such as name, address, phone number, fax number, e-mail address and how he or she heard about you. Do this with every new customer or prospect. This basic information will help pinpoint various ways you'll be able to communicate with them, audit the effectiveness of the marketing device that led them to you or thank or follow up with whoever referred them. Then, expand the information intake a little. By asking how they plan to use the end product or who it's for and making some notations about comments made, you position yourself to specialize your communication and offering to this customer. You should also use every encounter with customers to gather more information about them and build up the file.

You can use the database to monitor buying habits, and in turn, pinpoint your best customers. You'll then be positioned to shower special attention on those who contribute most to the profits of your business (see Survival Tip #83). You'll also be able to personalize your communication messages. The use of a database can put you on the path to optimizing your customer base and sales volume to attain the highest profitability. Don't delay. Start building a customer database today.

Survival Tip #86: Invest in a customer communications program.

Communicating with your customers (and prospects) on a regular basis contributes to the development of a relationship. Staying in touch helps reinforce your interest in the customer and your commitment to understanding and fulfilling their needs. You can develop a program that allows you to stay in touch by phone, mail, fax or e-mail, or in person. The avenue you choose should take into consideration your customers' preferences. For example, during your postpurchase follow-up call (see Survival Tip #81), you could inquire as to how the person would prefer to receive future mailings. Or you can develop a preferred customer application and explain to people that the information is for your database (see Survival Tip #85) and will be used to inform them of advance notice offers along with other mailings. The application can have a section for checking off their communication preferences.

A popular component in a communications program is a free promotional or customer newsletter. This can be effective in educating your customer, encouraging repeat business and expanding your customer base. It also works as a value-added tool when you provide readers with useful advice and information. Tips, statistics, resources, or client news catering to your customer's interest will ensure that the newsletter gets read. It need not be lavish; two to four 8½ x 11 pages will do. It should surely communicate your business identity. For example, a wordsmith's newsletter will be ineffective in inspiring confidence if it's full of grammatical errors. You can even make it interactive by inviting readers to send in questions for you to answer or include a savings coupon. A helpful resource: Elaine Floyd's *Marketing with Newsletters: How to boost sales, add members & raise funds with a printed, faxed or Web-site newsletter* (for ordering information, see page 158).

Postcards are effective for staying customer-connected. You could provide customers with a problem-solving tip of the month, a summary of upcoming events that cater to their interest, a special sales invitation or a service call reminder. Some business owners have created mini-newsletters on postcards.

Manning a phone program can also be effective in some relationships. An engineering consultant's program includes periodically calling customers to share industry information of interest; he also calls clients for their expertise on other projects he's working on. Your customer relationships may also lend themselves to staying in touch through occasional dining or get-together outings.

You'll be able to retailor the program as your customer relationships grow. When you learn more about people, your imaginative energy will work wonders in developing other communication strategies. Be sure the program complements your company's overall consistency in communication by contacting people in regular, steady intervals.

Survival Tip #87: Don't confuse a regular customer with a satisfied one.

People will patronize your business even though they're dissatisfied with your service. There are several factors that contribute to this behavior. A regular customer may not be aware of your competition, so the person believes that the service you're providing is as good as it gets. Or the customer may have gone through a slew of bad providers and you're better than they were, which may not be saying much. It may also be too inconvenient for the person to switch or shop around right now, so it's better to stick it out with you in the meantime. Or perhaps you're just cheaper than the rest—in which case you'll be quickly abandoned when an even lower-cost business, or a slightly more expensive one with much better service, comes along.

Does all this sound unbelievable? Then consider how many times you've shopped in a store where you disliked the service because you were too busy to drive across town.

All business owners should be concerned because a dissatisfied regular customer works against you in subtle ways. First, the person is unlikely to give you any referrals (see Survival Tip #91). The person knows deep inside that he or she is dissatisfied with you and wouldn't dare risk referring someone over to your business. Second, the person probably doesn't buy anything extra from you, which nullifies the 80/20 rule (see Survival Tip #83). Third, the person will probably dump your business when you least expect it. If your absence or unavailability ever forces the dissatisfied regular to go someplace else, you may be unknowingly signing your own release papers. The person may stumble into making a switch, and you'll then lose him or her for good. It's at this point the person will proceed to tell nine others of his or her dissatisfaction with your business.

A survey of dissatisfied customers revealed that they never complain because: They feel it's not worth their time; they feel the provider won't listen if they do complain; and they feel the company won't do anything about the complaint. If you're not getting referrals or unsolicited compliments from your customers, you may be nursing a dissatisfied clientele. A customer-driven business makes it a priority to satisfy its customers' needs. When you do, they'll think twice about switching away from you. Remember, though, you must provide service that is good from the *customer's* point of view. You can find out if you're on track when you flat-out ask them (see Survival Tip #88).

7 WAYS TO INFLUENCE CUSTOMERS AND WIN LOYALTY

1. Say thank you. Sound simplistic? Recount the number of times you paid for a product or service, were handed your change or receipt and sent on your way without a word of thanks. Always remember to express your appreciation to anyone who supports your business. Make sure your workers understand the thank-you drill, too. There will also be times when a customer's actions warrant a special note of thanks. This endearing principle also applies to your networking and referral relationships.

2. Respect your customers' privacy. Don't be so quick to make a buck off your customer database. People are becoming increasingly concerned about how private information they give is being used. Your customers may willingly share information with you, not expecting you to turn around and sell or use it outside your business. Always give your customers the option of not having their information released. By asking them first, you'll find that this courtesy will be appreciated in the relationship.

3. Give gifts. Incorporate some form of gift-giving to your best or regular customers. You can honor them with a gift of appreciation at year-end holidays, customer birthdays or anniversaries. A study by the University of Florida's advertising faculty revealed that the top gifts business-people give are office/business accessories, food and personal gifts. Survey respondents indicated that customers' responses to receiving gifts from these categories were the most favorable. Treat customer gifts with the same care as ones to a good friend. Try individualizing your gifts to avoid a wholesale appearance. You can find some useful tips in *The Creative Gift Giver* newsletter (see page 158 for ordering information).

4. Mind your manners. No matter how friendly your rapport is with a client, don't make the mistake of being too familiar with them. Speaking or joshing in an inappropriate manner can ruin a relationship and create a question mark in someone's mind about your professionalism. Absolute no-no's: using profane language (not *everyone* in the world swears!), mispronouncing or shortcutting customers' names, bemoaning about your personal problems and gossiping or bad-mouthing another customer or your staffers.

5. Stay customer-driven, not competition-driven. Many businesses feel pressured to install special features and services based on what their competition is doing or provide services based solely on their own preferences or considerations. But did you check with your customers to make sure it's something they will value? For example, because it seems customer-focused, a business may install a 24-hour faxback service, allowing customers to call in, listen to a menu of information they can have faxed to them, punch in their selection and fax number, and receive a fax within minutes. But prodding customers may reveal that a toll-free fax line is what's really needed. Whenever you forget your customers' needs you're merely giving lip service to the customer-driven philosophy.

6. Suppress a "full-stomach" attitude. Your business may have more than enough business. If you're not careful, you'll experience the downside of your success. Sometimes a full plate can create an apathetic attitude toward additional business. A client called a business owner with a referral lead. The business owner began spouting off about how busy he was and that he hoped the lead had the money to pay for the services. The client was appalled by this arrogant attitude and began giving referrals to a business that was hungrier—and more grateful. Don't abandon the strategies that made you successful.

7. Celebrate Customer Service Week. The International Customer Service Association (ICSA) sponsors a special week in October. You can get more information from ICSA at 800-360-ICSA (faxback: 800-203-ICSA; Web address: www.icsa.com). Although customer service is a daily priority, you can use the celebratory week to do something special for valued customers, raise awareness with your employees or jump-start a new campaign.

Survival Tip #88: Survey customers for valuable feedback.

Your assessment of your business's service may differ drastically from a customer's, particularly if you've adopted service strategies based on industry norm or past practices—void of customer input. Customers are the lifeline of any business; your business exists to meet the needs of customers, so their view of how well you're doing is vital.

Implementing an organized and systematic program for soliciting customer feedback can give you these advantages for remaining at the top of your customer service game:

1. You'll get a quick head count of how many dissatisfied regulars are on your books.

2. You'll get in touch with your customers' thoughts or unexpressed feelings about your business. You may find that someone appreciates your work but resents having to leave messages all the time or being charged a rush or cancellation fee.

3. You'll find out customers' priorities, ensuring that service is delivered in a fashion they value and need.

4. You can gain a head start on developing and offering new or better solutions to their problems, which can translate into other profit centers for your business.

5. You can clear up any gray areas that surface from their comments. For example, a customer may make a new service suggestion for something that's already part of your business. This could be a red flag that you need to invest more in educating customers about your overall operation.

You can approach the surveying process in a few ways. You could host a one-question poll, querying everyone during a designated week or month. You can have customer satisfaction cards displayed in your business and ask people to fill them out before they leave, or you can send them out under separate cover. You should also use each customer encounter as a feedback opportunity. Every order, confirmation or follow-up call can provide you with valuable insights. You have to proactively listen to what's being said and encourage the person into further conversation with you. A comment such as, "It's been a trying day" may mean your business had something to do with it. Or you can simply ask people, "How'd you like the service?" the way restaurants and other service providers do at the end of your visit.

A more formal approach is to conduct an annual survey. You can create a simple questionnaire of about five to 10 questions. You should ask a combination of questions: some that allow the customer to grade or numerically rate your business and some open-ended ones that'll give you ideas and comments to sift through. Some examples of rated questions: *How would you rate the quality of our work?* or *How well are we meeting your needs?* Some examples of open-ended questions: *What do you like best about our company? What do you like least? Share three ways we might be better able to serve you. Is there anything about our business you find confusing or unclear?* (By the way, if you own an established business and haven't ever surveyed your customers, shame on you!)

According to a recent International Customer Service Association membership survey, companies who measure customer satisfaction do so through written surveys or telephone interviews. You can follow suit with your program. If you choose phone interviews, contact your clients in advance to set up an appointment. Mailer surveys should include a postage-paid envelope for easy return. Follow up with a participation thank-you note. Some feedback may require one-to-one follow-up to clarify or address specific concerns. As you comb through the feedback, pat yourself on the back for things you're doing right. Unflattering feedback, however, should be swallowed gracefully and turned into opportunities to profit from change.

Survival Tip #89: Charm 'em with extras.

Give a little, and you'll gain a lot of customer loyalty. Amazingly, you can do this without putting a dent in your wallet. I've done so on a number of occasions, costing me time and a little postage. For example, a Staples representative gave me dozens of $10 discount coupons at an expo where I spoke. I picked up extra resource guides and product sample packages from each expo booth. Later, I bundled up the goodies and sent them to my best customers and a few to my personal and professional service providers. They all went wild over this unexpected (and useful) treat. Another time, I provided a client with a media placement lead that resulted in him receiving hundreds of product orders. The average person enjoys and appreciates receiving something pleasantly unexpected, and your patrons are probably no different. Your business is in a much better position to dole out "extras" than a larger business; your front-line contact gives you ample opportunity to take what you know about customers individually and shower them with personalized treats.

Another way to charm your customers is to make them feel like insiders. You can coordinate cooperative arrangements with other vendors that allow your customers to get discounts on their product or service. If you become privy to some information that a customer may be interested in, why not pass it along? If a vendor is offering you special pricing, explore the possibility of letting your customers in on the deal. You'll want to be sure it's clear to customers that the "extra" is a direct benefit of being associated with you. For example, consider being involved in setting up the contact appointment or working as the drop-off point for an item to be picked up. Your involvement will reinforce your standing as the beneficial link. It's a win-win arrangement, too. The vendor is getting introduced to new customers, your clients are getting a sweet deal and you're the wonderful middle person building loyalty on both sides.

The information you gather over time about your customer will position you to make other unexpected gestures. Listen. Stay alert. And the next time you come across a fabulous "extra," you'll know exactly who to send it to.

Survival Tip #90: Become an information source clients cannot live without.

Information is the currency of exchange in networking alliances; it can work in your customer relationships, too. You can begin to position yourself as a font of information by taking your customers' interests and matching them with sources they're not finding on their own. As others in your networking circle act as your eyes and ears (see Survival Tip #64), you can work the same way for your customers.

People have confidence in knowledgeable folks. Being conversant on topics outside your profession can indicate to others that you're someone in the know. In the course of educating yourself, you can keep your eyes peeled for information that'll be useful to your clients. It may be an article, a book or a press release. For example, I regularly receive press releases from the Census Bureau, a service available to professional researchers. There have been many occasions when I've passed the advance information along to my clients and colleagues.

A shining example of an information connector: David Wood, a copywriter, publicist and marketing consultant based in Weare, New Hampshire. Wood provides his services to the construction industry; he's made it his mission to connect construction entrepreneurs to resources they might otherwise bypass. Wood crams each issue of his quarterly newsletter with useful, entertaining and sometimes odd information. I even look forward to receiving it. One issue, for example, included tidbits on: caring for your pet dog; how to use golfing to solidify a client relationship or build one up; financial tips and statistics; and reviews of books on business and topics of general interest. Wood admittedly spends three hours a day combing through a potpourri of material. He sends the missive to clients, corporate friends, prospects and the like. (He'll send you one, too. Just call him at 800-HEY-WOODY.) Its high pass-along readership, coupled with word-of-mouth, has positioned Wood as a valuable information source in his audience's mind.

Consider working as your customers' concierge, building up a referral network. You can maintain your own ready reference database with everything from professional to personal service sources. Of course, you'll need to thoroughly screen out your referrals to ensure that you're sending them to quality providers. You can mention your referral database in conversation or include it in your customer newsletter or as a bill-stuffer reminder.

Big businesses aren't providing this type of personalized service to their customers, but you, as a small firm owner, can. The strategy works best when you know your customers and are clearly catering to their needs. Personalized service makes clients think twice about divorcing themselves from your business.

Survival Tip #91: Ask for referrals straight out.

Your customers hold the keys to the doors of business from other people they know who'll value their recommendation. You'll need to be assertive, though, as the average satisfied customer only tells five other people. You can encourage customers to talk up your business through a referral program. You should immediately enroll every person that patronizes your business into the program. You can introduce it through a letter sent out a few days after they're served by your firm, catching folks while they're still feeling enthusiastic about your work. A straightforward letter should explain to the customer that your business is built on providing quality service that leads to repeat and referral business. Include some business cards for them to distribute. Whenever people are in your office, you can also remind them about the program.

People are inspired by useful incentives, and your referral program should include some. Offering a percentage discount on their next purchase or a commission fee on leads that turn into actual sales is something to get excited about. You could even host an annual referral drive. One bootstrapper offered $1,000 to the customer who brought in the most referrals during a given period. Another bootstrapper's client has so many accrued referral dollars that it's been months since she's paid for anything. But what you're giving away in incentives can pale in comparison to what you're gaining in additional business.

There are a few tricks that'll make your efforts more productive. You'll improve the quality of your referrals by being specific in what you ask for. Rather than asking, "Do you know anyone who needs financial planning assistance?", ask "Do you know a two-income professional family with young children?" An online bootstrapper shared her scripted pitch: "I'm calling you today to make sure you know to pass the word that I'm looking for potential advertisers for a free multilevel marketing newsletter I am starting. The first issue—20,000 copies—will be out on January 1st. Who do you know that will want this exposure?"

If you feel that a client is reluctant to offer any referrals, don't dismiss his or her attitude as uncooperative. Sure, the person may not want to be bothered, but it could be something more. Confirm that he or she would indeed refer others to you. Your double-checking will help you root out any dissatisfied regulars (see Survival Tip #87).

Survival Tip #92: Act swiftly to correct a problem.

An irate, angry customer doesn't have to be a lost one. Studies have revealed that 95 percent of dissatisfied customers would do business again with a company if their problems were solved quickly and satisfactorily. It's up to you to turn the situation around. When a customer begins to explain a problem, control any impulse to react defensively. You can win back disenchanted customers just by listening, so let them do the talking. If your company is at fault, acknowledge the error and apologize. You can appease angry or annoyed customers when you let them know your willingness to correct the problem to their satisfaction.

Before you offer up remedies, be sure to ask the customer how he or she would prefer the problem be resolved. A customer may be amenable to your replacing an item or redoing the work, thus giving you a second chance. However, if a customer is adamant about a full or partial refund, it may be in your best interest to honor the request, even when it's not your policy to do so. Your yielding can help squash any bad word-of-mouth advertising. Once you and the customer have agreed on how to resolve the problem, quickly follow through on your word. Don't drag your feet. If you're given a chance to correct the work, make it a priority to get it done. Remember you're trying to win the client over again. If a refund is in order, then quickly refund the customer's money.

If your company is not at fault, don't rub it in a customer's face. Instead, after the customer has been able to vent, offer an explanation that focuses on helping the person avoid any similar situations in the future. And you should still express regret that the customer had that negative experience with your company. When employees are involved in the dispute, you should take time out to retrace the problem with them, providing them with the necessary retraining. You can adopt a similar approach for winning over a customer who expresses some dissatisfaction in your postpurchase follow-up calls (see Survival Tip #81).

Survival Tip #93: Stay close during the servicing process.

While postpurchase follow-up is important for all businesses, service providers should pay special attention to how they communicate during the service process. If you're working on a project that'll take 30 to 90 days or longer to complete, for example, you should have a communication schedule in place for checking in with the client. There are several reasons for doing so. First, you'll be able to ensure that the project is on track. Second, you'll be able to deliver a final product that's in line with what the customer requested. Third, periodic check-ins can help prevent a client from being unpleasantly surprised by an end result they feel is unsatisfactory.

When you're preparing for a long-term project, think about how to stay close to the client. One consultant calls mechanisms for doing this "timely client relations tools." Your mechanisms can include a phone call, fax or e-mail check-in. You should be prepared to present a schedule to the client as you're ironing out the details of a project and its delivery schedule. These briefings can benefit your relationship tremendously. You can use the session to provide the client with a progress report, communicate any problems that may have arisen, allow the client to communicate any desired changes or reassess the project entirely. For example, a consultant holds 60-second check-ins for budget updates. A professional trainer who conducts training sessions over a three-month period has participants complete an assessment after a few sessions. She reviews the reports and shares some of the workers' feedback with the company that hired her to train its employees. This process helps the company evaluate what it has already received for its expenditure.

Certain service businesses, such as massage therapy, hair salons or nail salons, would not use this particular strategy because of the shorter time frames involved in providing their services. However, these businesses can stay close to the customer by confirming if the customer would like to be served the same way as before. Of course, if you run this kind of business, you're going to need some notes of what that last time involved—a special color or curl pattern, perhaps. As an attentive service provider, you would have gathered this information from previous visits, right?

In developing your own schedule, keep in mind that the more money clients spend, the more they'll be watching you. By staying close, you can circumvent any buyer's remorse. Not only will you deliver what you promised, but more important, you'll deliver what they want.

Survival Tip #94: Avoid misunderstandings.

Customers' attitudes will quickly sour toward your business when they feel you should have explained an issue before a buyer's commitment was made. Miscommunication or lack of communication usually involves the pricing and associated policies of your operation. A common sticky point: a quote versus an estimate. Many businesspeople use the words interchangeably when they do not share the same meaning. A *quote* implies a fixed amount that the customer expects not be exceeded. An *estimate* refers to an educated guess that may change as work commences. It's commonplace to honor a quote for a specified time; be sure that's communicated to the customer. When a job begins based on a cost estimate, the customer should be contacted once you reach a certain dollar point inside the estimated range; this will allow the him or her to evaluate the cost of what's been done against the cost of what's left to do (see Survival Tip #93).

Let people know your policies up front. If you charge a cancellation fee, for example, the policy posted as a wall sign or on collateral materials isn't enough. When a customer cancels, then calls for another appointment, you should remind him or her of the previous cancellation. Don't just slyly add it to the tab. If you charge a rush fee, let people know in advance of your taking the order. This way the buyer can decide whether or not paying the premium is worth it. Other policies that should be discussed include special fees or surcharges, time restrictions on work revisions, how long incentive or refund credits are honored and whether or not a deposit is refundable or can be credited toward another job.

Some businesses find it appropriate to use a customer information sheet. This facilitating tool explains to customers the costs and procedures of doing business with you. The information is verbally explained to customers, and it should be presented to them in a manner that will make them feel they are being shown a cost-efficient way to work with your firm, rather than in a manner that will make them feel as if they're being schooled by a taskmaster. (They should be given a copy for their reference, as well.) Courteously say where you stand, and let customers choose their place in the workings of your business.

Survival Tip #95: Don't make guarantees or promises you can't afford to keep.

"I promise to make you happy," you say to a customer or client. What does that *really* mean? Are you verbalizing your explicit or implicit guarantee policy? An explicit guarantee policy clearly states what it is promising and what it will do if it fails to deliver. Federal Express, for instance, guarantees package delivery by 10:30 a.m. the next business day or it's free (contingent upon bad-weather delays, of course). Conversely, an implicit guarantee is not stated; rather it's the impression customers have that they can count on you to deliver. An implicit promise is earned through your track record of making good on customer dissatisfaction.

While a strong guarantee policy will help your business stand out from competitors and ease customer worries (see Survival Tip #79), failing to deliver on a promise could ruin your reputation. Carefully mull over your guarantee policy. Begin by honestly noting your reaction to possible customer problems. If a client asked you to redo the work several times, would you gladly comply with the requests? Or if a person bought something from your store, used it and brought it back a little worn, how would you feel about giving a cash refund? Making promises or guarantees simply to appease people without considering your own feelings or limits could cause you problems. You may find yourself begrudgingly following through, which will work against your customer service efforts.

What quality or characteristic of your business do you believe in most? Is it the product itself, the way you do the work or the end results it brings to the user? Avoid copycat guarantees (mimicking the service promises of other similar businesses); you may end up overextended. Your guarantee should play to the strength of your business, the factor you believe in most. When you guarantee or make promises around what you do best, your heart will allow your cash register to finance the policy.

Survival Tip #96: Carefully handle special requests.

Part of building a relationship with clients is making them feel comfortable with you. Goodwill feelings may inspire a customer to ask you for special concessions. Some possible scenarios: A regular may begin experiencing cash flow problems and ask you to waive your deposit requirements. Or one of your accounts may ask you to extend its 30-day terms to 90 days. New or prospective clients may weigh in with their requests, too. Psychologists and some physicians accept patients on a sliding fee scale and day-care providers will often work around a family's budget. Someone may inquire whether your business does the same.

How would you handle such requests? It's worth thinking about. First, consider the requester's value to your business. If it's a customer who's been with you for years, granting special terms may be in order. Next, consider the magnitude of the request. If the request is for extended payment terms, then consider how that will affect your overall cash flow position. You should also consider how much of your business comes from a particular requester. For example, if an account brings in more than 20 percent in payables, you may be courting danger. The same scrutiny would apply in instances where you agree to flexible pricing requests. Professionals who use sliding scales always maintain a strict balance between those who pay in full versus those who follow other pricing plans.

If you decide to honor the request, safeguard the arrangements (and relationship) by clarifying specific details. For example, if the request is a one-time proposition, make sure that's clearly understood by the requester. For example, if you're waiving the deposit this time, reiterate that the next job will require one. More complicated requests may need to be in writing. A letter explaining revised billing terms or differential pricing can reinforce that an arrangement is temporary. If you're offering flexible pricing, you may want to cap the arrangements with time restrictions.

Also, offer up some other solutions. You may be able to service customers at your usual fee, while setting them up to proceed on their own for services they can't afford from you. Say, for example, you run a full-service editorial business, providing writing, editing, layout and design. A customer can't really afford the whole package but really needs your writing and editing services. You could complete these services for the customer but deduct the layout and design, leaving that work up to him or her.

Survival Tip #97: Keep clients involved with your business.

Besides delivering quality work and service, customers' confidence can be further inspired by your business's growth and development. Many of the changes you introduce will indeed be prompted by customer feedback. However, there will be times when you follow trails based on other interests or passions. In this instance, you'll need to make sure your customers don't begin to feel alienated by your new direction. For example, my clients were delighted to hear that I was writing this book. However, in announcing the news, I explained to them how promoting the book and Research Done Write! would work in concert and how our working relationship would continue.

You can curtail the tendency of your customers to see your new direction as a sign of abandonment by involving them with your growth. Whenever you're adding new services, experimenting with other technologies or contemplating any type of change that'll affect your patrons, be sensitive to how it may be interpreted on their end. One bootstrapper, for instance, surveyed her clients about a name change she was considering. The owner was leaning toward a shorter moniker that had a more strategic alphabetical placement in the yellow pages and a better reflection of her expanded services. By polling clients through a newsletter and in face-to-face meetings, she discovered that many of them identified the business by her own name, so she was prompted to include it in her ads along with the new title.

Anxiety gets stirred up when customers aren't gingerly introduced to changes. Be prepared to educate customers on how new changes will benefit them. For example, say you start using e-mail to deliver completed projects to customers, rather than sending them by using overnight mail. You wouldn't just announce: *All projects are now delivered via e-mail*. Instead, you could announce the availability of the service in your customer newsletter, asking customers to respond with their preferences. You could also call customers and explain the new delivery system and how it can be a time- and money-saver—for instance: *E-mail eliminates the risk of lost packages, the inconvenience of waiting for a delivery person and delays caused by unfavorable traveling conditions due to bad weather*. Don't impose the change on people. Also, use your annual customer survey (see Survival Tip #88) to gain insights as to how people may respond to changes.

Another way to keep customers involved is to share the bounty with them. For example, if you're being profiled in an article, there may be an opportunity for you to refer the media to your customers or have one of them mentioned as a customer. Also, if you're in the business of publishing and depend on advertisers to keep your publication going, you could try strengthening their loyalty by sharing your publicity opportunities with them. The publisher of the newsletter *The Creative Gift Giver* (see page 158 for ordering information) helps her advertisers get publicity by sending out press releases to the advertisers' local papers announcing: *Local crafter is featured in an upcoming issue of national publication on creative gift-giving*.

So, as you grow, always remember to keep your customers involved with your business, and they'll, in turn, stay involved with you.

Survival Tip #98: Graduate from the "sole client" scenario ASAP.

An anchor client—one that generates the majority of your revenue—can smooth out the wrinkles of a fluctuating cash flow. However, you leave yourself open for disaster when you become dependent on one primary client. It's easy to do, especially if the client is your former employer or you're working with a downsized firm that's turned to outsourcing.

Work arrangements that monopolize your resources and prevent you from prospecting for other clients can be easy to rationalize. For example, one professional justified her arrangement by saying she'll have plenty of money when the project's over. Perhaps that's true. But how far will all the money you've stashed away carry you if the transition into finding new projects results in a drought?

There are other pitfalls, as well. Working with one client may make you a candidate for IRS scrutiny. Whether a self-employed professional has multiple clients is a factor the IRS uses to confirm one's status as an independent contractor (see Survival Tips #27 and #122). You also put yourself in danger of becoming professionally stagnated. You may become so focused on tending to one client's need that you become closed off from the needs of other clients. You'll miss out on the valuable and varied insights into marketplace needs that are revealed through interaction with a circle of clients. Also, people who become dependent on one client tend to neglect their marketing efforts (see Survival Tip #74). If you haven't been communicating your marketing message, it's difficult to turn on a dime. You'll essentially be starting over because some other diligent marketer may have captured your audience's share of mind.

Once you've landed one source of business, begin building on that base immediately. You can aggressively scout out referrals from this base client, and if you're in a position of working with more than one person in that company, enlist their referral support, too. In the meantime, follow your marketing plan and remain committed to its execution.

Keep in mind that most client relationships have a life span. Even if you work with people for several years, there are factors that cause a relationship to evaporate, such as death, relocation, retirement, shifts in priorities and more. When a relationship runs its course, a business that works with a pool of clients will fare better than one that relies on a single arrangement.

Bootstrapper's Follow-up File

50 Powerful Ideas You Can Use to Keep Your Customers, Second Edition, by Paul R. Timm, Ph.D. (Career Press, 1995); 800-CAREER-1 (201-848-0310 in N.J. and outside U.S.). $7.99.

50 Ways to Win New Customers by Paul R. Timm, Ph.D. (Career Press, 1995); 800-CAREER-1 (201-848-0310 in N.J. and outside U.S.). $8.95.

A Businessperson's Guide to Federal Warranty Law and *Writing Readable Warranties*, Federal Trade Commission, Public Reference, Room 130, Washington, DC 20580-0001; Web address: www.ftc.gov. Two **free** guides giving you practical suggestions for writing simple and easy-to-understand warranties. Includes guidelines on advertising satisfaction guarantees.

Creating a Client Newsletter, Best Impressions, 9847 Catalpa Woods Court, Cincinnati, OH 45242. An eight-page guide providing how-to information about story ideas, design and production considerations, uses and potential pitfalls for producing a customer newsletter. Also includes six sample newsletters. $5.95.

Customer Service and Retention, Clement Communications, 800-345-8101. A biweekly newsletter of tips and techniques on how to manage your customer service program. Also publishes *Master Salesmanship*, a biweekly newsletter on handling sales situations. **Free** sample copies available.

Customer Service on the Internet by Jim Sterne (Wiley Computer Publications, 1996); 800-225-5945. $24.95.

Customers First: A Practical Guide to Profitable Customer Relations, Dartnell, 800-621-5463. A biweekly newsletter. Also published by Dartnell: a series of 15 different business management newsletters, including *Salesmanship: Tips, Techniques, and Strategies That Get Results!*, *Successful Closing Techniques:*

Building the Sale from Proposal to Purchase and *Overcome Objections: Your Personal Guide to Success in Selling.* A complete listing and **free** samples available.

Guide to Business Gift Giving, 444 Whittier Ave., Suite 200, Glen Ellyn, IL 60137. A special mini-report. Submit request for a copy on company letterhead with SASE. $1.

How to Compile and Maintain a Mailing List, Quill Corporation, 800-789-6640; Web address: www.quillcorp.com. A **free**, 40-page guide providing helpful information about building and maintaining your own list.

How to Win through Great Customer Service, Quill Corporation, 800-789-6640; Web address: www.quillcorp.com. A **free**, 64-page guide of tips and ideas to help you make customer service a priority in your business.

Lotus Approach, 800-343-5414; Web address: www.lotus.com. A database software to track customer information.

Marketing with Newsletters: How to boost sales, add members & raise funds with a printed, faxed or Web-site newsletter, Second Edition, by Elaine Floyd. See page 123 of the Bootstrapper's Follow-up File in Chapter 5 for a full listing.

Microsoft Access, 800-426-9400; Web address: www.microsoft.com. Database software to track and monitor customer activity.

Service Breakthroughs: Changing the Rules of the Game by James Heskett and Christopher W.L. Hart (Free Press/Simon & Schuster, 1990); 800-223-2336. $35.

Strategic Database Marketing: The Master Plan for Starting and Managing a Profitable Customer Based Marketing Program by Arthur M. Hughes (Irwin Professional Publishing, 1994); 800-634-3966. $35.

The Creative Gift Giver, 444 Whittier Ave., Suite 200, Glen Ellyn, IL 60137; 630-790-9189; fax: 630-545-2417; e-mail address: CASwrite@aol.com. A quarterly newsletter of imaginative and creative techniques for gift-giving. Four issues: $15. Sample packet of two back issues and several special gift offers: $9.

The One to One Enterprise: Tools for Competing in the Interactive Age by Don Peppers and Martha Rogers (Doubleday/Currency, 1997); 800-323-9872. $24.95.

The One to One Future: Building Relationships One Customer at a Time by Don Peppers and Martha Rogers (Doubleday/Currency, 1993); 800-323-9872. $15.95.

Chapter 7

Managing Your Business

"In dreams begins responsibility."

—William Butler Yeats, Irish poet and
dramatist, *Responsibilities* (1914)

Survival Tip #99: Manage your business with respect and attention.

You treat your customers well, and they love you. But how do you treat your business? Many entrepreneurs believe exemplary service is synonymous with a well-run business. It's only part of the equation. It took one bootstrapper years to make this connection. Delivering quality work and service was her trademark; customers' unsolicited compliments confirmed it. But she was operating without a playbook; she handled situations as they arose. She often ended up on the short end of deals and agreed to arrangements that weren't in the best interest of her business. The business began to run her instead of vice versa.

What does a well-run business look like? It creates and uses an internal playbook for its foundation. Most big business offices have an operations manual (see Survival Tip #100). It's a vital tool and can work for small offices, too. How else are you going to know where to draw the line in challenging situations or what your policy is on bounced checks? A well-managed business doesn't cheat itself out of opportunities because it's disorganized; it has policies and services in place that make it run like a well-oiled machine (see Survival Tips #105 and #115). Owners of tip-top operations know that high sales and heavy foot traffic don't always equal profitability; they stay aware of their price position through testing strategies (see Survival Tip #106).

A well-managed business has a captain who's physically and emotionally healthy (see Survival Tips #116 and #117); it's hard to run a business when you're exhausted all the time or allow the business to rob you of life's pleasures. Your business needs to be nurtured; your respect and attention shouldn't only be reserved for your customers. When you neglect to manage your business well, you work against yourself, the dream and its survival.

Survival Tip #100: Live by a set of standard operating procedures.

As mentioned in Tip #99, an operations manual can serve as your management script. It provides you with a guidebook for managing your business. Your tailor-made manual can be as short or as long as you like. It'll benefit you most when you use it to govern your client, supplier and employee relationships. Referring to your manual will help you sidestep the problems associated with a "winging it" management style. It'll provide you with a foundation for handling problems, setting up new accounts and overseeing your business in general. It can rescue you in an overzealous moment when you may ignore an important detail. Use of a manual allows you to work from a responsive base, not a reactive one; you'll have guidelines in place to measure special requests against (see Survival Tip #96).

Your manual should allow you to respond without stuttering when asked what your policy is on a particular issue. For example, someone may call and ask: "Do you offer credit?" Some client relationships warrant billing terms while others do not; you'll need to clarify some guidelines for yourself to work from. Your manual can include any of the following:

- Information checklist for new accounts or for qualifying for credit.
- Payment policy—that is, deposit requirements, billing terms, etc.
- Billing and past-due collection procedures.
- Customer complaint procedures.
- Guidelines for selecting vendors—location, track record and turnaround times.
- Criteria for outsourcing projects and selecting and verifying information on other professionals.
- Guidelines for pricing, quoting or bidding on jobs.
- Etiquette for manning the phones.

These suggestions can be used as building blocks for putting together a manual based on your business type. Share the manual with your employees; it'll help them understand more clearly the workings of your business. Update and revise it as your operation grows, incorporating new sections or addressing issues that arise in your day-to-day experiences.

Survival Tip #101: Be detail-oriented.

Haste makes waste and skips every detail in between. When you focus only on *just do it, do it, do it*, you're bound to overlook a detail that'll come back to haunt you later. It isn't necessary to become a detail fanatic; however, your business should have an aura of detailedness to it. A client's excitement about launching a project can be contagious. But before you run with the assignment, have all the questions in your mind been answered? This is when your standard operating procedures can save you (see Survival Tip #100). Have you met everyone you'll be working with? Is it clear who will provide what kinds of materials for you to work from? Do you need a purchase order number to get paid? Ironing out details like these can help eliminate misunderstandings later (see Survival Tip #94).

Detail is important when you employ others or contract with self-employed professionals. It's amazing how many businesspeople hire workers or subcontract work out to others without checking references. It's like handing a stranger the keys to your home; you're granting them access to a cherished asset—your business. Have you verified the type of work the person has done in the past? Is the person truly an independent contractor? Do you have a copy of a current business license? Is a nondisclosure form appropriate for the working relationship? (A company may have an independent contractor sign one of these forms to keep the details of a developmental project from being leaked to the marketplace or competitors.) Even people who are recommended by referral should be checked out.

Whenever you commit to a financial obligation, the absence of one detail can lock you into an arrangement. One bootstrapper learned this lesson the hard way. She paid a cash binder to begin negotiating the terms for taking over a business. Once the deal was solidified, she discovered that the existing suppliers' contracts weren't transferable to the new owner—a major setback because the deals were needed to keep the business profitable. Whether it's a maintenance contract or special service purchase, make sure you understand what you're paying for and your options for terminating the relationship. What are you (and they) responsible for? What recourse do you have if they (or you) don't perform? If an arrangement is legitimate, others will appreciate your attention to detail.

Besides building confidence in your ability, developing an eye for detail will protect your business and relationships. "Just do it" may promote Nike well, but focusing on the details will work better for you.

Survival Tip #102: Tap into free and low-cost training networks.

Many entrepreneurs become certified in business management through the curriculum taught at "Mis-University." They learn lessons from the experiences of misemploying, miscalculating, mispurchasing and mismanaging. Mistakes such as these can be costly, and in some instances, deadly for the business. There's good news, though. You can minimize on-the-job mistakes through free and low-cost training opportunities available to novices and more experienced bootstrappers alike.

If you've been laid off from your job, you may be able to participate in a **free** job training program for displaced workers that offers an entrepreneurial training track. Title III job assistance programs for displaced workers are grant-funded by local and federal government departments. Displaced workers are usually referred to the programs through unemployment offices. To qualify for a Title III program, you must be unemployed and apply to a program serving your residential area. (Title III programs are not to be confused with the private out-placement services, workshops or training that your company may offer you upon terminating your employment; there's a cost to partici-pate in these.)

Title III programs provide eligible participants with training in business fundamentals over a set time period, and upon completion, some programs offer access to mentors and to loan pools for financing startup businesses. For example, the DownHome Washington pro-gram offers training along with mentorship follow-up and administers a special SBA Microloan Fund in 13 Washington state counties (see page 184 for more information). You may be able to connect with a program through your local Private Industry Council (PIC). There are more than 600 PICs nationwide (see page 186 for more information).

You may also be able to benefit from the Self-Employment Assis-tance (SEA) program. This federal provision allows states to establish programs in which qualified unemployed people can use their unem-ployment benefits as a self-employment stipend and receive entrepre-neurial training. Each state must pass legislation to establish the program. So far California, Connecticut, Maine, New York and Rhode Island have authorized SEA-type programs. Check with your local or state employment development department.

Don't overlook opportunities available through your trade, profes-sional or networking associations. Many offer members **free** learning opportunities. The Association of Black Women Entrepreneurs, for instance, offers the WIN TECH program—a one-year, mini-MBA pro-gram, underwritten by corporate sponsorships, that gives participants (both men and women) marketing-intensive training. (See page 184 for more information.)

Need to improve your technology skills? People 55 and older can learn computer technologies through SeniorNet's nationwide learning centers (see page 186). Others interested in tackling the Internet can take **free** online classes through the Spectrum Virtual University (calendar@horizons.org). Your local library may also be a source for training. Many libraries have received grant funding to set up public workstations and give one-on-one Internet training.

You can also create your own free training opportunity. Consider asking a business owner if you can work as an apprentice or volunteer. You'll be able see first-hand what it takes to run a particular operation. In your search to find or create opportunities, you may also find some other possibilities in the business startup package you ordered (see Survival Tip #26).

Survival Tip #103: Protect your profits with a business "filter."

The formula for profitability: Stay focused. You can safeguard your focus by having a "filter" against which you'll measure all your market-, product- or operational-related decisions. Think of a filter as a mesh screen made up of the strengths, customer base, purpose and market position you have defined for your business. Any opportunities that come along must be "filtered" through this screen; if they don't fit what you've defined for your business, you should pass on them.

Even when the most attractive opportunity comes along, a filter can help you make a business decision based on soundness instead of emotion. A filter will help your business stay on track in its development, progressing steadily toward fulfilling your goals.

One bootstrapper's business is completely driven by the filter of who his market is: small- to medium-sized businesses that have been in operation for two years. The businessman was asked to develop and teach a how-to seminar for home-based businesses. Once he passed the opportunity through his market filter, he determined that it would not be beneficial to the business. He did not work with startups; in fact, he had excluded them from his ideal customer profile. He realized that the project would work against his core business, so he passed on it.

Another bootstrapper had an opportunity to have her skin cream for pregnant women distributed to discount distributors. This was an interesting opportunity on the surface, but her product positioning filter revealed its possible downside. Her product was priced for an upscale market, and in a discount store, price would be a driving factor in determining which products shoppers would buy and which they would reject. The filter reminded her that her product would profit most from endorsements by obstetricians and distribution through specialty maternity and baby shop channels.

Operating without a filter is a form of mismanagement. Without one, your business may be prone to becoming unfocused, chasing inappropriate opportunities or forming unproductive ties. With one, you'll be better able to scrutinize opportunities not merely on their potential but on how they will directly benefit what you're doing.

Survival Tip #104: Learn when to say "no."

Saying "no" can be good for business. It's easy to say no to an annoying or difficult client. But your confidence shouldn't stop there. You can matter-of-factly say no when your answer revolves around important core issues.

Here are some points to consider:

Does the opportunity complement your business's direction? As one bootstrapper grew in visibility, so did her opportunities. There was a catch: She was becoming a magnet for low-paying projects. These projects, in the end, would bring her business down, slowing her pace toward plum, high-wage gigs, so she had to turn many of them down. In another example, a partnership of computer developers began doing repair work along with program development, but as it turned out, programming was more profitable, so making it their core business meant passing on repair activities. These bootstrappers were clear on their desired business direction; it became their policy to say no to opportunities that wouldn't advance them anywhere but forward.

Does your business have the resources in place to professionally handle the work? Phyllis Apelbaum of Arrow Messenger Service in Chicago was offered a six-figure service contract. The project (and the money) was attractive, but she knew at that point in time that her firm was too small to service the account. She admits it was painful to pass on the job, but acknowledges that her business couldn't do the work. There will be instances when it's better to refuse a job than risk poorly serving a customer. If the demands of an opportunity mean that you have to *hastily* hire people or buy equipment or become a quick-study overnight, consider saying no.

Does the project offer you just compensation? If the time and sweat don't match the dollar sign, say no. Some projects aren't worth your effort. Will involvement result in your values being compromised? If an opportunity contradicts your lifestyle and beliefs, no amount of money will ease your ill feelings later.

Politely saying no doesn't have to put people off. Explain that it's not the right opportunity for you now and consider offering a referral. You'll be respected for your honesty. Apelbaum's motto: "When you turn business down for the right reason and in the right way, very often it will come back to you." Or something even better will come your way.

Survival Tip #105: Maximize your resources with "just-in-time management."

"Just-in-time management" is an industry phrase that means manufacturing products as you need them. In lieu of stocking huge inventories of raw materials, businesses order them when needed, use them and then ship the finished product. This practice allows you to have what you need when you need it, reduce excess spending and expand your cash reserve. Bootstrappers can apply this practice to their businesses, as well:

First, look at your inventory. Think of excess inventory as idle money; it's just sitting on your shelf doing nothing. Even as a service business, you have inventory in the form of equipment, forms and supplies. Control your inventory by calculating how much and how often you use each item. Then set a minimum to be kept on hand, and reorder a predetermined amount each time the supply falls below this minimum level. Factor in the turnaround delivery time of your suppliers, noting any premium charges you may incur for a rush request that may be too costly.

Second, evaluate how you're using your computer. Many communication tools can be stored on your system—correspondence, marketing materials, proposals, contracts, budgets, invoices, thank-you notes, resumes, an operations manual and, of course, your mailing list. You'll be able to update and customize these materials at will, and you can recycle formats and phrases from document to document. If you farm out your writing, secretarial or desktop publishing projects, always request a disk copy so you can add them to your in-house system. You can also slice some of your printing costs by keeping your communication tools stored on your system and getting reproductions made only when you need to (rather than getting stacks of materials run off all at once, only to have them sit in your supply closet, collecting dust).

Third, look at your people resources. You'll be able to manage overflow work more efficiently when you have a network of professionals to call on. You'll need to spend time cultivating relationships with skilled individuals who are available upon demand (see Survival Tip #111). Let your peers know that you're looking for people to work with. Then check them out and test them on a few nonrush projects first (see Survival Tip #119).

Survival Tip: #106: Regularly test your prices against the market.

A well-managed business is a profitable one. You should always stay aware of your price position—knowing whether you fall on the high-, low- or middle-priced point on the marketplace scale. When you're aware of your price position, you can devise ways to protect or build on it. Maintaining your profit base will require that you monitor the basic costs of doing business, marketplace trends or competition.

Shifts in these areas may force you into a change. However, there are strategies you can use to keep pace with the market and stay ahead of your competition.

All pricing boils down to what the market will bear. Quoting higher on prospects' jobs will allow you to test the waters and see how high you can go without losing business. Try quoting a higher rate to new inquiries for a designated time period. Avoid using referrals as your guinea pigs, since they may already know your price position (people have a tendency to share what they paid for things). Or change the price of your product for a while. The sales or prospects' responses may lead you to a new price point. This approach keeps you in touch with your market's potential.

Consider your competition. You may have developed a price point by default. If your competitors are charging 50 percent less than you are, you automatically become the premium provider. In this instance, if your profitability began to drop, your business may be forced to add new profit centers or diversify to increase or maintain its profit base. Use prospects to find information. If a prospect indicates that he or she has been comparison-shopping, ask where and find out how much the quote was. Periodic competitor-snooping will give you an idea of where you fall in the pricing ladder and help you better evaluate options for positioning.

Regularly gathering this type of information can help you prepare to absorb any dips in profit. You'll gain an advantage when introducing changes to your customers—your presentation will be based on real comparison data, not off-based notions.

Survival Tip #107: Aim at having a project minimum.

An aerial photography service has a minimum order requirement of $75. A desktop publisher bills in quarter-hour increments. A doctor's appointment may cost you $60—it doesn't matter if you take up an hour or five minutes of the doc's time. Another professional bypasses projects that are under four figures. All of these small business professionals have calculated a minimum by which to do business. Of course, this strategy isn't appropriate for every type of business. However, working with a project minimum can be effective in helping you maintain or increase the profitability of your business. You may not start off with the confidence to work with a minimum, but as you grow in status and expertise, consider incorporating one into your operation.

You can begin to explore working with a minimum by asking yourself: *At what point does a project become unprofitable?* For example, the aerial photography service has to set up each reproduction job separately. In order to make money, the firm has factored in a minimum covering the basic expenses associated with each job. A desktop publisher may get several quick, one-minute change requests from clients, which can add up in a given day. Rather than lose out by calculating a small fee for each short request, the publisher makes sure customers understand that the minimum charge is a quarter-hour. Some professionals impose their own quota system, aiming to serve a set number of clients per day or to make a certain amount in sales. This is setting parameters for yourself for fulfilling the financial goals of the business.

Another way to increase your profitability is to develop skills that will enable you to provide services that are worth more. A person may begin providing basic bookkeeping, then become an accountant, then ultimately become a high-priced CPA. Or a printer may open shop with basic printing services and then graduate into more specialized projects, such as yearbooks and annual reports. Within virtually every profession, there are opportunities to improve your skills through certification or training (see Survival Tips #102 and #147). These can translate into more profitable services for your business.

Survival Tip #108: Introduce rate increases in stages.

Inevitably, you'll be faced with the task of raising your rates and introducing the change to your customers. You can avoid frequent rate changes by initially calculating your cost and profit margins at a higher percentage, giving yourself room to absorb any costly occurrences. You should annually review your rates in terms of the overall profitability of your business. A rate increase may not be in order; adopting a smarter-working management style may be the answer (see Survival Tips #107, #109, #113 and #115).

Rate increases can be tied to rising business costs, a transition into higher-priced products or services or the results of testing the market (see Survival Tip #106). If your increase is tied into skyrocketing business expenses, explain that to customers. For example, a U.S. paper shortage began in 1994 and prices rose between 11 and 28 percent; it continued into 1995, resulting in another 15 percent increase. Nevertheless, businesses continued to patronize their printers and office suppliers because everyone understood what was going on.

How customers, particularly your old-timers, respond to new rates will depend on how you handle it. You could begin by charging all newcomers the higher rates (if you've been testing the marketplace, the transition should go smoothly). But your existing clients may require more finesse. Introduce the change by:

- Giving an advance notice, say 30 to 60 days; this will allow them to take advantage of the old rate and save money.
- Explaining the increase, relating it to expanded services or economic conditions.
- Offering other pricing options, such as customized versions of your standard service, package deals based on volume or prepaid services, or retainer specials allowing the customer to use your service for a flat monthly rate for a set time period. (The longer the retainer agreement—a year, for example— the bigger the price break you could give the customer.)

If you're under contract, be sure your original deal specifies the possibility of a rate change. You may also find it effective to impose increases on a case-by-case basis, according to each customer's status. If a 10-percent rate increase will decrease a particular customer's volume by a sizable percentage, you'll lose money overall.

Raising your rates takes confidence, so prepare yourself to lose some customers. If you're providing a value-added offering with stellar service, your loyal customers will continue to use you.

Survival Tip #109: Tend to the business of collecting your money.

Don't be afraid to ask for money that you're due. You're setting yourself up for problems when you manage your receivables with a timid or lax attitude. Being lackadaisical about customers' payments may create a casual attitude in their minds about paying you. If you're ever faced with a delinquency, you may be ineffective in resolving it because you haven't been developing your assertiveness skills.

Be kind to your cash flow and communicate your payment policy in advance. Your payment terms should be discussed as soon as you secure a sale, and in some cases, as you're negotiating a deal. It's at this time clients may express to you their payment terms, telling you that they pay all accounts in 30 to 45 days. If you can afford to work under their suggested arrangement, that's fine. If not, explain your terms and work to reach a compromise. Trust me, everything is negotiable. For example, I've worked with some of the same clients as my colleagues, but my payment experiences have been quite different than theirs because I negotiated better payment terms for myself.

Follow up as soon as an account becomes past due. If a payment is due on the 15th, call on the 16th. When you contact your customers quickly, your actions communicate that you expect payments to be made promptly or you expect to be notified of any delays. Collection expert John Johanson of Mid-Continent Agency in Rolling Meadows, Illinois, points out that the period of 31-60 days following the payment due date is the most critical time, when your cash flow either maintains its momentum or breaks down. Customers whose accounts are 31-60 days past due are usually just slow payers—not collection problems. When you stay close to them through phone calls or letters, you can accelerate the payment process. Don't wait until the payment is more than 60 days late. Otherwise, you may have difficulty collecting the money.

Other safeguards to consider: Use your postpurchase follow-up call to reiterate payment terms (see Survival Tip #81). When you inquire about customers' satisfaction with your offering, you can wrap up the conversation by saying, "Since everything was okay, we'll look for your payment on the 15th." Also consider padding your cash flow by billing in cycles—having accounts due on different days. This way, if you're faced with a few delinquencies, you'll still have some cash coming in.

Survival Tip #110: Avoid lopsided contracts and terms.

My personal motto: Enter all negotiations prepared to walk away from a bad deal. This mind-set can be quite liberating. It's part of my business filter, and I use it to scrutinize every client alliance and project that comes my way. There may be times when you're approached with opportunities for which the arrangements are more beneficial to the other party. You may be tempted to go along with the deal because you need the work or believe doing it one time won't hurt. Consider this: You're setting a precedent that may be difficult to break away from. If you're in a contract-oriented profession (such as freelance writing), you drag your industry down when you accept unattractive terms because it makes buyers believe that they can make any offer and someone is bound to accept it.

Bad deals come in various packages. First of all, avoid letting clients dictate payment terms to you. That practice is particularly common if your clients are larger entities. Scores of businesspeople cringe as they agree to payment schedules they cannot afford for the sake of landing an account. Another scenario: taking on work that you won't make any money on. People confuse this with the toe-in-the-door strategy (see Survival Tip #80). Introducing your business on a smaller scale means making less money initially, not *giving* your talents away. When you don't make money on jobs, you're contradicting your price position. Also be careful about entering into work arrangements that will jeopardize your status as an independent business (see Survival Tip #122).

Don't be afraid to negotiate. One reason many self-employed professionals agree to poor deals is that they haven't honed their negotiating skills. Be prepared to offer some halfway solutions. For example, if a client tells you 60 days is its policy for making payments, you could counter by explaining that your normal terms are 30 days, but with a 50-percent deposit you'd be willing to carry the account for 45 days. Express to the other party that productive working relationships are built on win-win arrangements; this will set the tone for friendlier negotiations.

5 MANAGEMENT CRIMES NEVER TO COMMIT AGAINST YOUR BUSINESS

1. Undervaluing yourself in the market. Just because you're the new kid on the block, you don't have to be the cheapest. A home-based bootstrapper thought that because her business was part-time, it seemed right to charge less. Not so. Your fee structure should cover overhead expenses and be in line with the experience you bring to the market. Careful industry research will help you structure your pricing correctly. At worst, you would enter the market charging a moderate rate, regularly testing your prices before increasing them (see Survival Tip #106).

2. Failing to honor the policies of your business. Don't compromise your business standards just to placate a demanding customer. If your office is nonsmoking or whatever, make sure everybody who walks in the door abides by the rule. When you bend the rules, you set a precedent that someone will remind you of later. You also send a message to customers and employees that anything goes in your operation.

3. Disrespecting your time. You can't expect others to respect your time when you don't. If others see you lollygagging on the phone or socializing when you should be working, then they'll begin to think that what you're doing isn't that serious. Value your time by using it wisely. You'll set a tone for others to follow suit.

4. Mismanaging your hard-earned money. Haven't you heard that the excess of the 90s is gone? Even when you can *afford* to, it's foolish to become a spendthrift in your ways. You may find it difficult to begin tightening your belt again. Always manage your resources wisely. It'll help you maintain a responsive position instead of a reactive one.

5. Being lax in how you pursue business. If your business income isn't a necessity for your family's financial survival, be mindful of how that can negatively affect your drive. Entrepreneurs have shared with me that knowing they had spousal financial support affected their aggressiveness at times; they knew that if a deal didn't work out, their needs would still be met. If your business isn't a hobby, don't treat it as one. Even if you feel financially secure now, if you haven't been developing your business savvy, you won't have anything to fall back on when you really need it.

Survival Tip #111: Practice defensive driving.

Success happens when opportunity meets with preparation. Sometimes we work so hard to create an opportunity for ourselves that we neglect to prepare for it. Your wish may be "more business," but when it comes, you find yourself scrambling around, fumbling through the process. Instead of making money on an opportunity, you lose money. It's lack of preparation that makes a professional appear amateurish, a winner look like a loser and the most talented person question his or her ability. You can capitalize on opportunities by approaching them from a defensive point of view—asking yourself, "How can I prepare myself to respond when the other guy makes a move?"

Make it a habit to think several steps forward. For example, if you're working toward selling to the government, what management system do you need to have in place? Electronic data interchange (EDI) is the all-electronic method the federal government is moving toward to buy goods and services. You'll need access to a VAN (value-added network) to conduct EDI transactions. In this instance, you need to educate yourself on the costs of what's available and prepare to get the system in place. (A current listing of all government certified VANs can be obtained by calling 800-318-9223.) Let's say you've been courting an account that would require additional staffing. Have you been actively looking for people? Do you have a placement service or organization that you can use to connect to qualified people? Have you begun negotiating flexible pricing or payment terms for your volume order? Thinking ahead can help you save money and maximize the profit on each deal.

Sit down and review your business development goals. Although you may feel ready for an opportunity, scrutinize your existing resource network and your ability to expand it. How will you handle any sudden surge in business? Have you been comparison-shopping for new equipment? Have you begun to research the various loans available to you, so you won't be wiped out by a possible jump in business expenses? Write down all the details of your impending situation and begin to create your strategy for preparing for each one. Forward thinking is good management.

Survival Tip #112: Incorporate disaster planning into your operation.

The Northridge, California, earthquake of January 1994 wiped out Sue's Secretarial Service. The facility housing Sue Clamage's business was so severely damaged she was never allowed back inside. She lost important computer files, customer records and completed assignments. Her equipment losses included five computers, three printers, a Xerox machine and a phone dictation system, totaling about $65,000. Her standard insurance policy helped recoup some of the losses. The experience prompted Clamage to beef up her disaster-preparedness strategy; she now stores backup computer files off-site and maintains a line of credit to tap in an emergency.

Your recovery from a disaster begins with having adequate insurance coverage (see Survival Tip #29). However, your insurance coverage should be supported by a disaster recovery plan. If your office was affected by flooding, fire, an earthquake or another natural disaster, how would you bounce back? Your business can recover quickly when you plan in advance. Keeping duplicate records off the premises can be a lifesaver. You should be backing up your computer system regularly. You can keep duplicate copies of important records, documents and other important numbers in a safe deposit box.

Next, develop a communications strategy to prevent loss of clients or customers. For example, you can check with your phone carrier to find out about available service routing options to keep your business going. Consider alternative facilities you could use in the interim. You may able to coordinate some shared space arrangement with another business. You should also verify whether your equipment suppliers can provide you with loaners. Consider having an additional credit line so you can buy what you need while you're waiting for your insurance claim to be processed. Write up your plan and make sure your employees know who to contact and what to do if you're affected by a disaster. A helpful resource: *How to Survive a Catastrophe: A Guide for Businesses* (see page 185 for more information).

Survival Tip #113: Develop a smart shopper's mentality.

Did you know that less is more? It's a smart shopper's cornerstone: The less money you waste, the more you have to build your business, to make investments or just enjoy. Smart shoppers aren't nickel-and-dimers, though. They take advantage of the free and low-cost offers of business service providers who are fiercely competing for their dollars. A smart shopper has purchasing savvy and is dedicated to getting true value for every hard-earned dollar spent. Here are three areas where you can easily begin to incorporate smart shopping into your business:

First, avoid making shortsighted purchases. Buying equipment, products or services that you quickly outgrow creates a self-defeating cycle. Say, for example, you need an additional phone line in your office, so you pay to have one installed to fulfill your immediate need. Six months later, you need another line, and you pay an installation fee again. What you should have done originally was have the technician do the wiring for more than one line—you actually save on installation charges when you have more than line installed simultaneously. Or say you need a computer, so you buy a cheap one just to get started. Six months to a year later, you find you need more memory and more features than the barebone model you bought can allow, and you have to invest in a new, more advanced model.

When you buy quick fixes instead of making "investment" purchases, you end up chipping away at your profits. You start the cycle when you are unclear about your needs and the business's direction or when you just hastily buy "stuff" to get over an immediate hump. Always think your purchases through. Focus on funneling your dollars into business-building purchases that help you provide standout service for the long haul.

Second, think multipurpose. As with your marketing devices (see Survival Tip #72), think about multiple purposes for items you invest in. Many items are candidates for the "multipurpose test," such as brochures, collateral and office equipment, furniture and supplies. A foldout business card, for instance, can serve as a mini brochure. Or four-in-one office equipment can allow you to fax, copy, print and scan. Want to save multidollars? Then think multiple purpose.

Third, sample 'til your heart's content. Freebies are everywhere. U.S. businesses spend billions every year on giveaways. Whenever possible, try an item first. This will help eliminate your buying items that you really don't need or like. Avery Dennison (800-252-8379) will send you labels and stationery from its product line. Lotus (800-872-3387) has a working model on CD of its SmartSuites, an integrated software package consisting of several applications (a multipurpose item). For a sampler package of office supplies, you can also contact 3M Office Products (800-395-1223). In fact, whenever you're going to order *anything*, always ask whether a sample is available before you buy.

Begin embracing this philosophy today, and you'll wind up the owner of a well-managed business.

Survival Tip #114: Install convenience services and tools.

There are little things you can do to give yourself an advantage in managing your business. Your goal here is to use tools or implement services that make it easier for you to run the business and for employees, suppliers and customers to interact with you. Begin by evaluating who handles your mail. Whether you're in a storefront space or a home office, paying for a P.O. box or mail service can improve the handling of your incoming mail. For example, many P.O. box-holders can pick up their mail as early as 8 a.m., collecting checks so they can make an early deposit. A mail service, however, gives you a safe place to receive package deliveries when you're away. Shipping your packages can be easier, too. UPS's Quick Cost Calculator software allows you to compute shipment rates and compare costs for a variety of other shipping options; by the way, it's **free** (800-742-5877).

A number of other convenience services and tools can help you run your business more smoothly:

- Interested in opportunities to capitalize on customers' impulse-buying decisions and eliminate your bounced check worries? Then you can obtain merchant status, which allows you to accept credit card payments from customers. Merchant status is becoming easier for small businesses to secure because many professional associations now offer it as a value-added membership benefit (see Survival Tip #115).

- Your customers may also appreciate being able to use a dropbox outside your office, or at a centralized location in town, for depositing payments, work/projects and other items after hours.

- You can also make it a cinch to bill your clients for the phone calls you've made for their projects by taking advantage of a service offered by many long-distance carriers for **free** or a low fee. The feature, commonly referred to as "call manager" or "account coding," enables you to punch in a code you've designated to a particular client before you dial a long-distance phone number for that client's project. Your long-distance bill will then be itemized by client—listing the calls and their cost separately according to each client's code.

- Having trouble managing your follow-up schedule? Instead of relying on your memory or manual calendaring system, invest in a contact management software program. This program can remind you to make follow-up calls and send correspondence at specific times, as well as keep detailed records of all your contacts and business activities.

Make yourself more accessible with expanded contact options. For example, pager notification on your phone system will enable you to respond quickly to your customers' calls. Ensuring that you have an ample number of lines dedicated to voice calls and faxes also makes your operation run more smoothly. E-mail access is another convenience tool. An informal survey of my networking circle revealed that a large percentage of self-employed people subscribe to online services for e-mail usage only. You may discover more convenience options through your trade-journal reading and from suggestions in your customer surveys (see Survival Tip #88).

Survival Tip #115: Put value-added programs to work in your business.

The next time you get a solicitation in the mail from a business supplier, think twice about throwing it away. It may be your link to discounts on other valuable products and services. Business-to-business suppliers' offerings now have value-added programs attached to them. For example, a primary supplier, such as your phone carrier, may team with other suppliers that target the small business market to offer a special package deal on all their services. These kinds of co-op deals can include offers from banks, office superstores, trade associations and others. What's neat about some of the programs is that you may be gaining access to things you need that you've been unable to get on your own.

Many phone carriers offer model examples of value-added programs. US West has two programs aimed at its self-employed customers, The Home Office Network (800-898-WORK) and US West Business Start-Up Kit (800-603-6000). Both programs offer small businesses **free** office setup counseling, introductory discounts on phone services and products, a newsletter and business building re-source guides. Augmenting the program are more than $300 worth of certificates that can be used to save money on items from value partners, such as Microsoft and CompuServe. Bell Atlantic offers its customers technology education through its Knowledge Centers (800-867-6000). Small business owners can visit the facilities to pre-view and experiment with communications technologies and applica-tions at no charge. Another program example: the bank. Mine offers its small business customers 15- to 50-percent discounts on airline and rail tickets, car rentals and on a variety of other goodies. Also, associations are getting in on the act by offering members access to low-cost legal services, business and health insurance and merchant services (enabling small businesses to accept credit card payments).

These programs are big business's way of building customer rela-tionships. Whenever you're dealing with supplier companies, ask them about the existence of such programs. Frankly, many business owners aren't tapping into these networks because they ignore cus-tomer communications tools that are used to promote the programs, such as direct-mail promotions, bill inserts and newsletters. So the next time your supplier sends you something in the mail, read it to ensure that you're not tossing your ticket to a deal that can be put to work in your business. (You can learn more about value-added pro-grams from my special report, *How to Find Value in Value-Added Programs*. See page 185 for ordering information.)

Survival Tip #116: Protect your greatest asset—yourself.

There's a television commercial in which a woman business owner is shown working in her artistic studio. A narrator explains that the woman has opted for the independent lifestyle, but she worries end-lessly when she feels under the weather or has a recurring body ache because she doesn't have health insurance. The commercial goes on to advertise an insurance company that has affordable options so busi-ness owners don't have to worry about not being covered. Unfortu-nately, too many people in this country can identify with this com-mercial. Business owners will insure the assets of their business while neglecting their most important asset—themselves. Part of taking care of yourself means going to the doctor when you need to. When you're juggling the various expenses of your business, make having health coverage a priority.

If you've recently left a job, you're entitled to continue your insurance coverage under the Consolidated Omnibus Budget Reconciliation Act (COBRA). Depending on the circumstances, you can keep the coverage for 18 to 36 months. You pay for the premium at your employer's group rate, which may be substantially less than a private policy. You can use this time to look for other coverage.

Many self-employed people find affordable coverage through a health maintenance organization (HMO) or preferred provider organization (PPO). Many HMOs and PPOs provide quality care and accept individual members. Contact your local medical society or city's consumer affairs office. Also, consider any state plans or coverage pools. For example, self-employed Oregon residents have access to affordable health coverage through Oregon Health Plan. Your state department of insurance should be able to tell you about similar programs in your area. A professional or trade organization can be another source. Groups such as the National Association for the Self-Employed (800-827-9990) and Home Office Association of America (800-809-4622) offer coverage options.

Carefully scrutinize the stability of a carrier, the premium costs versus the benefits included and how premiums and rate increases are calculated. Remember that your medical history will usually affect your premium costs. Don't forget your tax deduction. The health insurance tax deduction for self-employed people has increased to 40 percent.

Survival Tip #117: Don't forsake the working lifestyle you adore.

Chances are that you didn't become self-employed to live in drudgery or discontentment. If you didn't mind that state of being, you would have kept your day job, right? Entrepreneurism is one of the few occupations that allow you to mesh your professional and personal interests together. It provides you with a working lifestyle that you can control, and it allows you to work toward your ultimate fulfillment (see Survival Tip #7). Business demands will require you to work long, dogged hours, but how you manage your business can help balance this out. When you forget that you're the captain, you become a slave to the business.

What key benefit does your working lifestyle enable you to enjoy? Is it the fact that you have flexibility to pursue personal interests, are more accessible to your loved ones or are able to participate in community activities? It's important to make a note of these benefits. If your business regularly interferes with these benefits, then there's a problem that may tie into your management style. The same is true if you're working toward a benefit and never get there. For example, you may be cutting your deadlines too close or overbooking your schedule, wasting too time much on the phone or just working against yourself in general.

As you grow, it's important to stay involved with the parts of the business that give you fulfillment. Delegation is part of smart management, but you can still have an active part in desired areas. For example, if you grow to the point that you must hire an independent sales rep to shop your product around, you can still periodically do drop-in visits with shop owners.

Part of good management is regularly taking some time off to rest and rejuvenate yourself. It may be as simple as a mental health day or an extended weekend. Make a regular habit of evaluating how you're managing the business. Is the working lifestyle you dreamed of a part of your reality? Are you moving closer to your desired existence or just farther away? You don't want to wake up and be managing a business that you don't enjoy.

Bootstrapper's Follow-up File

Accounts Receivable: How to Tame the Beast, Dun & Bradstreet Information Services, 800-333-6497. A **free** guide of helpful collection strategies.

Act! 2.0, 800-441-7234; Web address: www.symantec.com. Contact management software.

America at Work, Microsoft Corporation. A six-part video series dedicated to helping you learn how to better manage your business. Topics include: marketing your business, getting started with technology, doing business on the Internet and managing virtual offices and alternative workplaces. Series is available for viewing at Small Business Development Centers nationwide at no charge.

America Online, 800-827-6364. An Internet and online service provider.

American Collectors Association, Inc., P.O. Box 39106, Minneapolis, MN 55439-0106; Web address: www.member.com/aca. Sells publications on collection strategies; Web page includes collection fact sheet and frequently asked questions about the collection process.

Association of Black Women Entrepreneurs, P.O. Box 49368, Los Angeles, CA 90049; 213-624-8639. A professional networking association open to women and men. Offers a variety of educational opportunities to its members, including a one-year marketing-intensive training program.

Bank Card Solutions, 800-260-1500. Providers of merchant services.

CompuServe, 800-848-8199. An Internet and online service provider.

Consumer's Resource Handbook, Consumer Information Center, Pueblo, CO 81009. A **free**, 125-page guide designed to help consumers make informed decisions and avoid problems.

Corel WordPerfect Suite and WordPerfect Suite 7, 800-772-6735; Web address: corel.com. An integrated package of word processing, spreadsheet, graphics and presentation software.

Delhi, 800-695-4005. An Internet and online service provider.

DownHome Washington, Snohomish County Private Industry Council, 917 134th St. SW, Suite A-10, Everett, WA 98204; 206-743-9669. Provides **free** entrepreneurial training for dislocated workers in 13 counties in the state.

Energy Efficiency and Renewable Energy Clearinghouse, 800-363-3732. Handles information queries about energy efficiency issues related to your business. All information provided **free** of charge. Request **free**, 27-page resource guide, *Hands-on Solutions to Improve Your Profits and Productivity: Energy-Saving Tips for Small Businesses.*

Everything's Organized by Lisa Kanarek (Career Press, 1996); 800-CAREER-1 (201-848-0310 in N.J. and outside U.S.). $16.99.

GEnie, 800-638-9636. An Internet and online service provider.

Hammermill Papers, 800-242-2148. Provides **free** sample paper packs.

HMO SmartPages, Web address: www.buyerszone.com. Created by the publishers of *Business Consumer Guide,* provides information on more than 150 HMOs nationwide.

How to Find Value in Value-Added Programs by Kimberly Stanséll, Research Done Write!, Suite B261-BSS, 8726 S. Sepulveda Blvd., Los Angeles, CA 90045. A special report presenting a five-step strategy to evaluate the worth of a value-added program to your business. Includes a roundup of programs nationwide. $5 ($5.41 for California residents).

How to Save Money on Office Supplies, Quill Corporation, 800-789-6640; Web address: www.quillcorp.com. A **free**, 54-page guide providing helpful tips for cost-efficiently buying supplies for your business.

How to Set Your Fees and Get Them, Fifth Edition, by Kate Kelly (Visibility Enterprises, 1994); 800-784-0602. $17.50.

How to Survive a Catastrophe: A Guide for Businesses, Insurance Information Institute, 110 William St., New York, NY 10038. A **free** guide providing helpful information on how to develop a catastrophe recovery plan. Send SASE with request.

InfoAlert: Your expert guide to online business information, The Economics Press, 800-526-2554. A monthly newsletter of tips on how to use the Internet in your business. **Free** sample copy available.

InsWeb, Web address: www.insweb.com. A Web site offering links to health insurance carriers and agencies worldwide. Enables users to scout out price quotes for coverage online.

Microsoft Small Business Resource Center, 800-60-SOURCE; Web address: www.microsoft.com/smallbiz. Provides information on how Microsoft products can be used to help manage your business.

National Association of Private Industry Councils, 1201 New York Ave. NW, Suite 800, Washington, DC 20005; 202-289-2950. An association of the members of the 600-plus PICs in the country. Provides information, technical assistance and advocacy for its members. Contact for a referral to a local PIC.

National Public Telecomputing Network, 30680 Bainbridge Rd., Solon, OH 44139; 216-498-4050; e-mail address: info@nptn.org. Provides a nationwide listing of local Free-Nets, a community computer system that offers **free** and low-cost Internet access.

Postal Business Companion: Time-Saving Information for Your Business, U.S. Postal Service, M. Dempsey, Business Account Services, Room 8430, 475 L'Enfant Plaza, Washington, DC 20260. A **free**, 124-page book filled with resources and tips for managing your business.

Principles for Business, Minnesota Center for Corporate Responsibility, 1000 LaSalle Ave., Minneapolis, MN 55403-2005. An information package on guidelines for running an ethical business. $15.

Prodigy Information Service, 800-776-3449. An Internet and online service provider.

Quicken and QuickBooks Pro, 800-816-8025; Web address: www.intuit.com. Accounting/bookkeeping software programs.

Self-Audit Kit, Software Publishers Association, 800-388-7478. A **free** kit to help you perform a self-audit of your business's software practices and procedures.

SeniorNet, 1 Kearney St., 3rd Floor, San Francisco, CA 94108; 415-352-1210; fax: 415-352-1260; e-mail address: seniornet@seniornet.org; Web address: www.seniornet.org. Provides information on its local computer learning centers.

Share Communications Network, 800-247-0352; Web address: www.noncash.com. A service that allows merchants and businesses to accept noncash (credit card, bank debit card) payments and processes such transactions for them.

SideKick, 888-782-7347; Web address: www.starfishsoftware.com. Contact management software.

The Source, Mid-Continent Agencies, 3701 W. Algonquin Rd., Rolling Meadows, IL 60008. A quarterly newsletter with tips on credit and collection. **Free** sample copy available.

The Things Everyone Should Know About Point-of-Sale Software and Hardware by Wayne Philips (A-Z Business Services, 1996); 407-296-3274. $14.95.

U.S. Postal Service, National Customer Support Center, 800-238-3150; Web address: www.usps.gov. Provides a variety of **free** publications, software and information helpful for small businesses.

Using Prepaid Phone Cards, Consumer Action, 116 New Montgomery St., Suite 233, San Francisco, CA 94105. A cost comparisons survey of various cards, including tips on how to use the cards. Send SASE for **free** copy.

Waste Reduction Tips: For Your Bottom Line, Environmental Newsletters, Inc., 11906 Paradise Lane, Herndon, VA 20171; 703-758-8436; e-mail address: aso@aol.com. A bimonthly newsletter of tips and strategies to help businesses save money by reducing waste. **Free** sample available.

Women's Network for Entrepreneurial Training (WNET), SBA Office of Women's Business Ownership. A mentoring program matching successful entrepreneurial women with female business owners whose companies are ready to grow. Contact your local SBA office or Small Business Development Center for more information.

Chapter 8

Working with Others

"No one can succeed and remain successful without the friendly cooperation of others."

—Napoleon Hill, motivational
speaker and author

Survival Tip #118: Use self-knowledge to pinpoint how others can help you.

Other people can begin to help build your business from day one. You don't have to be a bona fide employer to begin using your people resources. In fact, you've already begun the process. It started when you used the research knowledge of your local librarian. Or when you picked the counselor's brain at the SCORE office or Small Business Development Center. I'm working for you right now as you highlight the strategies on these pages or order the information presented to you in this book. Your subconscious recognized that you were short on knowledge in an area and pointed you to people who could help pick up the slack.

You can consciously go a step further by taking inventory of your strengths and weaknesses. Be honest. You'll need this information to help you handpick your support team of peers, contacts, suppliers, mentors and employees. Write down the areas in which you excel. Do you have strong verbal presentation skills? Exceptional technical knowledge? These are the areas around which you will build your business. Next, note the areas where you are deficient. You may be weak in getting your ideas across on paper or limited in your computer skills. Use fearless self-knowledge to identify the abilities and resources you'll need to look for in others, who then can be put to work in your business. Be open to ways of working with others without necessarily employing them.

Your clarity will help you stay focused; you'll know when a "people resource" is better than an organizational one. For example, hiring someone to do telemarketing may not be as effective as signing up with a professional referral service. You can also decide whether to improve in a desired area or use another person's talents instead. If you don't like to sell your product, for example, and have no interest in learning how, then a working relationship with an independent sales rep may be a viable option. The same is true in your peer relationships. A marketing extrovert and a computer introvert could cook up ways to barter based on each other's attributes. A strategic approach will be at work here: You're aligning yourself with people whose strengths complement yours. Consider it. Embrace it. You'll form more productive relationships and discover the most suitable people to work for you.

Survival Tip #119: Consider hiring alternatives.

Manning your business without an employee payroll doesn't have to stunt its growth. There are countless bootstrappers running profitable businesses solo while incorporating others' talents into the process. Many business owners create an army of contractors (see Survival Tip #121). You can create your own network of other self-employed people whose talents, knowledge, resources and skills can be used to handle the demands of your business. Besides helping you with overflow work, the collaborative talents of your team can help you obtain larger projects and grow with your clients' needs.

The manpower behind your network may vary. For example, a Web page consultant may have a team of writers, graphic designers and other technical experts in place to handle projects. A product designer may use a manufacturer's representative to sell his or her wares. A newsletter publisher may use a subscription management service. A cataloger may use an order fulfillment house. A road warrior may use an answering service to cover the phones. You'll need to determine the feasibility of any arrangement based on your support needs and the costs versus the investment of hiring in-house staffers.

Bob Mastin of Aegis Publishing Group in Newport, Rhode Island, doesn't rely solely on his part-timers to manage his firm. He uses a strategic alliance as his defacto sales team. The Telecommuting Advisory Council, an association for companies interested in the telecommuting movement, sends him a monthly list of new members (who are usually eager to get their hands on information about working more productively and comfortably from home). Mastin, in turn, sends the new members books on the subject of telecommunications, along with information on placing bulk orders of the book.

Make sure your network is reliable. You'll need to consider others' availability as you begin to rely on them to facilitate opportunities. Consider working on a trial basis before committing yourself to a work arrangement. If someone fails to deliver for you, it could put you in a bad position with your customers. You may discover or feel that your business would benefit most from having a staff devoted to you. In this instance, you should begin to evaluate the responsibilities associated with becoming an employer (see Survival Tip #120).

Survival Tip #120: Be sure it's the right time to hire.

Faced with a crunch work period or finding it difficult to manage business growth? Hiring an employee may appear to be an obvious solution. If you hire prematurely, what seemed like a good idea could turn into a burdensome expense. It's estimated that the employer's taxes, worker's compensation insurance and administrative paperwork will cost you an additional 30 percent of your payroll. Some businesses try to sidestep the expenses by dubbing everyone they hire as independent contractors, which can turn into a disaster when done incorrectly (see Survival Tip #121). Hiring an employee is an investment in your business and in another person. Your decision to become an employer should be scrutinized carefully.

Before you begin the recruitment process, you can avoid a costly move by filtering your decision against some important factors:

What are my business needs? Keeping a daily routine journal can help you pinpoint duties to delegate. The information may help you distinguish between a cyclical or sustained growth period. You can also use the notations to clarify the skills your worker will need and create job descriptions and placement announcements.

What is my hiring objective? Are you looking for someone to help handle tasks associated with a new account or take over your mundane duties? For example, if you need someone to handle word processing, then paying an outside business to handle the work may be a more cost-efficient move.

Do I have the resources in place to support another worker? You'll need to provide proper workspace, equipment and supplies so that a staffer can work productively. If you work from home, you'll need to be sure that your zoning allows nonresident workers (see Survival Tip #33).

You should also consider the short- and long-term advantages of your decision. It isn't always easy to find qualified workers, so you need to be clear about how much time you can afford to invest in the process. If you need to have a worker lined up by a set date, consider ways to use the services of other self-employed people in the interim. Whatever you do, don't rush through the hiring process, winding up with someone you wish you'd never met.

Fair Measures, a management law consulting group, has an "ask the lawyer" section on its Web site (www.fairmeasures.com), where business owners can get **free** legal advice. Browse through the area. Reading through others' hiring blunders and predicaments may provide you with food for thought. (You can learn more about managing employee turnover from my special report, *How to Hire Right the First Time and Avoid Costly Turnover Problems*. See page 202 for ordering information.)

Survival Tip #121: Beware of the independent contractor trap.

Many businesspeople try to minimize their responsibilities as an employer by hiring independent contractors. The arrangement can cut your paperwork in half—you don't have to withhold taxes and only file tax Form 1099 for those to whom you've paid more than $600 in a year. But beware: The Internal Revenue Service (IRS) is watching you. Uncle Sam has made it a priority to audit businesses suspected of misclassifying workers. If you get caught, the repercussions, such as back taxes and stiff penalties, can bankrupt your business. A notable example is Microsoft Corporation, which recently was ordered to pay employee benefits to hundreds of workers it had been classifying as independent contractors. The software giant plans to appeal the ruling; a small business, however, may not be able to bankroll a lengthy legal process.

The key distinction between an employee and an independent contractor is control. Merely allowing a worker some discretion or freedom in the job or having a signed independent contractor agreement on file does not camouflage an employer-employee relationship when one, in fact, exists. An individual can be considered an independent contractor when he or she is regularly engaged in the independent trade or business related to the service performed and is free from control and direction in the performance of the job.

You should keep this in mind as you work through the steps of deciding whether or not to hire (see Survival Tip #120).

The IRS has a new document, *Independent Contractor or Employee* (Section 530, Relief Requirements). The simple, one-page document explains your rights under the law when the agency questions your classification of workers as independent contractors. Other IRS publications include: *Circular E: Employer's Tax Guide* (Publication 15), which includes all the IRS's legal definitions and guidelines, and *Employment Taxes* (Publication 937), which includes 20 factors used to determine proper classification of an independent contractor. Request **free** copies of these documents from 800-TAX-FORM or download them from the Web at www.irs.ustreas.gov.

Protect yourself when working with outside professionals by getting copies of their business license, home occupation permit, client references or any documentation that verifies they're operating as an independent. Carefully monitor how much time the person is devoting to your business; you need to avoid the trappings of a full-time employee scenario.

Survival Tip #122: Protect your own independent status.

Conversely, you don't want to become a casualty in a reclassification battle. You need to protect your status as an independent, self-employed person. If the IRS determines you're a participant in an employer-employee relationship, your client will shoulder the expense of back withholding and Social Security taxes, interest and penalties. There's a downside for you, too. You may have a bigger tax bill as the result of losing deductions such as health insurance premiums, home office allocation, mileage, equipment and more. What's more, you may even lose your client; it may be too expensive to carry you on the books as an employee. Be careful and monitor how entrenched you become in your client's operation.

Take some clues from the independent contractors at Microsoft. The court found that Microsoft had fully integrated the workers into its workforce. Although the contractors were hired to work on specific projects, many of them had worked on successive projects for two years. They billed the company for their hours and were paid through accounting, not payroll. They had no supervisory or delegation authority, were excluded from official company functions and wore identification badges of a different color to distinguish them from the regular staffers. However, they often were involved with employee work teams, performed identical duties as other workers and shared the same supervisors. See any similarities in your existing relationships with your clients?

Some of the hallmarks of a legitimate client relationship: establishing and maintaining your distinct business identity (see Survival Tip #27); being compensated for your work on the entire job, not hour-by-hour; controlling your work schedule and how the work is done; and having multiple clients (see Survival Tip #98). You should refer to IRS Publication 937 (see Survival Tip #121) and govern your behavior accordingly.

Survival Tip #123: Family, friend or foe?

You're buried in work. Your relative, friend or neighbor needs a job. Should you marry the two opportunities together? It depends. Hiring family members and friends is a delicate situation. Some business owners have done it with no problem, but for others, the jury is still out. You can protect the relationship and your business from a hiring nightmare by considering what may go wrong and preparing for it.

Don't hire your relative or friend just because you feel sorry for him or her. If the person doesn't have the skills that you need, you may resent him or her later when the situation becomes shaky. Evaluate the person's abilities as you would an outside candidate's. Take into consideration the person's previous work experience. You may have firsthand insights into his or her working personality. For example, if your friend disliked her last supervisor who was "too bossy" or has said that she hates taking instructions from morons, consider how receptive she'll be to your management style.

Establish a professional tone for the working relationship. You should present to the person a job description or an outline of work duties along with your procedures manual. Even if your office has a relaxed or casual atmosphere, you need to head off possible misconceptions. For example, one bootstrapper hired her best friend to handle clerical tasks, and although the two women's children were playmates, the business owner explained that the kids were not allowed in the office under any circumstances. You should also set some boundaries about how you'll both behave during work; talking too much about personal issues can affect the relationship's professional tone.

Treat the person with respect at all times, clarifying up front how performance issues will be handled. You should also avoid asking him or her for a personal favor that you wouldn't dare ask another employee. If you behave as a professional, your relative or friend will be encouraged to do so, as well.

Survival Tip #124: Expand your recruitment venues.

Placing a newspaper ad is often the knee-jerk reaction of a business that needs to find job applicants. But this can be expensive and often produces a pile of unqualified or undesirable applicants. Consider some other sources for matching your business with skilled people. You can reach the qualified crowd nationwide through Internet databases (www.bestjobsusa.com) or through Jobtrack's online service (www.jobtrak.com; 800-999-8725). The type of work you're offering may be a hands-on experience that's fit for a college work-study or intern program. One bootstrapper has had great success in hiring college freshmen to work in the business up until graduation. If your opening is suitable for a college student, contact placement offices at local colleges and universities.

Consider community workplace programs—opportunities to help improve your community employment base while meeting the needs of your business. For example, the Metropolitan Transportation Authority in Los Angeles (213-922-5255) sponsors an employment and training educational program. The program places high school students in transportation industry companies for a 10-week internship. Another program called "Worklink" (800-253-7746) helps employers evaluate the workplace skills of local high school students. And the National School-to-Work Learning and Information Center (800-251-7236) helps facilitate opportunities for students to gain skills through local employers.

Use your professional affiliations as sources, too; they could point to some reliable contractors. For example, the HomeBased Business Association of Arizona (www.softrain.com/hbba) publishes the semi-annual *Independent Contractors' Outsource Network* directory, listing local self-employed professionals, and distributes it to sources most likely to need the services of these professionals. You can also expand your recruitment pool by offering your colleagues or suppliers incentives for new hire referrals.

Survival Tip #125: Train people to retain them.

Nothing will eat up your profits faster than employee turnover. Your role as an employer isn't limited to issuing directives and being able to meet payroll. Your job includes being a nurturer and mentor to your employees. It's an ongoing process and begins on the first day of employment. Set your workers up for success by providing them with ample equipment, materials and supplies to do the job. You should also give them a job description or checklist to eliminate any ambiguity about their responsibilities.

You should establish a timetable for acclimating the worker to aspects of the job. Avoid overwhelming a person with everything at once. You should set aside blocks of time to introduce and work through various tasks. You might include a sample packet that illustrates how forms or letters are to be completed or procedures for answering the phones. Encourage the worker to ask questions as you go along, and set aside separate times to talk about how things are going. When you're dealing with a performance issue, always tell the employee how to improve. For example, rather than saying, "You need to take better messages," explain that a complete message includes name, company, alternative phone numbers and times to reach the caller, along with a brief description of the call's purpose. This type of feedback provides the employee with a clear path toward improvement. Provide your workers with positive reinforcement. If your employees feel good about working for you, it'll come through in their customer service. (You can adopt a similar approach when you use the services of a temporary worker.)

Remember that hiring employees is an investment not only in your business but in other people. The only way to have productive and profitable relationships is by developing people's ability along with your business. Helpful resource: *Choosing the Right Training Program: A guidebook for small businesses* (see page 201 for ordering information).

Survival Tip #126: Make your business an attractive place to work.

You may not be able to compete with the benefits of a blue-chip employer. Frankly, you may not have to. Small businesses are in the enviable position of being able to offer their workers unique incentives that a big business might ignore in its quest for uniform policies and regulations. Here are a few examples of the advantages that you, as a small business employer, can offer your workers:

- Try to pay the most competitive rates to employees that you can afford because you'll save money overall. A printer who is concerned about waste taking place in production, for example, would probably see the waste factor reduced if he paid for quality staffers. Weigh your wage scales against going rates in your community. You can get compensation information from trade associations, the unemployment office or those in your networking circle.

- You can boost your pay offer with other incentives. For example, one bootstrapper offered a clerical staffer an additional per diem to her hourly wage for projects in which she handled advanced tasks. The business owner didn't have to commit to paying the extra money regularly, plus it gave the worker an incentive to improve her skills. You can also offer a delivery bonus for meeting a deadline on a big job. Or create a special discount program, such as offering regular discounts on your merchandise or services.

- Include your workers in special events that you're invited to.

- Consider time and convenience benefits. Workers are hungry for flexible work arrangements. If it jibes with the needs of your business, try offering flextime, personal emergency days or telecommuting arrangements.

- Just like you charm your customers with extras (see Survival Tip #89), do the same for your employees. If you have access to any deals that can be passed along to your employees, then pass them along.

YOU MAINTAIN FRIENDLY COOPERATION WHEN YOU...

Listen to those around you. Your secretary or anyone who works with you can be a source of inspiration. How attuned you are to other people's feedback is a self-esteem issue (see Survival Tip #11). When you close yourself off from others' perspectives, you may be missing out on opportunities with potential benefits. You may not use other people's exact ideas, but their thoughts may plant seeds for concepts of your own. So listen.

Avoid pigeonholing your providers. You want your customers to use more of your offering menu; your providers would appreciate the same from you. For example, many people use their accountant only at tax time. You can use his or her professional service to strategize and plan year-round everything from business financing to purchasing decisions to retirement planning. Don't overlook your printer's expertise; he or she could advise you on the best paper to buy for your office printer and tell you which paper houses have the best deals. Consider your providers part of the business family.

Respect others' professional abilities. Your time demands may require outsourcing work that you can very well do yourself. Since you're capable of doing the work, you may not place as much value on another person's abilities. Resist the urge to nitpick at the work, thinking you could have done a better job yourself. Review the work with an objective eye. It doesn't have to be done *your* way for it to be considered good. If it's done *well*, appreciate the effort.

Don't irk others the way customers irk you. Doesn't it annoy you when a client uses the "check is in the mail" line? Or when clients don't return your phone calls? Or when they try to pull a fast one on you? Your people network feels the same way when you behave this way toward them. So don't do it. And if you're tempted, remember: Do unto others as you would like them to do unto you.

Survival Tip #127: Create a championship circle.

Put the expertise and wisdom of others to work in your business by creating a board of directors. Your board can include a mix of professional peers, legal or financial advisors, or mentors. Some business owners opt to have a peer group of selected professionals. Since you'll be soliciting advice from the group, your members should include people that you respect and with whom you share similar philosophies and business practices. It helps when some of the members are more experienced or conversant than you in a particular area.

You can use the group to provide you with feedback on aspects of running your business or you can bounce growth and development strategies off of them. You should meet with them periodically in person. You can also send them an informal quarterly update about your business. A bootstrapping publisher uses her circle to discuss editorial issues related to her publication. Another bootstrapper meets bimonthly with a peer group of six others to discuss problems and brainstorm about new ideas. The advantage of such working relationships is that the members can point out blind spots in your thinking and give you objective feedback because they don't have the emotional attachment to issues of your business that you do.

Another option is to work with a business coach. A coach helps you set goals and grow your business through problem-solving sessions—duties similar to your board's functions, but for a fee. Your board, peer group or coach relationships are set up separately from your other networking groups. You should always host or pick up the tab for any gathering where people are advising you for free. Though it may take time to develop your board, it's a component of your people network that you can start building today.

Survival Tip #128: Get in on a trade secret exchange.

Trade secrets can be invaluable. No, I'm not talking about proprietary business information that is protected by intellectual property laws. I'm talking about secrets of your trade, the kind of knowledge that can be gleaned from other businesspeople who have front-line information that a newcomer, novice or outsider may not be privy to. It's another form of networking, but the more bonded you are with a person, the deeper the information you'll get. It's not about creating a gossip exchange. And it goes beyond asking people what type of software they use or what is the best association to join. It's about gaining an advantage in a situation because of the information you heard straight from the mouth of an insider.

For example, one bootstrapper received an offer to do some spokesperson work for a national corporation. She was inexperienced in these matters and didn't want to be overzealous in negotiating the offer's terms. Fortunately, she had a relationship with someone who had experience in this area. The person openly explained the fine art of such deals, including how much money and the type of perks to ask for. She was wide-eyed while listening to all this information but followed the instructions and landed a plum deal for herself. The trade secret clearly gave her an advantage in handling the situation.

People who trade secrets are great networkers. But it takes a great networker to know one. It's a dividend from relationships built over time. Secret-swapping will begin to happen as you earn people's confidence through actions that reveal your character. As people become comfortable with you, they'll open up and share valuable information that you'll be hard-pressed to find elsewhere. Confidence is important, since trading a secret often involves sharing intimate details about one's personal situation. It requires give-and-take, too. So, as you begin to give of yourself, you'll become the recipient of some trade secrets, too.

Bootstrapper's Follow-up File

101 Questions to Ask Your CPA, American Institute of Certified Public Accountants, Division for CPA Firms, 201 Plaza 3, Harbor Side Financial Center, Jersey City, NJ 07311-3881. A **free** guide offering tips and suggestions for using a CPA as an integral part of your business. Send SASE with request.

Choosing the Right Training Program: A guidebook for small businesses, Government Printing Office, Superintendent of Documents, P.O. Box 371954, Pittsburgh, PA 15250-7954; 202-512-1800. A 42-page training guidebook. $3.25.

Employer Information Hotline, U.S. Department of Justice, Office of Special Counsel, 800-255-8155. A 24-hour hotline providing employers with **free** tips and information packets on how to comply with the employment eligibility verification process, featuring prerecorded information, a faxback option and the opportunity to speak with a representative.

Equal Employment Opportunity Commission, Publications Information Center, 800-669-3362. Provides **free** resource booklets and fact sheets on hiring and employment practices.

Hiring resources: *ADA Enforcement Guidance: Preemployment Disability-Related Questions* and *Medical Examination and Job Advertising and Preemployment Inquiries Under the ADEA*, Equal Employment Opportunity Commission (EEOC), Office of Communications and Legislative Affairs, 1801 L St. NW, Washington, DC 20507. **Free** guides outlining permissible preemployment inquiries under the 1990 Americans with Disabilities Act and the Age Discrimination in Employment Act of 1967.

How to Hire Right the First Time and Avoid Costly Turnover Problems by Kimberly Stanséll, Research Done Write!, Suite B261-BSS, 8726 S. Sepulveda Blvd., Los Angeles, CA 90045. Special report presenting a five-step plan for hiring employees. Includes tips on interviewing, testing and training staffers and a list of additional employer resources. $5 ($5.41 for California residents).

National Association of Temporary and Staffing Services, 119 S. Saint Asaph St., Alexandria, VA 22314-3119; Web address: www.natss.com/staffing. Provides legal and legislative advocacy, public relations, education and industry-related information to its membership of staffing services companies. Offers referrals to local firms in your area. Send SASE for a **free** copy of *How to Buy Temporary Help Services.*

Occupational Safety and Health Administration, Publications Office, P.O. Box 37535, Washington, DC 20013; 202-219-4667; fax: 202-219-9266; Web address: www.osha.gov. Provides a bevy of **free** resource guides, such as *How to Prepare for Workplace Emergencies, Working Safely with Video Display Terminals, Consultation Services for the Employer* and *Employee Workplace Rights,* as well as a **free** complete listing of the agency's holdings titled *OSHA Publications and Audiovisual Programs.*

OPAC System Keyboarding Test, 800-999-0438; Web address: www.biddle.com. A software program containing three different timed typing tests. Promotional copy, available for $6 handling fee, can also be downloaded for **free** from Web site.

Paychex, 800-322-7292. Provides payroll services to small businesses.

Stay Out of Court: The Manager's Guide to Preventing Employee Lawsuits by Rita Risser (Prentice Hall, 1993); 800-922-0579. $18.95.

The Job Accommodation Network, 800-526-7234. Provides **free** advice to businesses on how to accommodate disabled workers.

The Manufacturers' Representatives Educational Research Foundation, P.O. Box 247, Geneva, IL 60134. Provides **free** listing of industry-specific rep associations and guidelines for interviewing and working with a prospective rep.

The Motivational Manager: Strategies to increase morale and productivity in the workplace, Ragan Communications, 800-878-5331; Web address: www.ragan.com. A monthly newsletter. **Free** sample copy available.

The President's Committee on Employment of People with Disabilities, 1331 F St. NW, #300, Washington, DC 20004; 202-376-6200; fax: 202-376-6219. Provides a **free**, comprehensive information package about ADA compliance, including material on tax and hiring incentives.

The Virtual Office Survival Handbook: What Telecommuters and Entrepreneurs Need to Succeed in Today's Nontraditional Workplace by Alice Bredin (Wiley, 1996); 800-225-5945. $16.95.

Chapter 9

Coping with Adversity

"Each of us has the right and the responsibility to assess the roads which lie ahead, and those over which we have traveled, and if the future road looms ominous or unpromising, and the roads back uninviting, then we need to gather our resolve and, carrying only the necessary baggage, step off that road into another direction. If the new choice is also unpalatable, without embarrassment, we must be ready to change that as well."

—Maya Angelou,
poet and author

Survival Tip #129: Prepare to pick yourself up when you stumble.

Everybody stumbles over bumps during their bootstrapping journey. Your survival will depend on how well you pick yourself up and move on. The bumps will include setbacks brought on by inexperience, lack of forethought or uncontrollable influences. Setbacks can be unsettling, rocking your confidence or threatening your professional and financial well-being. But the experience doesn't have to deter you from pursuing your dream. How well you rebound will depend on your attitude. You can train your mind to manage disruptive occurrences so that you don't succumb to paralysis. The process begins by adjusting your perspective on setbacks.

First, understand that setbacks aren't failures. Failing to persevere is a failure. You may be on the verge of turning the corner of success. If you retreat with discouragement, you'll miss out on what you've been working toward.

Second, setbacks provide you with an opportunity to learn about yourself. You may discover a character flaw, such as being inflexible or resistant to change, that is hindering your success.

Third, setbacks will reveal how committed you are to your vision. If you delve into the personal histories of successful bootstrappers, you find that many of them endured extraordinary challenges. However, their commitment to make the business successful was stronger than their desire to quit, thus sustaining them through the difficult spots.

There is no absolute formula for eliminating the inevitable highs and lows of running a business. Instead, there are strategies you can use to turn stumbling blocks into steppingstones to more success. During my bootstrapping tenure, I've stumbled into all sorts of predicaments. Nevertheless, I persevered. The following tactics (Survival Tips #130 through #140) have contributed to the development of my mental toughness. Each one has helped me get up, dust off, put one foot before the other and move forward. You, too, can use them to emerge stronger and become a better businessperson.

Survival Tip #130: Analyze your situation.

Curb any impulse to reach for a Band-Aid cure when faced with adversity. Instead, stop and begin to analyze your situation. Make some mental or written notes; this will help clarify your reality. Money experts always advise people to first list all debts to determine their financial position. The same approach will serve you well, too.

Ask yourself: *How deeply am I buried in this situation?* You need to know exactly where you stand.

Your notations should define your problem. List the events that have created the situation and the consequences you're experiencing, and express how it makes you feel. For example:

> **Problem:** I can't meet my overhead expenses.
>
> **Event:** I haven't had any billable work in 60 days.
>
> **Consequence:** My suppliers are threatening to discontinue services.
>
> **Feelings:** I'm snapping at everyone, and insomnia is my nighttime companion.

Now dig deeper by determining if you're faced with a short- or long-term problem. If you haven't had work for 60 days, why is that? Do you have something in the works that's being delayed? Let's say that you landed a new contract, but it was pushed back by the client. The projected delay time will determine its effects on your current situation. A 30-day postponement is short-term compared to a six-month one. Or is the 60-day dry spell the result of marketing negligence due to overdevotion to one project? In this instance, you're leaning toward a long-term situation—it's difficult to drum up work when you've ignored your marketing pipeline (see Survival Tips #74 and #98).

When faced with an adverse situation, it's easy to feel like you can't see the forest for the trees. An assessment of the situation helps you grasp the bigger picture, break it into manageable bites and begin to resolve it accordingly. You'll be free to untangle yourself from a situation and focus on realistic and appropriate solutions.

Survival Tip #131: Focus on solutions to rework a situation.

As a novice bootstrapper, I used to have one response to my setbacks: Quit! It always seemed that just as my business was gaining momentum, something would come along to disrupt its progress.

Every setback increased my internal pressure; I felt that everyone was watching and still wondering what possessed me to quit "that good job." I was no stranger to hard work, but I wasn't used to trying so hard to make something work. So quitting always seemed like the best solution. But I never did. I would walk away from the problem for a day or two, come back and take a stab at reworking my approach. After a few years, my automatic reaction to a problem was the thought: "Rework the situation." A shift in my mind-set had occurred; my natural inclination was to focus on solutions no matter what I faced.

Once you've clarified the long and short of your situation, ask yourself: "What do I need to get over this hump?" Don't get stuck staring at the problem—it won't change anything. Shift your energy toward resolving it. What steps can you take to bring it to an end? Jot down all possible solutions—even farfetched ones. If money is the issue, you need to focus on all the ways you can generate some. Let's say that slow-paying clients are wreaking havoc on your cash flow. Don't let their bad habit persist. Possible solutions: Request deposits or payments in installments, or charge a rebilling fee to discourage late payments. "Relief" solutions—intended to take out the sting of the problem in the immediate term—may require you to swallow your pride and be more flexible. For instance, you could resolve a 60-day dry spell by taking on less desirable work or offering to do overflow jobs for a competitor.

There is a solution to every problem you'll face in business. Some solutions will be obvious, whereas others may require creative footwork on your part. Your action-oriented mind-set will help you work through any feelings of discouragement. Inactivity only intensifies the consequences of your problem, and you'll begin to feel hopeless as things deteriorate. Putting solutions into action is the only way to build a bridge to the other side of a problematic situation.

Survival Tip #132: Distinguish between a money problem and a strategy problem.

Many setbacks you encounter will not be money-related, although they may appear to be on the surface. A timely cash infusion *can* give new life to a business on its last leg, but money itself will not rescue you from the results of following a bad idea that is eating up your funds.

Let's say that you've been testing a direct-response ad for three months. The results have been marginal. Your budget is running low, and you need to keep testing. The advertising outlet has offered you a special new promotion; however, the cost exceeds what you have available. You begin to brainstorm for ways to get more money to throw into this strategy. Stop. Are you about to pursue a dead end? Your results have been marginal, and all the outlet is offering you is another opportunity to drag the process out for a reduced rate. Before you make an additional commitment, examine your approach. You may discover that you've been advertising on low-response days (such as Wednesdays and Saturdays instead of Sundays or Tuesdays, which are high-yield days). Perhaps you overlooked a detail such as this in your planning. Throwing more money into advertising on more "off" days would not solve your problem; tweaking your strategy will.

When you automatically think money is the solution, you'll be prone to throw good money after bad. When evaluating a setback as it relates to your financial base, first examine what you're doing. Do you understand the direction or strategies that you're using? Are you making decisions with outdated information? Do you need more information, training or knowledge? Approaching your problems this way will help build discipline.

Before you go looking under your mattress for your stash, ask yourself, "Is money really my problem?"

Survival Tip #133: Call on the counsel of a select few.

When you're going through a difficult time, you need a safe place to vent your thoughts and feelings. You can build a "safe house" with "pillars" such as your family members, friends, colleagues or championship circle (see Survival Tip #127). You won't call on them to solve your problems but to serve as a sounding bound, to help you gain perspective and to make you feel less isolated. Talking through your problems can unclog your thinking and clear the path to solutions.

Your intimate circle should include people who are familiar with your background, who understand you and what you're doing and who are great listeners.

For example, one pillar in my safe house is my best friend, Jamis. She's my childhood friend and a fellow entrepreneur. Venting with someone who has known me for so long has contributed to my success journey; she reminds me of my attributes that I tend to forget. You'll get the best feedback and support when you have honest and secure people rallying around you. They have insights into your character and an unfailing way of helping you see overlooked solutions.

Don't discount the value of being active in an online newsgroup or other forum, either. Although the communication is faceless, people use message boards and forums to forge professional bonds. When you actively participate in an online forum, you're building up a form of loyalty and support. I've witnessed a countless number of occasions in which an active member has posted a problem he or she is having, and regular troopers have responded, providing valuable feedback and insights based on similar experiences. The dialogue is candid and open.

If you don't have someone to talk to, all is not lost. My favorite line in the movie *Shadowlands* is: "...people read to know they're not alone." Reading books by and about accomplished businesspeople can help clarify your thinking in a situation. Articles in entrepreneurial periodicals that share others' survival strategies and struggles can be helpful and inspirational. Read, clip, file and refer to these pieces. They may be your life jacket when you're drowning.

Survival Tip #134: Don't be afraid to change directions.

Setbacks are often red flags, flashing signals that you're traveling in the wrong direction. It's tempting to ignore the signs if you have a predetermined picture of what your business should look like. Rather than considering a directional change, you will probably want to clamp down and persist in handling the setbacks the way you always have. But a business that never seems to sustain its momentum is a candidate for directional scrutiny. The problem may be that you're trying to gain entry into the wrong market, courting the wrong customer or marketing the wrong message (reread Chapters 5 and 6).

Setbacks may also be signaling you to go back to the direction that gave you your first success. A graphics supply firm, for example, enjoyed early success selling high-quality graphics supplies to advertising agencies and artists. As the operation grew, its owner began to dabble in other areas of the industry. The company began to experience a series of financial setbacks because the owner, who was a salesperson by nature, took over financial and administrative tasks and strayed from the strength that built the company—his contact with the customers. The business got back on track by aligning everybody in the company with duties that matched their talents.

Give yourself permission to change your direction. You may feel that you'll appear foolish to others, be ridiculed or have to hear, "I told you so." But it's your business and you're in control. You'll find it easier to reroute your direction when you're not in heavy financial debt (see Survival Tip #44). But don't let your worries influence your decision to make a change; you'll have more difficulty dealing with the internal voice that you've ignored. Misplaced determination or pride won't pay your bills or move you any closer to building a better business, so feel free to modify your business accordingly.

Survival Tip #135: Consider downsizing solutions.

Stumbling blocks may be the result of using too many cylinders to build your business's engine. Big chain retailers, for instance, accelerate their growth through a blowout strategy, opening multiple locations as fast as possible before they're copied by competitors. Your business may have adopted a similar strategy to create marketplace dominance or boost profitability. Your success, however, will depend on the management resources you have in place to support the demands of this approach. Otherwise, you're bound to experience problems because of your inability to juggle all the responsibilities.

Consider the concept of downsizing to reduce what you're doing to a more manageable size. Are you losing money? A downsized business that is well-managed will make more money. Are you trying to manage too many profit centers? For example, if your consulting business has speaking and publishing components, the demands of your two secondary components may be pulling you away from consistent follow-through on your customer contacts and leads to the point that your primary practice—consulting—isn't really growing. Begin to dissect the areas responsible for the breakdown. For example, your speaking component is a combination of paid and in-kind speaking engagements. You could downsize by limiting your *pro bono* engagements from 12 per year down to, say, six. If your publishing component includes a promotional newsletter, reduce its size, rather than decreasing its frequency. If you offer free consultations, designate a certain day to conduct them, rather than doing them upon request.

The downsizing concept can be applied to your overall business or to specific areas. This concept allows you to leverage yourself and eliminate some of the problems you're experiencing. Be careful not to shrink your business to the point that it becomes anorexic. Your goal is to be able to manage and grow the business at a sustainable level that allows you to minimize the adverse effects associated with trying to do too much.

Survival Tip #136: Try suspending your operation before you walk away.

When the oil industry went bust in Texas, so did Jan Triplett and Dan Diener's Austin-based business. The partnership duo produced customized slide-tapes for oil companies' in-house training programs. The once-lucrative business struggled along through year's end until the demand for its services evaporated; its primary customer market stopped hiring and training. What's more, other local industries slowed down as they held their breaths waiting for the ripple effects of the bust to hit them—so Triplett and Diener could not turn to *them* for business. Down to their last $36, Triplett and Diener started to think that closing the business was their best bet. But it wasn't—their services could be offered to another market, not just oil companies. They decided to suspend their full-time operation for a few months and use the time to restrategize.

Your circumstances may be overwhelming, and you may want out. You may just need some time away from the situation, or you may be facing personal issues that require a release from your responsibilities. Rather than close your doors entirely, give yourself some breathing room and temporarily suspend the operation. You can use the suspension period to reevaluate your situation and create a comeback plan. You may not need to suspend the business completely but reduce your activities to a minimal level. Diener and Triplett, for instance, took workplace jobs, did odd projects and still networked to form other alliances, which led to new contracts.

When deciding whether to suspend or to terminate your business, ask yourself:

- *Is there still a market for my offering?* You may need to change directions or reinvent your presentation to the market (see Survival Tip #134). These modifications may still be able to work under the guise of your current business.

- *Do I still enjoy the work and the business?* If not, then closing it to pursue another avenue may be the best solution for you.

- *What is the core issue I am facing and how can it be resolved?* Triplett and Diener faced the problem of losing the target market for their services. They could resolve their problem by finding a new target market and taking some time out to accomplish this since the overall economic climate of the city had declined.

A suspension puts your business in a state of readiness to be revived. If you don't leave your customers hanging, you'll lessen the fallout from your decision. Explain to them what you're doing, why and for how long. Give them as much notice as possible with some alternative suggestions, perhaps making some arrangements for another professional to serve them. If you still have passion for being your own boss, quitting isn't the solution. Taking time to reforge is.

5 THINGS TO DO WHEN BUSINESS IS DOWN

1. Keep your marketing engine running. Don't abandon your marketing plan. Many businesses cut back on marketing during hard times. It's wiser to slash another fixed cost. Studies have shown that businesses who maintain or increase their marketing outlay during slow periods wind up outselling competitors who cut back. Consider adding some short-term marketing tactics, such as sales or price promotions, to ride out a slump. Whatever you do, don't turn off your marketing engine.

2. Donate a few hours of your services as a door prize. Louise Kursmark has donated her desktop publishing services as a prize for golf tournaments sponsored by her business association. The winner gets a certificate good for specific services such as layout or design, which Kursmark advertises as a $100 value. This gets the winner into Kursmark's office and stirs his or her imagination, usually generating a project for more than the certificate value. A giveaway can be a business stimulator for a startup as well as an ongoing tactic to expand a business's customer base. You can also tailor this strategy to products you may sell; it can be a great way to increase a storefront's foot traffic.

3. Get a temporary gig. Don't be ashamed to work in someone else's business as a temporary worker. If you need the money, this can be a quick way to generate some cash. You'll find that the temporary work force is full of other self-employed people. You can sign up with a temporary employment service, preferably one that serves your local community so that commuting costs don't eat up the money you earn. You can also offer to do overflow work for a competitor when you're slow. It'll keep you involved with work you enjoy while funneling some cash into your business.

4. Comb the classifieds. Perusing the classifieds can help you in two ways: You may find an independent contractor opportunity or you may be able to create an opportunity for yourself to fill a need. Go through the classifieds and mark the ads that interest you. Contact the company and offer your business as the solution to their temporary problem. Be sure to emphasize how your special skills and talents can save the company money in the interim; they're getting an experienced person who they don't have to train. Some companies think they need to hire a regular worker, when in reality they really need a qualified contractor—which could be you!

5. Offer incentives for paying in advance. Try offering discount incentives to customers who prepay for long-term commitments. For example, some online service providers provide you with savings when you prepay your service for a year. You can apply this concept to your business, as well. A financial advisor, for instance, could offer clients six one-hour planning sessions at $100 an hour to be used over a given year. Preselling this way can generate cash quickly. Limit your preselling program to a period of one year, leaving yourself room to introduce any rate increases. A word of caution: Be sure that when business picks up again, you're still able to manage all the prepaid accounts (see Survival Tip #149).

Survival Tip #137: Don't allow stress to overwhelm you.

There will be times when your stress system is tested. If you're not careful, your mind and body will short-circuit. When you're working through a difficult situation, particularly a prolonged one, don't ignore physical systems, such as headaches, body aches and pains, chronic fatigue or inertia. This is your body talking, alerting you that it's possibly about to conk out before you resolve your current problem. You may be tempted to keep hammering away at the problem, thinking you're close to finding a resolution. Don't do that to yourself; you may not make it.

In a survey I conducted, bootstrappers said that their number-one strategy for surviving a tough time was *taking a break*. Not going on vacation, but taking a moment to step away from the problem. Setting the problem aside for a brief moment frees your mind to concoct possible solutions. A put-it-on-the-shelf mentality can help you better manage stress. For example, one home-office bootstrapper takes time out to garden for a while and comes back refreshed to tackle the issue at hand. Another bootstrapper takes on one-day temporary assignments through a service to get away from the office. You can renew your spirit through inspirational or devotional reading. You know what your body and mind respond favorably to, so gravitate towards that which will rejuvenate you.

Psychologist Maynard Brusman has a tip for managing high-stress periods. At the end of the day, do a quick review in your mind of what you've done. Rest in the fact that you've done everything possible for one day. Appreciate your efforts. Appreciate the day. Relax your mind and go to sleep because tomorrow is another day. You'll have another chance to work on the problem.

Survival Tip #138: Don't ignore your financial obligations.

A bootstrapper's absolute survival skill: proficiency in juggling expenses. If you become entrenched in a cash crunch, you need to know how to manage your financial responsibilities without ruining your credit and vendor relationships. Prioritize your bills based on your legal and credit obligations. If you employ others, you should always meet payroll. Credit cards, bank equity lines, insurance premiums, utility bills, and auto, equipment or office space leases merit top attention because delinquencies are reported on your credit report and you can lose service or possession of your assets. You should always pay at least the minimum to these creditors.

You should also avoid missing your IRS payment obligations, such as payroll deposits or your quarterly estimated taxes. You'll be penalized, and trying to catch up on payments can be difficult. You may find more leeway with your smaller vendors, such as a printer, bookkeeper or other professional service provider. Don't be afraid to communicate. You may feel embarrassed that you're in this position, but failing to notify your debtors can result in needless heartache. If you're in a prolonged cash crunch—say, for 60 to 90 days—get on the phone and start negotiating. Explain to your debtors the situation, your absolute willingness to pay and your need for some special arrangements. You may be in for a pleasant surprise. A bootstrapper was in a 90-day cash crunch and unable to make her car payment. She called the creditor and explained how she had miscalculated her cash return on the opening of a new facility. The creditor suspended her payments for three months without repossessing the business van. Her solid payment history with the company prompted this cooperative arrangement.

Drastic times may require that you let go of those "nice to have" things and keep the bare necessities. You can reduce your expenses by scaling back on services—for example, unlimited usage of your online service, which generally costs more, or work you have outsourced, such as your office-cleaning. You may be able to entirely eliminate some of these services. You should also make a list of quick cash alternatives, noting all the sources you pull money from in an emergency. You'll have a ready supply of solutions when your capital is thin. (You can learn more about juggling your expenses from my special report *How to Pay Your Bills When You Don't Have Any Money*. See page 218 for ordering information.)

Survival Tip #139: Make mental notes all through the trial.

Adversity can guide you into a better understanding of yourself. But if you're not paying attention, you'll miss it. Dr. Martin Luther King, Jr., said that the best time to judge a person's character is in a time of adversity. It can be an opportune time for you to judge your-self and use those observations to become a savvier businessperson. You can develop this self-awareness by making a concerted effort to note your reactions as you're going through a trying situation. One bootstrapper asked her employees to evaluate her performance and discovered that she didn't communicate or give directions well when she was particularly busy with clients, which made it difficult for her staff to work independently.

When asked what the self-employment journey has taught them about themselves that they didn't realize before, many of my survey participants cited *inflexibility*. This quality often surfaced in the midst of adversity. Many respondents said that had they been more flexible in their attitude, a problem could have been resolved sooner. Many of them were guilty of having an "it's my way or no way" attitude.

Ask yourself: "Why am I in this situation?" or "What is the lesson of this experience?" It may be the result of a personal weakness. If you ignore it, you'll find yourself in the situation again or in an even more intensified one. Be open with yourself, exploring your flaws and your motives. Are you judging people too quickly? Then you need to be more open to others' suggestions. Are you reacting this way because of a lack of confidence in yourself? Then you should try to remedy this area through self-development (see Survival Tip #147). You should note everything that went right and things that went wrong during a difficult period. Note your positive attributes and examine ways to apply them to the counterproductive parts of your character.

Survival Tip #140: Use the experience to put safeguards in effect.

You can neutralize some of the lows of running a business by us-ing what you learned from previous slumps and working to sidestep them in the future. First, acknowledge any mistakes you made that brought hardship into your business. You'll continue to stumble over your ego if you can't admit you made a mistake. Admitting your mis-take opens you up to learning from the experience. Sort through the mistake or setback and examine the facts, looking for areas where you can apply some preventative measures.

Let's say that a dissatisfied customer demanded that you refund a portion of your consulting fee...but you've already spent it. Depending upon the financial state of your business, you may be facing a precarious situation. Now is the time to figure out how to prevent such a quandary from happening again. Retrace how the project was secured and examine the source of the customer's discontent. Were you clear on the specifications of the job? Did you stay close during the servicing process, checking in when you met certain benchmarks (see Survival Tip #93)? Next, examine ways you could have prevented the situation. Preventative measures could include using a project intake form (see Survival Tips #82 and #94). In the past, I've used a project strategy form, which includes all of the specifications of the work I'm doing for a client. In this instance, the use of one could have been a lifesaver. Another safeguard would be to make it standard procedure to check in with clients while you're working on a job, particularly on long-term projects. As for the issue of not being able to refund the money—you have bills to pay, I understand. But it's critical to have something to fall back on, such as a line of credit you can use in an emergency.

With each adverse experience, you'll develop into a seasoned self-employed professional. It'll become natural for you to look for remedies to your problems and develop your business so that the lows don't always push you back to square one. You may not exactly *delight* in your struggles, but you'll have a more positive outlook. You'll be looking for ways to use the experience to pave your way to future success.

Bootstrapper's Follow-up File

100 Ways to Motivate Yourself: Change Your Life Forever by Steve Chandler (Career Press, 1996); 800-CAREER-1 (201-848-0310 in N.J. and outside U.S.). $13.99.

How to Pay Your Bills When You Don't Have Any Money by Kimberly Stanséll, Research Done Write!, Suite B261-BSS, 8726 S. Sepulveda Blvd., Los Angeles, CA 90045. Special report presenting a five-step plan for handling your financial obligations when you're in a cash crunch. Includes tips and strategies for developing a cash cushion and negotiating your debt without ruining your credit. $5 ($5.41 for California residents).

Insights and Inspiration: How Businesses Succeed, Blue Chip Enterprise Initiative, 800-367-2234. A collection of case studies on businesses that have overcome extraordinary challenges and emerged stronger. Profiles hundreds of businesses from a variety of industries. Book: $8.95; three-volume video: $50.

Making it on Your Own: Surviving and Thriving on the Ups and Downs of Being Your Own Boss by Paul and Sarah Edwards (Jeremy P. Tarcher/Perigee, 1991); 800-788-6262. $10.95.

Succeeding in Small Business: The 101 Toughest Problems and How to Solve Them by Jane Applegate (Plume/Penguin USA, 1992); 800-331-4624. $12.

The Accidental Entrepreneur: for Self-Employed Corporate Refugees, 3421 Alcott St., Denver, CO 80211. A bimonthly newsletter. Send SASE for **free** sample. $24/year.

The Power of Positive Thinking, The Peale Center, 800-274-5097. A **free**, 50-page, condensed version of the best-selling book by Norman Vincent Peale.

Winning Ways: The newsletter for people living and working with passion, P.O. Box 39412, Minneapolis, MN 55439. A bimonthly self-employment newsletter. Sample copy: $4; one-year subscription: $31.

Working Solo: Reaching Independent Entrepreneurs, 800-822-SOLO; Web address: www.workingsolo.com. Quarterly newsletter. $24/year.

Chapter 10

Managing Your Growth and Development

"If one advances confidently in the direction of his dreams, and endeavors to live the life which he has imagined, he will meet with a success unexpected in common hours."

—Henry David Thoreau, American
writer, philosopher and naturalist

Survival Tip #141: Take pride in the legacy you leave behind.

How do you want to be remembered in your lifetime? What is the mark you'd like to leave on society? Journalists often ask presidents how they'd like to be recorded in the history books. It's an area of concern; no president would relish the thought of his term being dubbed a lame-duck tenure.

You can shape your legacy through a mission statement that defines the aims, goals and purpose of your business. You can combine it with a personal mission statement that speaks to your life's direction, values and beliefs. The dynamics of these statements can contribute greatly to your business's success.

A company mission statement will keep your business focused. It will work as the guiding principle for growing and developing your business. The statement will remind everyone working in your business what your business stands for. Here's an example of a media producer's mission statement: "...produce quality educational materials, dealing with health and social issues, to serve students and teachers..." A publisher's statement: "...provide affordable and practical financial information to help women become financially independent..." These statements are clear, direct and easy to follow.

You can also use your *personal* mission statement to guide your business practices. Combining the two kinds of statements will help you behave in ways that reflect your values. It will prick your conscience, helping you avoid becoming concerned only with *your* bottom line and ignoring the effects your decisions may have on people to whom you're committed. When a factory owner's facility burned down, he continued to pay his workers. He chose not to be remembered as the factory owner who made money off all the locals and left town. The public applauded his behavior but viewed it as unusual because we live in times when companies choose profits over people.

Ask yourself, "What do I want to be remembered for?" Use and grow your business in a way that promotes the legacy you want to leave behind.

Survival Tip #142: Etch out a growth plan.

A fledgling business becomes a thriving one through the deliberate planning of its owner. Your business may have unlimited potential, but you'll never realize it without a plan for unleashing what's there.

First, examine what you want for yourself. Someone once urged me to grow my business so large that it would become a problem. An interesting thought, but not for me. I've envisioned another working lifestyle, so I quickly tossed the advice. You're building a business around your dreams and desires, not someone else's. Clarify your position immediately, because it will influence the growth choices you make.

Look at your business from many different angles. Does it lend itself to going national or global? Even the smallest local shop may have hidden broader geographical appeal. Consider other audiences who could use your offering. There may be room for you in other markets. Can you redress your offering? For example, high-end fashion designers can create a lower-end line under a subsidiary label to capture the dollars of another audience. Are there other distribution channels for you to use? A local television program repackaged its format into a radio show. A product manufacturer marketed its wares through a catalog. Think of your business as a prism in your hands. When you look at it from various angles, you'll see other ways to expand what you're doing.

Next, identify the resources you'll need to move into growth areas. For example, if exporting interests you, then begin educating yourself through the National Export Center (800-872-8723). If you're planning to increase your distribution channels, you'll need to identify qualified outlets. If you plan to launch a Web site, you'll contact technology developers. You etch out your plan by addressing the *who*, *what*, *when* and *how*. Your plan should include implementation timetables, perhaps introducing each phase in annual or biannual time frames. Leave yourself room to make changes. You may begin exploring an area and discover that it's not for you. Your plan will become a reality through a goal-setting program (see Survival Tip #143).

Survival Tip #143: Use goals to bring your vision to life.

Bill Griffeth, the former of host CNBC's *Money Club*, gave viewers a prescription for feeling uneasy about their lives when they reach certain milestones: setting goals. If you never set goals or fail to follow through on your desired achievements, you begin to dread turning points, such as birthdays or a new year. It's difficult to assess your life or appreciate your travels because you don't have a solid reference point. Goals give you something to measure your life against. Studies show that only 2 percent of the population has written goals; interestingly, those people are the ones who achieve success.

Goals are an amazingly powerful tool. They turn your thoughts of "what might be" into "what will be." If you want to have a purposeful direction, to realize your business's potential or to develop into a business champion, you need to set goals. You can bring the vision for your business into fruition through goal-setting. A business without goals may progress aimlessly and end up in detour directions. You can use goals as a road map, defining paths with specific plans and ideas. This is the best way to capture the future you've dreamed for yourself.

Goal-setting need not be complicated. Begin by writing your goals down. Your goals should be specific and measurable, have a timetable and be divided into manageable pieces. For example, saying you want to increase revenues is too general, but saying you want to increase sales by $75,000 within the next 12 months is targeted. You would break this into achievable parts. I assign quarterly steps that must be accomplished in order to achieve my overall goal. My quarterly accomplishments help create momentum into the next quarter. This approach sometimes results in me reaching the goal earlier than I had planned. Motivation experts encourage you to write down the personal benefit or reward associated with your goals. This works as your reminder of what's important. The $75,000 increase, for instance, may translate into a one-month vacation. Regularly review your goals to ensure you're on track, possibly posting them prominently in your office.

You must commit to working at your goals. Otherwise, the exercise is futile. Don't overwhelm yourself; start with a few small goals. However, once you realize each one, savor the feeling of having drawn success from inside yourself and having persevered. Use the achievement as a reminder of what you can do, and move on to set more goals for yourself and your business. A helpful **freebie**: *Personal Goal Planner: Your Monthly Companion*, available by calling 800-731-GOAL. This a special offer to readers of *Bootstrapper's Success Secrets*, so be sure to mention this book!

Survival Tip #144: Generate some energy through diversification.

Here's a bootstrapping adage: "It's easier to make $1,000 per month from 10 businesses than it is to make $10,000 from one."

Although reaching your financial goals may not require a conglomerate of 10, diversification can be an excellent way to grow your business. You can increase your product or service line with one or more closely-related activities. Your profits can increase dramatically while overhead costs stay virtually the same. Diversification works as an income stabilizer. If one aspect of your business slows down, you have other sources to pull from.

There are many ways to diversify a business. A service firm can diversify by adding a retail product. A product line can be diversified with new applications. For example, a manufacturer of quick-fitting pipe couplings for oil fields sells one for construction and public work applications. But diversification doesn't stop here. It can include changing your marketing methods, moving from direct selling to consumers to wholesaling to shops or taking your person-to-person services and offering them to the business-to-business market. Diversification can also work as an antidote to business boredom. One business owner always loved to write. She was able to diversify her business by penning articles in her field of expertise.

Granted, some businesses are easier to diversify than others. Give your business a chance. Start by identifying other markets where you fit in, asking: *Who needs what? How can I modify my existing product or service to make it appealing to another target audience? What else might I offer that would help or benefit my clients or customers?* Some businesses have grown nicely on a one-stop shopping concept, providing their clientele with a primary offering supported by related ancillary ones. A business that relies on one widget for one purpose may die. Think about ways you can use diversification to keep life in your business.

Survival Tip #145: Create passive income opportunities.

Nancy Michaels of Impression Impact in Concord, Massachusetts, was able to double her income while limiting the scope of her services. How? By repackaging herself into a product. Her firm provided full-service marketing services, which included designing and implementing plans for small businesses in the New England region. Good pay, but the implementation was grueling. Michaels decided to cut back and offer plan design only, but she needed to do something to make up for the lost income. She was already using public speaking to promote her practice, so she took the meat from her presentations and packaged it into a marketing cassette series, *How to Be a Big Fish in Any Pond* (800-BIG-FISH). The product served two purposes: Michaels is able to make money without being present, and it's an effective marketing tool.

You, too, can make money in your absence through passive income opportunities. You can "clone" yourself and work and earn money when you're not around by taking what you know people are willing to pay for and packaging it into another format. It's considered a passive income opportunity because you invest in the initial production and let it start working for you. It's a low-maintenance form of diversification. A newsletter, for example, is high-maintenance—you have to produce it in regular intervals. But a cassette series, such as the one Michaels created, is low-maintenance. She made the initial investment, and she doesn't have to make any revisions to it for years if she chooses.

A passive income opportunity also gives others who otherwise can't afford your offering, or who are out of your market's physical location, access to you. The income is often generated by products such as books, audiocassettes, videos and software. You can also use fax-back services, allowing users to tap your information base from a menu of reports or fact sheets. A 900 number is another device. A lawyer, for instance, can dispense legal tips on a 900 line.

Your passive income item or service is promoted along with your core business. The difference: It works for you while you're working for your clientele.

Survival Tip #146: Continually invest in your business.

According to a national survey I conducted, the number-one investment bootstrappers make to grow their business is an investment in technology—technology in the form of better equipment and advanced features. Survey respondents invested in resources that helped them provide better service, do more work in less time and branch off into different areas. These resources can include everything from bookkeeping software to voice mail to color printers to designing a Web page. You, too, should continually look for ways to build a better business through equipment investments.

Resist the "If it ain't broke, don't fix it" mentality. You may be selling your operation short. Face it: The office you started off with shouldn't look the same five, 10 or 15 years down the line. There should be some semblance of growth. That begins with investing in better tools.

Your investment strategy should complement your business's growth and goal plan (see Survival Tips #142 and #143). For example, once her business turned the corner, one bootstrapper decided that her policy was to buy a new computer system every two years. This investment has helped her enjoy 25- to 30- percent growth each year. Your investments may include a deluxe printer or copier. Investments such as these allow you do more work in-house, thus increasing your profits and eliminating trips to the corner store. As you expand with regular employees, a networking communications system may be necessary. Another investment may be refurbishing your office, creating a workplace setup that better complements the way you work. For instance, you may decide to ditch a makeshift desk and replace it with an ergonomically friendly, roomier workstation that acts as a central location for all your work *and* your tools (computer, printer, etc.).

The next top investment bootstrappers make to grow their businesses is an investment in people. Your people investment will pay off most when you help employees grow with your business (see Survival Tip #125). Recent studies have shown that one of the top reasons employees quit their jobs is that there is no opportunity for advancement or personal development. You'll get more from your people investment when you give workers flexibility in their work, a say-so in how they work and closer contact with you and your customers, according to recent studies.

The third best bootstrapper investment is in personal growth and development (see Survival Tip #147).

Survival Tip #147: Continually invest in yourself.

Avoid getting too comfortable with success by neglecting your own personal growth and development. It's a fatal mistake, making you vulnerable to changes in the world around you. Create and commit to your own lifetime learning program. You'll keep your skills sharp, stay current, maintain your prosperity and be in step with our ever-changing society. You should earmark funds from your business to invest in various self-development vehicles and tools.

Make reading a priority. There's a lot of good information on the market, and you should regularly be feeding your mind with some of it. Rely on a combination of resources that are tailor-made for your information needs. For example, you could subscribe to an entrepreneurial magazine, newsletter and newspaper, creating a mixed balance of general management or industry-specific resources. My startup strategy included checking out from the library all the back issues of various publications to determine which ones were best for me. You can also stay current by scheduling library reading days. Save yourself some money by taking advantage of publication trial offers or ordering subscriptions for up to 90 percent off the cover price through a wholesaler such as Below Wholesale Magazines (800-800-0062). I've put together the *Bootstrappin' Entrepreneur Newsletter Bundler Package* to help jump start your reading program (see page 233 for ordering information).

Also, *associate* with your associates! Hands-down, bootstrappers will tell you that their best sources of information and learning have been other people. You can connect with fellow bootstrappers through local and national associations. Gale Research's *Encyclopedia of Associations*, which can be found in most libraries, lists more than 20,000 groups nationwide. You can find other networks by scouting them out online or asking your local SBA office or Small Business Development Center. You'll benefit most from an association membership when you actively participate and work with its members.

Regularly attend seminars, conferences or workshops. You can learn a lot at functions sponsored by associations or educational management companies. Commit to attending at least one major annual conference or trade show. Or attend at least two mini-workshops or seminars annually. You don't have to leave your office to learn. Online courses are growing in popularity, allowing you to participate from the comfort of your computer desk chair. Also, consider programs through local universities or colleges, such as the University of Southern California's Business Expansion Network (213-743-1726). You'll find other educational programs and events in the various trade publications you read.

Survival Tip #148: Put some money to work for your future.

Many business owners wait for their business earnings to soar before they begin stashing away some retirement cash. They hope that future profits will make up the difference for what they're not saving. Avoid delaying the investment process. Besides robbing yourself of valuable tax deductions, you're reducing your greatest investment ally: time. Financial experts and advisors repeatedly encourage people to put their money to work as soon as possible so they can benefit from the effects of compound interest.

A few retirement savings options are available to you as a self-employed person. Vehicles you can use to plan for your future:

- Individual Retirement Account (IRA).
- Simplified Employee Pension Plan (SEP or SEP-IRA).
- Keogh (self-employed retirement plan).
- Savings Incentive Match Plan for Employees of Small Employers (SIMPLE Plan).

Each plan has its own nuances. Depending on your selection, you can tax-defer anything from $2,000 to $30,000 and can include your employees. Helpful primer information includes the following IRS booklets (call 800-TAX-FORM): *Individual Retirement Account* (Publication 590); *Self Employed Retirement Plans* (Publication 560); and Form 5305-SIMPLE. Retirement planning kits for the self-employed are available from T. Rowe Price (800-638-5660) and Fidelity Investments (800-544-4774). You can also speak with a financial professional to aid you in your decision.

Look for other ways to make your working capital grow. For example, the United Services Government Securities Savings Fund (800-873-8637) has a couple of account options that come with unlimited checkwriting and pay daily competitive interest on every penny of your balance. Another helpful resource: *Money Smart Secrets of the Self-Employed* by Linda Stern (see page 234 for ordering information).

Survival Tip #149: Monitor your commitment level.

There's a fine line between expanding your business activities and spreading yourself too thin. You need to leverage the business to avoid becoming overextended with commitments you're unable to fulfill. You should constantly monitor what you're doing, how you're doing it and the effects it has on your operation. You're entering the over-commitment zone when the quality of work is compromised. Think of your work as a self-portrait. If commitment levels begin to paint a satisfactory picture versus excellent one, you need to reconsider what you're doing.

You can keep pace with your commitments when you have a reliable support system. Carefully monitor your support channels (see Survival Tip #119 for examples of a support network). Should there be a breakdown in your system, you're headed for trouble. For example, if you're experiencing persistent employee turnover, take time out to address what's going on in your business. The same attention should be given to any outsourced portions of your business. Your priority should be stabilizing problem areas first. It's foolish to bypass them. Your business will not grow unless it's adequately supported.

I was once contracted to do some consulting work with a software developer—a well-financed, two-man partnership that had received a couple of product development projects. The partners jumped at these opportunities—this was what they'd been working toward. They had hired several contractors to work on various aspects of each project, in addition to investing in new equipment to streamline work done in-house. In the beginning, every project progressed nicely. Then each project began to take on a life of its own, each having a different set of problems. The demands of each project began to overwhelm the hands-on owners, making it difficult for them to work cohesively with all the teams. Eventually the poor planning and lack of infrastructure halted one of the projects; the owners were unable to deliver on their commitment. They tried to do too much too fast, without the proper support.

It's good to test the boundaries of your business. That's what growth is all about. However, sustained growth is the result of delivering quality work consistently. You can only do that when your business is running on all cylinders.

Survival Tip #150: Relocate with the "portable" parts of your business.

Your entrepreneurial journey may transplant you into another community. We're a mobile society. Census Bureau statistics show that since 1975 nearly three-fourths of all households had changed residences. Economic conditions or changes within your family circumstances may dictate a change in your location.

Leaving your local community doesn't mean you have to abandon or disband your business. If your business is driven by a local clientele, think about parts of it that you can take with you. If you've been diversifying or expanding your distribution channels (see Survival Tip #144 and #145), you may be able to run some of those activities from your new location. A travel agency, for example, began with a local customer base. Through years of advertising in national travel magazines, its clientele was broadened, so when the owners decided to relocate from California to Oregon, they were able to take the business with them. Your growth strategy (see Survival Tip #142) could include adding a "portable" profit center to allow you some flexibility in the event of a move.

As a growth-minded entrepreneur, you may be tempted to run to where business prospects and the quality of life are better. You can make lifestyle changes more easily when your *entire business* is portable— able to be operated regardless of its location. For example, my business, Research Done Write!, can be operated from any place that has an adequate number of phone lines and good phone service.

Relocation may also be an opportunity to reimplement an idea that floundered in your old neighborhood. A home-based digital computer imaging firm struggled for three years in Montana, where the demand for high-tech graphic design was low. The owner moved to Phoenix, known for its thriving home-based business community, and set up shop. The business flourished locally, eventually building up a local *and* global clientele, including London, Brazil and China.

Louise Kursmark, a certified professional resume writer and desktop publishing professional, was relocated by her husband's job. She quickly introduced her business to the new community. Her savvy move: volunteering her services to a group that would connect her to her target audience. She hooked up with the Job Search Focus Group in Cincinnati and offered to teach resume-writing workshops, thus getting a chance to help others while helping herself.

It's important to let your new community know you're there. You can accelerate the process by sending out press releases (see Survival Tip #62) and joining associations. Some communities even profile their new small business residents in the local paper. (You can learn more about relocating your business from my booklet, *The Entrepreneur's Relocation Guide*. See page 235 for more information.)

Survival Tip #151: Develop success qualities.

The past four years of writing, consulting and developing projects aimed at small business owners have given me an opportunity to meet some of the most intriguing and fascinating people. They haven't graced the pages of *People* magazine, but they have definitely shaped the content of this book. Those people are entrepreneurs. Their stories have inspired and encouraged me in my own personal journey and make me proud to count myself as one of their crowd.

Those interviewed for this book were asked to share the one personal quality that has helped them become or remain successfully self-employed. The most popular responses were: perseverance, tenacity, enthusiasm, persistence and sincerity. But it doesn't stop there. There are a few other things you need to know about what it takes to make it as a bootstrapping entrepreneur:

- You must be willing to do research; it's one thing to come up with a good idea, but it's another to follow through on bringing it to life.

- Never promise more than you can deliver. If you don't accept shoddy workmanship from others, you shouldn't expect your customers to accept it from you.

- The ability to stay focused on your goals is critical.

- A commitment to excellence will help you stand out from the crowd.

- You'll remain steadfast when you have an absolute conviction that there's no happiness working for someone else.

- It is my belief that you absolutely need faith in God.

These are the qualities that have served hundreds of bootstrapping veterans across the country well. They can work for you, too.

I've presented to you the tips, tactics and strategies that will help you build a more profitable business, but please do not overlook the important character traits you need to have enduring success. They're already inside some of you, waiting to be unleashed. Some of you may need to develop them by reshaping your perception about yourself and life. Whatever you do, be your best. Be courageous. Be honest in your dealings. And never give up on your dream. Until the next book...

Bootstrapper's Follow-up File

900 Know-How: How to Succeed With Your Own 900 Number Business by Robert Mastin (Aegis Publishing Group, 1996); 800-828-6291; Web address: www.aegisbooks.com. $19.95.

Apple Computer seminars, Web address: www.seminars.apple.com or www.smallbusiness.apple.com. Seminars for small business owners nationwide. Past topics have included "Grow Your Business Electronically," "How Big Do You Want to Be" and "Leverage Technology to Your Competitive Advantage." Locations, times and dates available on Apple seminars Web site.

Black Enterprise, 800-727-7777; Web address: www.blackenterprise.com. A monthly magazine. $16.95.

Bootstrappin' Entrepreneur Newsletter Bundler Package by Kimberly Stanséll, Research Done Write!, Suite B261-BSS, 8726 S. Sepulveda Blvd., Los Angeles, CA 90045. A package containing the most popular four issues from the newsletter collection. Timeless information, including more marketing tips, business-building strategies, networking contacts nationwide, success stories, case studies and dozens more resources. $20 ($21.65 for California residents).

Business97, Group IV Communications, 125 Auburn Court #100, Thousand Oaks, CA 91362; 805-496-6156. A bimonthly publication offering information on small business management and marketing. Sample copy: $4.50; one-year subscription: $21.

Creativity Success Journals, Spotlight Publications, 800-527-7625. A personalized entrepreneurial journal to log the growth plan or goals for your business or other projects. $19.95.

Edward Lowe Foundation, 800-232-LOWE; Web address: www.lowe.org and www.edgeonline.com. Sponsors, organizes and develops courses for a variety of educational conferences, seminars and workshops held across the country for small business people and entrepreneurs.

Encyclopedia of Associations, Gale Research, 800-347-4253. A library reference book listing more than 20,000 groups nationwide.

Entrepreneur: The Small Business Authority, 800-274-6229; Web address: www.entrepreneurmag.com. A monthly publication. $19.97.

Francorp, 800-372-6244; e-mail address: francorp@aol.com. Provides consulting on franchising to entrepreneurs.

Home Office Computing: Solutions for Today's Small Business, 800-228-7812; Web address: www.smalloffice.com. A monthly publication. $16.97.

Inc.: The Magazine for Growing Companies, 800-234-0999; Web address: www.inc.com. A monthly magazine. $19.

Money Smart Secrets of the Self-Employed by Linda Stern (Random House, 1997); 800-726-0600. $20.

Moving Expenses (Publication 521) and *Change of Address* (Form 8822), Internal Revenue Service, 800-TAX-FORM; Web address: www.irs.ustreas.gov. IRS information on relocating and moving.

National Center for Financial Education, SASE Section, P.O. Box 34070, San Diego, CA 92163; Web address: www.ncfe.org. Provides information to help people do a better job of spending, saving, investing, insuring and planning for their financial future. Send SASE for information package.

Self-Employed Professional, 800-366-7857. A bimonthly publication. Sample copy: **free**; subscription: $19.97.

The Entrepreneur's Relocation Guide by Kimberly Stanséll, Research Done Write!, Suite B261-BSS, 8726 S. Sepulveda Blvd., Los Angeles, CA 90045. A 32-page guide providing you with a six-step plan for relocating yourself, your family and your business. Includes money-saving tips, research strategies for evaluating a new location, relocatee profile and directory of small business assistance agencies nationwide. $9.50 ($10.28 for California residents).

What Are Your Goals?: Powerful Questions to Discover What You Want Out of Life by Gary Ryan Blair (Wharton Publishing, 1993); 800-731-GOAL. $14.95.

Directory of State Resources for Small Businesses

Alabama Center for Commerce
Small Business Office of Advocacy
401 Adams Ave.
Montgomery, AL 36130
334-242-0400
>   Publication: *Doing Business in Alabama* (**free**)

Alaska Trade and Development
P.O. Box 110804
Juneau, AK 99801
907-465-2017
>   Publication: *Establishing a Business in Alaska* ($8 plus $3.50 shipping and handling)

Arizona Business Connection
Arizona Department of Commerce
Bldg. D, 3800 N. Central Ave.
Phoenix, AZ 85012
602-280-1480
>   Publication: *Small Business Book: Guide to Establishing a Business* (**free**)

Arkansas Industrial Development Commission
One State Capitol Mall
Little Rock, AR 72201
501-682-1121
> Publication: *Starting a Business in Arkansas* (**free**)

California Office of Small Business, Office of Permit Assistance
California Trade and Commerce Agency
801 K St., Suite 1700
Sacramento, CA 95814
800-353-2672
> Publication: *California Permit Handbook* (**free**)

Colorado Business Assistance Center
1625 Broadway, Suite 805
Denver, CO 80202
303-592-5920
> Publication: *The Colorado Business Start Up Kit* (**free**)

Connecticut Department of Economic Development
Office of Small Business Services
805 Brook St.
Rocky Hill, CT 06067
860-258-4200
> Publication: *Starting a Business? Start With Our Help* (**free**)

Delaware Development Office
Small Business Advocate
P.O. Box 1401
Dover, DE 19903
302-739-4271
> Publication: *Small Business Start-Up Guide: A Blueprint for Beginning Business Operations in Delaware* (**free**)

District of Columbia Office of Business and Economic Development
717 14th St. NW, 10th Floor
Washington, DC 20005
202-727-7100
> Publication: *Washington Business Guide* (**free**)

Florida Department of Commerce
Division of Economic Development
Collins Bldg.
107 W. Gaines St., Room 443
Tallahassee, FL 32399
904-488-9357

>Publication: *Florida Business Guide: References and Resources for Florida Business* (**free**)

Georgia Economic Development Department
Information Department
P.O. Box 1740
Atlanta, GA 30301
404-586-8403

>Publications: *Small Business Sources of Capital; Starting a New Business; Management Services and Technical Assistance: Small Business Resources Handbook* (**free**)

Hawaii Department of Business and Economic Development
Business Action Center
1130 N. Nimitz Highway, Suite A254
Honolulu, HI 96817
808-586-2545

>Publications: *Starting a Business in Hawaii; Hawaii's Business Regulations; Checklist for Employers in Hawaii; All About Business in Hawaii* (**free**)

Idaho Department of Commerce
P.O. Box 83720
Boise, ID 83720
208-334-2470

>Publication: *Starting a Business in Idaho* (**free**)

Illinois Department of Commerce and Community Affairs
First-Stop Business Information Center
620 E. Adams St., 3rd Floor
Springfield, IL 62701
217-785-7546

>Publication: *Starting a Business in Illinois* (**free**)

Indiana State Information Center
402 W. Washington St., Room W160
Indianapolis, IN 46204
317-233-0800
    Publication: *General Information Sheet for New Businesses in Indiana* (**free**)

Iowa Department of Economic Development
Small Business Division
200 E. Grand Ave.
Des Moines, IA 5309
515-242-4700
    Publications: *Iowa Small Business Resource Guide; Business License Package* (**free**)

Kansas Department of Commerce
Business Development
700 SW Harrison St.
Suite 1300
Topeka, KS 66603
913-296-3481
    Publication: *Steps to Success* ($3)

Kentucky Cabinet for Economic Development
Small and Minority Business Division
Small Business Start-up Packets
23rd Floor
Capital Tower
Frankfort, KY 40601
502-564-4252
    Publication: *Steps in Establishing a Business in Kentucky* (**free**)

Louisiana Department of Economic Development
Office of Commerce
P.O. Box 94185
Baton Rouge, LA 70804
504-342-5893
    Publication: *Six Steps to Starting a Business in Louisiana* (**free**)

Maine Department of Economic and Community Development
Office of Business Development
State House Station #59
Augusta, ME 04333
207-287-2656

Publication: *Answers: A Guide to Doing Business in Maine* ($4)

Maryland Department of Economic and Employment Development
Regional Development Department
Redwood Tower
217 E. Redwood St.
Baltimore, MD 21202
410-767-6300

Publication: *Maryland Guide to Business Resources* (only obtainable online at www.mdbusiness.state.md.us)

Massachusetts Office of Business Development
One Ashburton Place, Room 2101
Boston, MA 02108
617-727-3206

Publication: *Small Business Assistance Packet* (**free**)

Michigan Jobs Commission
Business Start-up Assistance
Victor Office Center, 4th Floor
201 N. Washington Sq.
Lansing, MI 48913
517-373-9808

Publication: *Business Start-Up Package* (**free**)

Minnesota Small Business Assistance Office
500 Metro Sq.
121 7th Place E.
St. Paul, MN 55101
612-296-3871

Publications: *A Guide to Starting a Business in Minnesota; An Employer's Guide to Employment Law Issues in Minnesota; A Manufacturer's Guide to Products Liability Law in Minnesota* (**free**)

Mississippi Department of Economic and Community Development
P.O. Box 849
Jackson, MS 39205
601-359-3593
   Publication: *Entrepreneur's Tool Kit* (**free**)

Missouri Business Assistance Center, Community and Economic
   Development
P.O. Box 118
Jefferson City, Missouri 65102
573-751-4982
   Publication: *Starting a New Business in Missouri* (**free**)

Montana Business Development Division, Department of Commerce
P.O. Box 200501
Helena, MT 59620
406-444-3814
   Publications: *A Guide to Montana's Economic Development and
   Community Development Programs*; *Start-A-Business* (**free**)

Nebraska Department of Economic Development
Business Assistance Division
P.O. Box 94666
Lincoln, NE 68509
402-471-3782
   Publications: *Checklist for Starting a Business in Nebraska*;
   Financing Alternatives for Nebraska Businesses; *Management and
   Technical Assistance for Businesses* (**free**)

Nevada Small Business Advocacy Office
2501 E. Sahara, Suite 100
Las Vegas, NV 89104
702-486-4335
   Publication: *Small Business Start-Up Package* (**free**)

New Hampshire Business Finance Authority
Industry Development Authority
14 Dixon Ave., Suite 101
Concord, NH 03301
603-271-2391
   Publication: *A Guide to Doing Business in New Hampshire* (**free**)

New Jersey Department of Commerce and Economic Development
SWMB Division
20 W. State St.—CN 835
Trenton, NJ 08625
609-292-3860
> Publication: *Doing Business in New Jersey* ($5)

New Mexico Economic Development Department
P.O. Box 20003
Santa Fe, NM 87504
505-827-0300
> Publication: *Starting Out: A Guide to Creating Your Own New Mexico Business* (**free**)

New York Business Assistance Hot Line, Empire State Development
633 3rd Ave., 32nd Floor
New York, NY 10017
800-782-8369
> Publications: *Your Business, A Management Guide* ($5); *Small Business Start-Up Package* (**free**)

North Carolina Small Business and Technology Development Center
4509 Creedmoor Rd., Suite 201
Raleigh, NC 27612
919-571-4154
> Publication: *New Business Start-Up Kit* (**free**)

North Dakota Department of Economic Development and Finance
1833 E. Bismarck Expressway
Bismarck, ND 58504
701-328-5300
> Publications: *Economic Development Guide*; *New Business Registration Forms* (**free**)

Ohio One-Stop Business Permit Center
Department of Development, Economic Development Division
P.O. Box 1001
Columbus, OH 43216
614-466-4232
> Publication: *Starting Your Business in Ohio* (**free**)

Oklahoma Department of Commerce
P.O. Box 26980
Oklahoma City, OK 73126
405-843-9970
> Publication: *A Guide to Doing Business in Oklahoma* (**free**)

Oregon Business Information Center
Public Service Bldg., Suite 151
255 Capitol St. NE
Salem, OR 97310
503-986-2222
> Publication: *Oregon Business Guide* (**free**)

Pennsylvania Small Business Resource
Department of Community and Economic Development
374 Forum Bldg.
Harrisburg, PA 17120
717-783-5700
> Publication: *Pennsylvania Small Business Operations and Resources Guide* (**free**)

Rhode Island Economic Development Corporation
One W. Exchange St.
Providence, RI 02903
401-277-2601
> Publication: *Starting a Business in Rhode Island* (**free**)

South Carolina Department of Commerce
Enterprise Development
P.O. Box 927
Columbia, SC 29202
803-737-0400
> Publication: *BusinessLine* (**free**)

South Dakota Economic Development
711 E. Wells Ave.
Pierre, SD 57501
605-773-5032
> Publication: *Business Start-Up Package* (**free**)

Tennessee Department of Economic and Community Development
Office of Minority Business Enterprise
Rachel Jackson Bldg., 7th Floor
320 6th Ave. N.
Nashville, TN 37243
615-741-2545
> Publication: *Small Business Guide* (**free**)

Texas Department of Commerce, Business Information and Referral
P.O. Box 12728
Austin, TX 12728
512-936-0081
> Publication: *Business Information and Referral Package* (**free**)

Utah Business and Economic Development Division
324 S. State, Suite 500
Salt Lake City, UT 84114
801-538-8800
> Publication: *Doing Business in Utah: A Guide to Business Information* (**free**)

Vermont Department of Economic Development
109 State St.
Montpelier, VT 05609
802-828-3221
> Publication: *The Vermonter's Guide to Doing Business* (**free**)

Virginia Department of Economic Development
P.O. Box 798
Richmond, VA 23206
804-371-8100
> Publications: *Let Us Guide You; Virginia Capital Resource Directory; Guide to Establishing a Business* (**free**)

Washington State Business Assistance Center
P.O. Box 42516
Olympia, WA 98504-2516
360-753-5632
> Publications: *Operating a Business in Washington State: A Business Resource Guide; Business Resource Directory: For Financial and Technical Assistance* (**free**)

West Virginia Development Office
Department of Commerce
Capitol Complex, M-146
Charleston, WV 25305
304-558-2234

    Publications: *Going into Business in West Virginia; Minority Owned and Women Owned Business Directory* (**free**)

Wisconsin Department of Commerce
Business Helpline
P.O. Box 7970
Madison, WI 53707
608-266-1018

    Publication: *Going into Business in Wisconsin: An Entrepreneur's Guide* (**free**)

Wyoming Economic and Community Development
6101 Yellowstone Rd., 4th Floor
Cheyenne, WY 82002
307-777-7284

    Publication: *A Guide to Business Permits and Licensing in Wyoming* (**free**)

Bootstrapper's Survey

Calling all bootstrappers! The following is part of an ongoing research project to gather feedback from self-employed people across the country. There's no form to fill out. Simply send in your responses to the following questions. You can answer all of them or selected ones. Your feedback may be used in various articles, books and other projects under development and could lead to your business being prominently profiled in a future project.

1. What questions would you like to see answered in a book for small business owners?

2. What parts of running a business present you with the most challenges?

3. What strategies have you used to graduate from a struggling bootstrapper to a prosperous one?

4. Share three things self-employment has taught you about yourself that you didn't know while in the workplace.

5. What is the most imaginative approach you've used to get new business or a client, to promote your business or to boost profits?

6. Which strategies in this book did you find the most or the least useful, and why?

7. If you won a private coaching session with a small business expert, what problems would you have him or her help you work through?

Your participation is appreciated. Please include a brief description of yourself and your business and how we may contact you. Send to:

Kimberly Stanséll
Research Done Write!
Suite B261-BSS
8726 S. Sepulveda Blvd.
Los Angeles, CA 90045
e-mail address: Ibootstrap@aol.com

Thank you!

About the Author

Kimberly Stanséll bagged her job as a corporate personnel director in 1989 and hasn't looked back since. She reinvented herself into an information specialist and small business coach. She runs Research Done Write! from her home in Los Angeles. Companies and organizations across the country use her research, writing and consulting services to develop reference materials and products aimed at the small business marketplace. She published the national quarterly, *Bootstrappin' Entrepreneur: The Newsletter for Individuals with Great Ideas and a Little Bit of Cash*, for four years and now helps others learn the ins and outs of entrepreneurship through her personal coaching service.

Kimberly's bootstrapping techniques have been featured in *The Los Angeles Times'* weekly business column "Small Talk" and a variety of publications, including *USA Today*, *Home Office Computing*, *The Chicago Tribune*, *Bottom Line/Personal*, *Woman's Day*, *Black Enterprise* and *Entrepreneur's Business Start-Ups*. Her bootstrapping column regularly appears in *Self-Employed Professional* magazine. Kimberly has also provided instructional and motivational television spots to *Making It! Minority Success Stories*, which airs on three California stations and more than 100 cable stations nationwide.

For more information about her services, contact:

Research Done Write!
Suite B261-BSS
8726 S. Sepulveda Blvd.
Los Angeles, CA 90045
e-mail address: Ibootstrap@aol.com

Index